For Curtis and Milo
who have endured being endlessly quoted
with more grace and good humor than I would have.

Emoji Created by Vecteezy.com
Pictures of Chester 8/20/2019, taken by Billie Kolpack
ures of the concert at The Music Room East Aurora 1/23/2016, taken by Donna Halle

Introduction

Many posts have been lightly edited from their original form. In addition, many original posts contained asterisks or _underlines_ to imitate italics. Some now appear as actual italics in this book.

A handful of posts have comments included. Unless otherwise specified, all of the comments are my own words, and the context is clear.

This book carries a Content Warning for strong language and discussion of sensitive topics. Beginning in 2016, violent events and experiences are acknowledged but never described.

Contents

Preface

When I was a child, I had these distant relatives, Nadyne and Mac, who I saw every handful of years at family reunion cookouts. They were my dad's aunt and uncle, and they were old and faded.

I had a child's understanding of them, and I'm sure it's wildly inaccurate. They seemed dusty and decayed, like people who were only slightly alive.

I genuinely liked Nadyne. I think I stood taller than her by the time I turned 10 years old. She wore no makeup, and she kept her hair in a self-cut pageboy. She appeared to have made a conscious decision to age with not one single attempt to slow it down. She had a high, baby's voice, and giggled nervously throughout all interactions. Her demeanor was pleading. And because she seemed so fragile, you loved her. Of course. She didn't really seem to know how to talk to children (or maybe not anybody), but she very sweetly tried.

Mac was skinny and stooped. His face had settled long ago into permanent frown lines. So, he may or may not have been a grumpy man, but he looked like one. He was the type who would nod at and greet a child if one made eye contact, but he didn't seem to have much use for them otherwise.

In my mind, they were hermits, wasting away inside their house. I imagined stacked piles of books lining their home's walls that released dust clouds when someone picked one up to read. I imagined closed curtains and low ceilings. I imagined silence. Like their home was a mausoleum buried under time.

We never dropped in on Nadyne and Mac, though we drove through their town every week. And when I was a child (long before cell phones and cell phone etiquette), my mom and my mother's side of the family were the kind of people who dropped in on everybody. --They're actually still like that. I think more than half of my extended family is personally offended by a day with nothing going on. I know this because their pictures on Facebook tell me so (and I love their pictures!).

In the first half of my life, I was just like my mom – extroverted and engaged. But as I began to approach the second half, I became much more like Nadyne and Mac (and again, I should emphasize that Nadyne and Mac may not have been hermits. It's totally possible that they were dazzling, community-minded joiners who only seemed partially mummified to a child. It's totally possible there was some other reason why we rarely saw them).

I think about them a lot because for the last batch of years, I've had agoraphobia. I leave my house occasionally (a practice that my beloved Zoom shrink celebrates every time), nearly only for doctor's appointments or other tasks that can be completed – leaving my driveway and then returning to my driveway – within 10 or 15 minutes.

And now when I think of Nadyne and Mac, I have to rewrite the story in my head. Because I'm a hermit the way I assumed they were hermits. But I feel like I have a full, happy, rich life! I don't feel like I'm wasting away inside my tomb. I feel like everything I need and want is right here, and it's only when I need to go someplace else that I become aware of and bothered by my mental illness.

For years, when people have suggested to me that I should publish my Facebook posts as a book, I would scoff. What finally convinced me to make this, is I asked myself to think of all the prolific random social media users I follow. If any of them made compilation books of their posts, would I read them?

And there are quite a few people whose compilation books I absolutely would read. There are so many weirdly wonderful social media writers. And all of us creative and chatty posters would say that we clearly didn't intend to end up with a product, but after all of these years and thousands of posts, we've made one all the same.

Recently, I had what I thought was a perfect idea for the title of this book. I was going to call it "Sort of Like Erma Bombeck but Not Really." I had it all planned out. I was going to have 2008-2015 be the "Sort of Like Erma Bombeck" chapters, and 2016-2022 be the "But Not Really" chapters.

It's likely that I would have done just that, except that when I ran the idea by my husband, he said, "Who's Erma Bombeck?"

I suppose she *was* known only to a very specific audience. If you or your mom didn't have a subscription to Good Housekeeping magazine or Reader's Digest in the 70s and 80s, you may not have heard of Erma Bombeck either.

But she wrote about marriage and family with humor and affection. She clearly liked her family, and she liked the absurdities of family life. I've always been pleased when my writing has been compared to hers.

But in recent years, there's been a ribbon of criticism implied: "*Sometimes* your writing reminds me of Erma Bombeck's!" "Those Erma Bombeck-type posts are my favorites!" "The other ones are a little too strident for me." Etc.

Most of my posts from 2008-2015 are warm, everyday, nice-y life-y reflections. And after that, I do still have funny and silly posts. But the world has changed, and my life has changed. My son grew up, went to college, and got his own place. Our beloved dog and cat both died. My health got worse, and then my health got a lot worse. There just wasn't as much absurdity to notice.

I will mention that there is one post that made the Final Cut, from 2018, where I brag about my son's new album being so amazing. And with every editing pass-through that I did for this book, I've thought, 'this post really doesn't fit. It's not think-y or funny or relatable, it's just braggy.' But every time, I've followed up that thought with, 'Heck, I've used this kid's life as 'post fodder' for years. I think he's earned a shameless plug (or two) for his album! After all, his music is available on all the usual platforms!'

Seriously though, throughout this whole project, I've been so grateful that my son is a creative person himself. Through all of these years, I have told the world *my* version of Milo. But my version doesn't count any more than anybody else's mother's version counts. I'm so glad that Milo has plenty of ways to share his own version of himself.

So you'll notice that the percentage of funny posts goes down over time and the percentage of longer and more serious posts goes up. There's even a smattering of angry posts. Lots of my followers have stayed with me and embraced the changes, but not everybody. And I get it.

I've classified this book as a memoir, because it really does have a story arc. It also serves as a completely random historical document. For example, I deleted most but not all of my posts on April the giraffe.

Because Facebook was so new in 2008, I didn't know how I wanted to use it yet. I've scaled back my posts from the earliest years pretty radically, and mainly just used them as character building. I hope you find this book –both the *Erma Bombeck* years and the *But Not Really* years- fast-paced and enjoyable. It was never my intention to turn my Facebook posts into a book, but I've had so much fun compiling it.

Shelly Duhn

October 10, 2022

2008

Tuesday, June 3, 2008 8:03pm

We're waiting for contact from the architect to tell us if we can renovate this really great house in East Aurora. Cross your fingers for us!

Wednesday, October 29, 2008 10:49pm

I'm tired, sore, and living in my new (very old) house. Best day ever.

Friday, December 5, 2008 7:48pm

Moment of zen: tromp to the plaza across the street for a hard plastic sled. Then follow behind, watching husband pull son through quiet, snow filled streets. Bliss.

Tuesday, December 9, 2008 6:45am

Such a 'Buffalo' experience:

We took the car through the car wash to get the weeks of salt off my car.

As I took the car out of neutral and pulled out of the bay, I said, "Wow! My windshield looks huge!"

And Kiddo said, "I don't know why, but it makes me feel so happy!"

Saturday, December 27, 2008 2:11pm

One last Christmas party today. Tomorrow the tree comes down and we start learning to love a house where the staircase stays right where it is. **Sigh**

2009

Saturday, January 17, 2009 12:32am

Just now, walked the Netflix out to the box & stopped to bask in my sleeping town, tucked in under a thick quilt of sparkling, glorious, still falling snow.

Tuesday, January 27, 2009 2:14am

We had the great fun task of going through every single money transaction since June. They were ALL wise and well thought out. Every one of them.

Sunday, February 8, 2009 12:59pm

We somehow went from agreeing on a guinea pig to agreeing on a dog. A dog. A dog.

Tuesday, February 24, 2009 4:21pm

I want movers to come carry every item out of this house, and then I won't allow anything back in until I know where to put it.

Wednesday, April 1, 2009 10:20am

Kiddo and I have been rallying hard to name our future dog "Scooby" (as in, Scooby Duhn. Cute, right?). I think we'll wear Curtis down any day now...

Sunday, May 10, 2009 11:40pm

Curtis is taking Milo to his first all-ages punk rock show this Thursday in Cleveland. It's a surprise, so don't say anything!

12

Wednesday, June 10, 2009 11:17pm

I love that my writer friends all think of me when they want a dirty story critiqued.

Thursday, June 11, 2009 4:41pm

On June 23rd, we're having an Invisible Fence installed! We *might* be getting a Corgi puppy in early July! But Corgi or no Corgi, it appears you can't promise your 10-year-old a dog and then hope he'll forget. Eventually, he will insist that you keep your promise.

Saturday, June 13, 2009 11:05am

My son hasn't stopped singing, dancing, bouncing, giggling. We've been promised the corgi! Taking name suggestions!

Saturday, June 27, 2009 11:55pm

Kiddo isn't taking guitar lessons right now, so his playing isn't as good as it was. But lately he's into writing songs, so we're just letting him go with that. I hope he starts lessons back up in the fall!

Saturday, July 4, 2009 1:05pm

I had my THIRD "sexy" dream about Keith Olbermann last night! More ridiculous than sexy - last night, he was my chiropractor and the adjustment involved him laying perfectly still on top of me.

Monday, July 13, 2009 4:41pm

This latest Amazon.com order included a leash, collar, and puppy chew toys! It won't be long now! Just a bit over a week! The latest name frontrunner is Johnny.

Friday, July 17, 2009 12:02am

This is how cool I am: A friend just asked me if I text, and I replied, "Like with cell phones?"

Friday, August 7, 2009 10:39pm

Today at the Eden Corn Festival, Kiddo was traumatized by the forces of gravity on The Muzik Express ride (like a super-fast merry-go-round). No single riders allowed, so they paired him with a cuuute 11-year-old girl. When the ride got up to top speed, she was practically in his lap. All of his gracious good manners left him immediately. He couldn't get off that ride fast enough.

Monday, August 10, 2009 11:42pm

Chester was running all over the house, getting into MUCH mischief and then, practically mid shenanigans, dropped like a stone and went to sleep.

Tuesday, August 11, 2009 1:16pm

[Summer vacation]:

Kiddo: "Mommy, why does anyone wear clothes? It's no different from looking at hands."

Me: "I agree! Should we become nudists?"

Kiddo, giggling: "Noooooo!"

Thursday, August 13, 2009 9:10pm

Poor Chester. We're all hot and grumpy over here and so he keeps flopping down on the floor, limbs every which way. Then 2 minutes later, when that spot's hot, he moves a few feet away and flops down again. It's all very dramatic.

Friday, August 14, 2009 9:46pm

I'm driving an hour each way tomorrow morning to get a $30 window AC unit from a guy on Craig's List. Something tells me we'll all be camping in the living room until fall! :)

Saturday, August 15, 2009 1:20pm

The $30 AC is a titch stinky, but it works great! You can tell because we're all smiling at each other, and the dog is floffing all over us.

Friday, August 21, 2009 3:39pm

Oh my goodness, Twilight. I haven't had so much fun reading a book in years and years and years and years.

Saturday, August 22, 2009 12:40am

It's been many many years since I've read a 500-page romance novel in two days (I'm too embarrassed to be seen reading romance novels with those cringeworthy covers. I was an English major! I'm an intellect, darnit!).

I loved every second of it. So delicious and forbidden and teenager-y! Returning to books that feed my mind is going to totally suck. :) Oh..but there are three more books in the saga, aren't there?! I'll make an exception.

Monday, August 31, 2009 12:00am

Curtis and Milo in an NYC comic book store, as told by Curtis:

Curtis: "Kiddo, do you like Spiderman?"

Milo: "No."

Curtis: "Do you like Iron Man?"

Milo: "No, I don't really like superheroes. Do they have any Garfield comic books?"

Curtis: "No."

Milo: "Well, that's stupid! Why do they call it a comic book store?"

Sunday, September 20, 2009 7:14pm

Parental pride: Today, driving back from Jenna's Bday party, the whole family was singing along to "Sheena is a Punk Rocker," and at the end, Milo started singing an interesting and note-perfect harmony. Curtis and I smiled at each other in the front seat.

Sunday, September 20, 2009 7:28pm

Just remembered that I had YET ANOTHER Keith Olbermann dream last night! This time he was my college professor and he'd pulled some strings to get me into Harvard Law, and I hugged him and then I hugged him again and held on a little long and then I whispered, "Is this okay?" And that's the dream.

Curtis said the same thing he always does: "Did he give you a Special Comment?"

Tuesday, September 29, 2009 4:06pm
Homework totally fries my kid. :(

Friday, October 2, 2009 8:26am
Kiddo's been pestering us for a new microphone for months and yesterday Curtis finally caved. They went to the Radio Shack across the street and got a $50 one.

This morning, I woke up to him repeating, over and over and over: "Check. Check One Two. Check. Check One Two."

Monday, November 30, 2009 9:21pm
Today, with absolutely no advance warning, my child asked me for hair gel. Then he gelled the BACK of his hair, I guess to make it look longer.

And then he asked me if I thought he looked like Jim from The Office now. And he spent the rest of the day checking himself out in whatever reflective surface he could find.

Wednesday, December 9, 2009 8:36pm
Curtis' astute observation about our son: "I don't think he's capable of exhaling without talking or singing."

Thursday, December 10, 2009 9:12pm
Nothing cuter in the world than watching a corgi run through a foot of snow. *Now you see him! * *Now you don't! * *Now you see him! * *Now you don't! *

Sunday, December 13, 2009 8:25pm

Curtis wins the bad parent award of the day. He bought a huge HDTV off a guy on Craig's List, and today, Mom said, "What made you decide to get a TV now?" And Curtis said, "Well, since we're getting the PS3 for Christmas," which was the point when Milo burst out, "WE'RE GETTING A PS3?????"

2010

Sunday, January 3, 2010 8:21pm

(Milo was in the kitchen getting a drink)

Curtis, playing Wheel of Fortune on the PS3: "They have the ugliest avatars on this game."

(Milo returns and sits down. A few minutes go by.)

Milo: "Hey Daddy, that avatar looks just like you only with different hair!"

Thursday, January 7, 2010 9:02am

Curtis saw the famous East Aurora albino deer in our yard last night! The deer was with a few of his friends and Chester was going apeshit. Curtis didn't know we had a famous albino deer in town, so when he came in, he said "It must have just been the light, but I would swear that one of those deer was white..."

Monday, January 18, 2010 8:03pm

Complete flake moment: Walking out of Moe's and see an old guy wearing a Bills cap.

And I said, "Hey, Buffalo! Oh wait--I'm IN Buffalo. Never mind!"

We've lived here for 2 years. I see Bills/Sabres attire many, many times a day.

Who knows where I go when I leave my brain?

Wednesday, January 20, 2010 2:15pm

It's true that I think in Facebook updates. And now, to make things even more silly, every time I hear a song, no matter what it is, I can see what it would look like if I were singing it in Rock Band.

Thursday, January 21, 2010 3:14pm

One of Kiddo's teachers assigned a BRILLIANT task: Write two papers about what you want to be when you grow up - one for what you want to do to be famous, and one for if you're not famous.

Kiddo is so sure that he's going to be famous, he blew off the second, 'not famous' paper and said, "I don't know. Maybe manage Taco Bell or something?"

Monday, February 22, 2010 10:53am

Buffalo in February: Where if you happen to be outside often enough, you just might see a pickup truck with a snowplow on the front, towing a boat.

Friday, February 26, 2010 1:19am

Very, very grateful that my mother is still with us after her genuinely terrifying experience today.

#1, I'd really miss her.

#2, I'd have a new most shameful secret: That just a small part of me could see the humor in my mother being killed by a vacuum cleaner.

Saturday, February 27, 2010 10:15pm

Reason #479876 why it's useful to have Curtis around: He's the only one willing to play all of our Rock Bands (Lego this time) in such a way that the really good songs get unlocked. Hooray!

Tuesday, March 9, 2010 5:07pm

There's a tired old saying her that we only have three seasons: Winter, Summer, and Mud.

I never appreciated this phrase until I got a low-rider doggie. 3 baths in 4 days.

I already told Curtis that I'm changing my renovation plans again (you know, that renovation that's going to happen any day now) to include a bathtub downstairs.

Friday, March 12, 2010 3:03pm

My next dog is going to be a dainty little germophobe. :) har har har

Thursday, April 22, 2010 9:42am

I was standing off to the side in a ridiculously crowded Tim Horton's, waiting for them to finish making mine and Curtis' sandwiches.

A man who looks a bit like Larry the Cable Guy (not good looking, not young, not monied) comes in to flirt with one of the women working there (a female Larry, so to speak).

They chat for a minute or two about nothing in particular and then they say goodbye and he heads toward the door.

She calls out, across that ridiculously crowded Tim Horton's, "Love You!"

He stops, turns slowly, and with unabashed, delighted, THICK, smooth, deep lust in his voice, says "Love you."

It totally made my day.

Mar 25, 2010 10:53:32am

Milo sings the Canadian National Anthem like a good American hockey fan: "oh Canada! Hmm hmm hmm hmm hmm hmmmmmmm!"

Tuesday, April 27, 2010 9:52pm

Two reasons my child is on my last nerve tonight:

1. Apparently 5th grade boys do *not* take superhero towels for swimming in gym class, which is a problem, since those are the only clean towels in the house.

2. He spent some time watching YouTube videos tonight and now, over and over, he's chanting "Happy Birthday to the GROUND"

Wednesday, May 26, 2010 8:50am

When I dropped Kiddo off at school this morning, the crossing guard had traffic stopped and a squirrel crossed with the children. It was adorable mayhem!

Saturday, May 29, 2010 9:28pm

I just OBLITERATED the Rock Band drums. Was walking into the room, slipped on the doggy's bone, and fell, boobs-first into the drums.

Monday, June 14, 2010 6:57pm

Me, singing along with the radio: You touch me and I'm weak, I'm a feather in the wind, and I can't wait to feel you touching me again!"

Milo: "Oh. Eww."

Monday, June 21, 2010 10:23pm

We practiced for Doggy's Graduation tonight (it's next Monday). We are *So Totally* going to pass this time!

Thursday, July 1, 2010 11:48pm

Today's lesson of the day: Want to make two 11-year-old boys laugh so hard you worry they'll both pee their pants? Drive down Dick Road.

Thursday, July 15, 2010 6:18pm

That's it. Until this clumsy phase of mine ends, no one's allowed to have glassware anywhere around me. I'm so damn sick of cleaning it up!!

Tuesday, August 3, 2010 5:55pm

Today we went to the store to get Curtis a new iPhone. We decided Milo's old enough to get the old one. He's THRILLED.

As we were walking back to the car, Milo said, "You know what I can't wait to do? The next time we're in a movie theater and they tell you to silence your cell phone, now I can do it too!"

Monday, August 23, 2010 12:31am

My poor, sweet kiddo can't sleep. That 4-hour time difference hasn't worked itself out of him yet. So, I just told him the Trisha the puppy story (Trisha was Milo's first toy and she was small enough to spend 2 months in the hospital NICU with him), and my sentimental little baby shed some tears and went upstairs to sleep with Trisha for the first time in years. /sniff

Friday, August 27, 2010 5:28pm

OMG, I love living in a walkable village! I swear this is true: Kiddo went to Blockbuster to get us a movie and just called me and said "Um, Mommy? I'm right next to Tops and we're out of milk so is it okay if I use my change to buy some?"

Of course, now I'm totally wishing I'd sent him with A LOT more money! We're out of WAY more than milk!

Monday, September 20, 2010 4:24pm

Today I was driving down a nice side street and I saw a pretty, expensive-looking wingchair out at the road.

As I drove past, I slowed down to see why on earth someone would throw it away. The back two corners were perfectly shredded.

A fine reminder to us all: Love your animals more than your furniture.

Saturday, September 25, 2010 5:50pm

Oh goodness. Kiddo's mad at me. I can hear him out in the yard, angrily listing my flaws to the dog.

Friday, October 1, 2010 4:48pm

You know how some parents have to hide the sweets and snacks in places that no one else in the house would think to look, so they don't instantly disappear?

I'm thinking about doing that with iPod cords.

Friday, October 8, 2010 10:16am

Watching a commercial for "The Shed Vac," and I said, "Oh, we NEED that!" And Curtis said, "That's right, because if there's one thing our dog would love more than a motor, it's having a motor rubbed on his body."

Tuesday, October 19, 2010 2:32am

Just one more reason to rejoice in the return of pomegranate season: Finding bonus bits in your bra hours later.

Wednesday, November 17, 2010 1:06pm

Once upon a time, I thought I could maybe lure my in-laws up to WNY, and it wasn't the promise of family. It was Wegmans. ;)

Tuesday, November 30, 2010 3:45pm

Milo, wishfully shopping for cruises online, reading about one on Carnival's site: " '..And ladies, treat your husband to the ultimate shave, right here in our spa'.. Mommy, what does that mean?"

Me: "I don't have a clue, Honey."

And I don't. Because it's not clear – is the lady or the husband getting the "ultimate shave?"

Friday, December 3, 2010 9:59am

Most car rides go like this: I hear the opening notes of my favorite songs on my shuffling iPod, and my kid says "Veto!" and this goes on until we find a sufficiently not-too-pretty song.

But this morning, with the roads clear, the sun shining and the gorgeous trees heavily weighted down with snow, the Carpenters "Top of the World" came on.

And Milo said, "This is exactly the right song for this ride."

Saturday, December 25, 2010 8:32am

OMG. I got a Kindle!!!!

2011

Wednesday, January 12, 2011 6:18pm

I love the movie, Ace Ventura so much!! It absolutely breaks my heart, though, that there's so much homophobia throughout. I know 'that's just how it was back then,' but it still breaks my heart. Him singing "AssHOLomiooooo" through his butt cheeks cracks me up every time.

Monday, January 31, 2011 8:41pm

Tonight at Game Nite, Plain Gramma said her favorite Dr. Seuss book is "Ham and Green Onions."

Monday, February 7, 2011 3:27pm

No one on the planet intimidates me as much as the crossing guard outside Milo's school. He yelled at me AGAIN! I swear, I never take my eyes off that man, and I still screw up! :(

Friday, February 11, 2011 10:16pm

O..M..G. My child just had his first slow dance.

Wednesday, February 16, 2011 10:05am

You already know this, but *everybody* loves my dog.

Thursday, March 24, 2011 6:08pm

Almost time to leave for Milo's talent show! He's singing a parody of Taio Cruze's Dynamite, It's really cute and he plays it really well. I'll post the video later. He's in Act 2, so it'll be a little while. Send him brave thoughts!

Saturday, April 9, 2011 5:20pm

I know my kid is famous for his parodies, but sincerely, his real talent lies with his 'real' songs. I envy that kid his song-writing ability. He's, like, GOOD.

Saturday, April 16, 2011 6:33pm

30 Songs in 30 Days, Day 8: A song you know all the words to: American Pie

One of the sweetest things Milo said to me when he was little was, "Mommy, Do you know ALL the songs?"

Thursday, April 21, 2011 6:19pm

Snoozing in the chair. A light, panting noise followed by the sensation of a slobber-filled tennis ball being dropped on my hands. Kept my eyes closed. Tossed the ball. Wash, rinse, repeat

Sunday, April 24, 2011 8:37pm

We just saw the famed East Aurora Albino Deer!! So NEAT!!

Sunday, April 24, 2011 9:04pm

Albino deer in our back yard!

Sunday, May 1, 2011 10:49pm

WOW. Bin Laden dead. WOW.

Sunday, May 1, 2011 11:56pm

Curtis just said "Can you believe it? When all this happened, we had a little toddler. If someone would have told me on that day that 'when we finally catch the guy who did this, your little baby is going to be *twelve years old*, I wouldn't have believed it. This took a long time."

Sunday, June 12, 2011 3:18pm

You could write such a fun snl skit about all the crazy pantomimes and code words parents and hairstylists have to interpret in order to give a middle school boy the Justin Bieber haircut without him ever saying that name...

Thursday, July 7, 2011 3:18am

I just fell HARD in the yard. Was crossing over the Invisible Fence line, carrying Doggy, and my foot went in a dip and twisted, and I went down and dropped the dog. He's fine. What a *good boy*, he shook off his surprise and then came and sat next to me until I could get up.

Friday, July 8, 2011 6:54pm

You know what sucks the most about catching your cold from someone you live with? They've already used all the tissues in the house, so you're stuck using toilet paper.

Wednesday, July 20, 2011 8:36pm

Someday when we're loaded and decide to rebuild this house starting with the basement, I'm putting my water meter on the OUTSIDE. Wading through spider webs to get to it is soooo icky!!

Friday, July 22, 2011 5:56pm

When Curtis was my boyfriend, I was very clear that I don't like punk music. And he was disappointed but accepting.

Now, I'm being very clear with my child that I *still* don't like punk music, but he doesn't take no for an answer. He thinks he just needs to find the magic song that will make me say "oooooh, now I get it!"

Friday, July 29, 2011 2:02pm

Today was the last day of Milo's summer writing camp. Hearing child intellectuals read their pieces was so heartwarming. And my goodness: At least 5 girls wrote poems about butterflies.

Friday, September 9, 2011 6:51pm

Was just at the gas station buying 'Charlie the Butcher' roast beef sandwiches for supper, and I was behind a dirty young guy who had an angry scowl on his face. A couple of minutes later, I returned to my car to find the same man standing at my car having a love-fest with my dog.

Thursday, September 11, 2011 6:42am

Where were you on 9/11/01?

Curtis and I were in bed in our rental house in Carrboro, NC. The bus had already picked Milo up for half-day preschool at The Children's Learning Center, a place where they had on-site therapists for the special needs kids (which he was at the time because of his prematurity).

Curtis and I were waiting for it to be 9AM to have a phone call with my parents' financial planner, a Smith Barney guy in Buffalo. He was supposed to call us. But at about 9:10, he still hadn't called, so we called him.

And he said "Sorry guys, I can't talk. There was a plane crash at the World Trade Center, and we have offices there. We'll reschedule for next week some time."

Curtis turned on the news - it was when we still had a TV in the bedroom, and we watched in bed in our jammies. The people on TV kept insisting that it was a terror attack, but I refused to believe it was anything other than an accident (for days, I felt that it had to have been an accident, a computer glitch or something).

Finally, I decided I needed to go get my baby and bring him home so I could hold him.

Someone knocked on our door. It was a construction worker that I knew fairly well and liked a lot (they were putting in an extension to our development that started right outside our door. And our baby boy loved construction, so we knew all the construction guys).

We talked for a few seconds about the crashes and the worker said, "This is all because of the Jewish people."

30

I took a few seconds to sincerely wish he hadn't said those words to me, and then told him that I was on my way to pick up Kiddo. And that is how I remember 9/11. We spent the next days glued to CNN like everyone else.

It was also the first time that I had one of those absolutely certain, 'Voice of God' thoughts that came from deep, deep inside me. The thought was, "I'm not supposed to be here." Meaning, in North Carolina.

Wednesday, September 21, 2011 8:27pm
Milo's alarm clock was going off for a while, so I went upstairs and said, "Get up Kiddo! It's a perfect day!" (it's cold and rainy, which, IMO, is absolutely a perfect day}.

Kiddo sleepily says, "A perfect day to sleep!"

Me: "No, a perfect day for LEARRRRRNING!"

Kiddo: "Nooooooo!"

Thursday, September 22, 2011 9:38pm
The sentence that most effectively sums up my evening: "Okay Kiddo, will you please help me figure out what changes we need to make so we don't have any more nights like this?"

Sunday, October 2, 2011 2:34am
Every year at this time, I'm reminded that my cat (who I've barely seen for the last few months), is a full-contact kitty when she's cold. /snuggle snuggle snuggle

Sunday, October 2, 2011 9:45pm
[Friday]:

Me: "Kiddo, you really need to start wearing the pants that fit you - those go straight up your butt."

31

Kiddo: "Ehhhhh, but they're too biiiiiiig!"

Me: They're fine. You just need a belt. Do you need a new belt?"

Kiddo: "No. I have one."

[Saturday]:

Me: "Kiddo, should we buy you a belt right now?" (we were at Target)

Kiddo: "Mom! I have a belt!"

Me: "But Kiddo, are you 100% sure it fits?"

Kiddo, cutting me off: "Mom!Mom!Mom!Mom! I HAVE a belt! It's fine. It's fine!!"

[Sunday night]:

Kiddo: "Ummmm, Mom? It turns out that belt doesn't go all the way around me anymore."

::simmer::

Sunday, October 16, 2011 2:45pm

Curtis just said clearly, and with great authority, "Wake me up in 15 minutes."

And I was a little taken aback and was ready to say something along the lines of "I'll do it, but a little sweetness goes a long way, you know,"

But then I realized he was talking to his phone. I'm not used to it yet. :)

Friday, October 21, 2011 12:00am

Like any other night that I come to bed, and Curtis is already asleep, I tiptoed in, put a flashlight under the bed so I could see well enough to get ready for bed, and moved his computer off my pillow to put on the dresser.

32

But tonight, unbeknownst to me, he had fallen asleep with his ear buds in, so when I picked up his computer, I ripped his earbuds out and scared the crap out of him.

Greatest Hits

So, this afternoon, Curtis starts snorting and snickering over the Broadway episode of South Park and, as he's hitting 'restart' on the TV, says, "You're either going to LOVE this episode or absolutely hate it." (for those who haven't seen it yet, the basic premise is that the men who take their wives to Broadway plays automatically get sex).

So we watch it, it's quite funny, and when it's over, he says, "Well?"

So I take my 'joking-but-not-really tsk tsk' tone and say "Sounds about right – and just think, you made me go to that Acappella show by myself last Sunday…you didn't join the Gay Men's Chorus when I asked you to…you didn't join the UU Choir when I asked you to…you won't watch Glee…. Your life could have been a whole lot different this past year…."

And he has the most wonderful stricken look on his face, and then, just as fast, he replaces that expression with a beautific, angelic one, and in his best former-voice-major-in-college voice, sings, "On my ooooooooownnnnnnnn, pretending he's beside meeeeeeeeee.." #myhusbandcracksmeup

What could be worse than standing in a Spirit Halloween, waiting for your kid to choose his Halloween costume among strobe lights, fake S&M gear, and Katy Perry's Firework blasting??

NOTHING

Tuesday, November 29, 2011 1:06pm

Greatest Hits

Heartbreaker of the day: So, I live in one of those glorious villages that time forgot, and, right on Main Street, there's a shoe repair store that's been there longer than I've been alive (I'm pretty sure they've had the same light-up shoe in the window since I was a kid).

And in the summertime, there are two chubby lab-type dogs who lay on the steps. You know the kind - you walk up to them, they open their eyes and their tail thumps once and they let you pet them, all without ever raising their head.

Anyway, today, for the first time ever, I had a reason to go into this place. And it was exactly how you'd picture it - there were time-faded signs all over the place, that were clearly done long before the daisywheel printer was ever thought up that say things like "Credit will only be extended to those over 80 and then only when accompanied by their parents."

The customer space was itty-bitty tiny, and there were two dog blankets covering about 75% of that floor space. But there was only the one dog laying on a blanket.

So after I finished my order, I said to the sweet grey haired old lady, "Only one dog today!" And in her best brave voice, she said "We had to put the other one down. She gave us the sign last Tuesday."

Which was sad enough on its own. But then she looked down at the remaining dog and said, "She's just..... She'll snap out of it sometime, I think..."

And then that poor, sweet lady was tearing up and feeling all embarrassed because she cried in front of a stranger, and it was the SADDEST thing. Hug your pets, folks!

Wednesday, December 7, 2011 9:21pm

Today's 'and what language do You speak?" moment came at my mother's dinner table (swiss steak night...mmmmmm).

Mom was talking about a holiday guest she'd seen on Ellen: "And she was a professional wrapper, real cute and young.."

and then Milo cut her off and said "Nicki Minaj?"

And then Mom looked horrified and said, "*WHAT* about a ménage??"

And then my brother Joe leaned over to Milo and said, "wrong kind of rapper."

Greatest Hits

Milo needed to write something about his father's hands for English class, using simile or metaphor. And so he's looking at Curtis' hands and he's like 'uh, they're white. There's 10 fingers..."

And I said, "She's probably looking for something like, 'are they manly?' 'Are they calloused?'"

And Milo said, "No... they're not really manly. They're soft and kind of....um...fat."

So, then he tried to get poetic about how fast Curtis types when he's programming. And he said, "how about, 'they dance across the keyboard like break dancers?" Then he burst out, "or Dance Dance Revolution!"

So here it is, the perfect sentence that had us all laughing and Curtis looking both sheepish and proud:

"His fingers dance across the keyboard like ten soft, fat white kids playing Dance Dance Revolution."

My son just finished writing a song that isn't 'good for a 12-year-old.' I'm pretty sure he just wrote his first hit song.

2012

Sunday, January 15, 2012 5:25pm

I'm listening to wonderful, snoozy music and I have two snuggy animals on/next to me and frankly, I don't feel like getting up to fix dinner At All!

Tuesday, February 7, 2012 3:36pm

Report card day!! Here's the very best comment ever:

Art: Adequately completes assignments with moderate effort.

Thursday, February 9, 2012 7:55pm

Watching 'That Thing You Do' with Kiddo. It's one of my all-time very favorite movies, so he's seen it before, but this time, it's as if he's watching his destiny or something.

Friday, March 23, 2012 7:07am

We live ridiculously close to a gas station. Probably less than a quarter mile.

And Curtis needed to be up all night, so he and Doggy walked to the Mobil Station in the middle of the night for Red Bulls (shudder).

And this was the quote from Curtis this morning: "We had a nice walk to the Mobil Station....and a nice drag back to the house...."

I know EXACTLY what that's like!! When the dog is doing *everything in his power* to communicate, "NOOOOOOO, You're going the WRONG WAYYYYYYY!!!"

Saturday, March 24, 2012 7:45pm

Milo's having a sleepover with his most entertaining friend.

36

We walked over to Great Buffet for a seriously mediocre dinner, then to Tops for Pop Secret Butter Popcorn, "Because it's just a higher quality popcorn, Mrs. Duhn."

I guess our 2-year-old Boy Scout fundraiser popcorn just wasn't working with his advanced taste buds.

Friday, March 30, 2012 5:41pm

Milo's entertaining friend: "I don't buy my own toothbrush. I just use the one from the dentist because he knows the best kind for people to use, Mrs. Duhn.

Saturday, March 31, 2012 12:32am

The guys went to see Cursive Band in Buffalo. They just got home and Curtis said he had Milo standing in front of him, the way daddies do when they take their children to concerts. Only this time, Kiddo had grown so tall that Curtis said his head was in the way and Curtis couldn't see.

Guess it's time to graduate to standing side by side.

Friday, April 13, 2012 5:09pm

"My flat Yoda ears are so cute, barely can stand it, you!"

Friday, April 13, 2012 10:26pm

Greatest Hits

Milo's Friend: Ummm, Mrs. Duhn, I just threw up.

Milo: And yeah, some got in my shoes.

Friend: Well, it would be a bigger deal if any had gotten in my shoes because my shoes are extremely rare and expensive.

Me: *sigh* Well, that's very lucky then, dear.

Wednesday, April 18, 2012 9:45am

The crossing guard outside of Kiddo's school (who looks like a cross between Crankshaft, Wilford Brimley, and my dearly departed grandfather) is pretty notorious for keeping cars waiting while he lets more kids cross. And he makes sure that the kids who arrive late to his party are stressed and hustling as he races them across the street while the cars sit at a green light.

Anyway, these poor kids have such heavy backpacks nowadays that it's really quite comical and cute (and sure, a little sad) when you see how their little bodies adapt when they have to hustle without actually running (because that wouldn't be cool) across the street.

So I'm sitting at the red light this morning and watch the usual progression of children strolling past the crossing guard. Enough seconds pass and my light turns green.

These two boys approach the crosswalk. They're talking to each other (like folks do), going slow, enjoying their morning because there's still 7 minutes before the bell rings and it's a nice day.

But instead of having them wait for the next light, -like those kids and all the cars were assuming would happen-, the crossing guard stays put in the middle of the road, puts his angry frown on and motions to these boys with great annoyance to Moveit! Moveit! Moveit! Moveit!!

So, they bend at the waist, creating about a 45-degree angle and shuffle/march quickly, while somehow managing to not bend their knees or elbows much, and it's all very military in that every kid's body does the exact same thing when they have to "run" while wearing a backpack.

It doesn't matter if you're the one walking or driving, or if you're a kid or adult: When you encounter the Main Street middle school crossing guard, you're meek, intimidated, and, without fail, he's going to find fault with *something* you're doing.

Thursday, May 3, 2012 12:29pm

Well, as long as you're comfortable, Dear!

Tuesday, May 15, 2012 3:21pm

Milo's got Michael Bolton singing about Captain Jack Sparrow (SNL skit) going through his head, and he just asked if a cinephile is someone who molests animals.

(a cinephile is someone who likes movies, just in case you didn't know that off the top of your head).

Saturday, June 2, 2012 3:09pm

Is there anything more hilarious to watch than a pissed off 13-year-old vacuuming the floor?

Tuesday, June 5, 2012 9:58pm

Greatest Hits

Here's the scene:

Game Nite at Gramma's house.

Milo is 13.

His great grandmother is 89.

We were playing 'The Game of Things.' Gramma was the reader, meaning we all submitted our answers to her, and she reads them and we guess who wrote what.

The question was "Things you shouldn't use as a pick-up line."

Here's the answer my son wrote, and which Gramma had to read out loud to the table (Thankfully she thought it was funny. I was mortified):

"If your right leg is Thanksgiving and your left leg is Christmas, can I visit you between the holidays?"

Wednesday, June 13, 2012 4:43pm

Before they discover boys, little girls discover animals.

So, I drove past The Caboose ice cream parlor (with Chester in the car as usual), and there were a few pre-teen girls in Catholic school uniforms standing on the steps.

And, with all of the volume and excitement that only a little girl who's just spotted The Monkees/The Backstreet Boys/Hanson/ Justin Bieber can muster, one of them screamed "OH MY GOD YOU GUYS, A CORGI!!!!!!!!!!"

Wednesday, June 13, 2012 6:12pm

I wonder if the inventor of headphones/earbuds knew that for the rest of eternity, parents would be speaking to themselves and only to themselves?

Sunday, July 29, 2012 3:38pm

Curtis and I just finished watching the Olympic opening ceremonies.

So, Paul McCartney finishes Hey Jude, Curtis hits stop on the remote and starts singing (to the tune of Hey Jude, btw), "Shelly Duhn! Go make me a sandwich! I am hungry! So make me a sandwich! Remember! Just ho-ow much you love me! Then you will start! To make me, a sandwich!"

I haven't decided yet if I'm going to do it. It was adorable but I never heard 'Please.' :)

Friday, August 31, 2012 9:01pm

Here's when you know your kid is really a teenager: So we ate our dinner and watched an episode of Castle, and when the show was over I said, "Okay, I need to put dinner away."

And Kiddo turned to me and said, "Ooh, dinner?"

To which I replied, "Yes. You remember - that meal we JUST ATE?!"

Sunday, September 23, 2012 10:44pm

You know what's silly and wonderful? At our house, the game Rock Band could easily be renamed the 'Happy-marriage-o-matic 5000.'

Most days, Curtis and I are your standard, pleasantly married couple who don't have a whole lot to say to each other. Then we play Rock Band and we get all smiley and shy, "I love it when you sing." "I love it when you sing too," and then, just like that, we're sweethearts again. :)

Thursday, September 27, 2012 7:04pm

I cooked real dinner (dirtied a pan) a few days ago and yesterday I vacuumed the couch and washed all the blankets that Curtis snuggles under, and he just sighed happily at me and said, "I love housewife season!"

Sunday, September 30, 2012 3:33pm

Chester just "braved" the new dog wash across the street! He's so fluffy now!

Friday, October 12, 2012 3:34am

"You're clean enough. Go away."

Thursday, October 25, 2012 8:05pm

Kiddo was just describing why he likes his (male) science teacher so much. One of the reasons is that, when the teacher calls on one of the kids, the teacher points and says, "You. Whaddya got?" I can totally see kids eating that up! :)

Monday, November 5, 2012 7:55pm

Now that I've got my Kindle, I have a hopeless addiction to romance novels. I just love them. And with reader comments, I can usually find pretty decent stories on Amazon for .99 or even free.

Every now and again, though, a real stinker finds its way through my filter. Friends, I offer you the most groan-worthy and unintentionally hilarious line (so far, at 3% read) from MIDNIGHT'S WILD PASSION:

"Seducing this woman would be like training a wild leopard to eat from his hand. She hissed and snarled now, but under a master's tutelage, she'd learn to purr."

Wednesday, December 5, 2012 4:50pm

Greatest Hits

Kiddo just asked Curtis to help him because the homework question was something like, "in the Declaration of Independence, Thomas Jefferson stated that the power to govern comes from the _blank_."

And Milo said, "Dad, I've looked all over the place, and I can't find anything. But when I've heard phrases like this, the answer is usually 'from the heart.' Does that sound like the right answer?

"I'm Totally not supposed to have this pen! You should probably chase me through the house or something."

Friday, December 28, 2012 4:35pm

Curtis got the game Skyrim for Christmas, and he read up on it and determined that it was fine for Kiddo to play too. Kiddo's been playing it almost constantly ever since, and it looks like a World of Warcrafty-type game - not my kind of entertainment at all, but no big whoop.

So just now, I came into the room, and on the TV screen, Milo's character is in a room and there are three women tied up with hoods over their heads. Which was NOT COOL WITH ME.

So, I said, "Milo, if there's torture in that game, you either need to find a way to avoid it or you can't play that game anymore."

and he said, "Oh, it's not torture, Mom, it's just the Dark Brotherhood."

and I said, "Okay fine. If you ever encounter the Dark Brotherhood again you have to get away from it or you can't ever play the game again."

He was agreeable and now he's back to running through the woods and doing whatevers.

The very, very best part of this story? Curtis was in the room when it happened, and he never said a word. This is big you guys! The only times that Curtis and I disagree on parenting is with regard to violence in movies and video games. And I always back off because Curtis is such a good man and a good father, and I don't pretend to understand the male fascination with violence (like, I really have a problem with the male fascination with violence). Anyway. It's a small victory...It's not like Kiddo will give up those games and switch to Farmville any time soon...but I'll take it.

Monday, December 31, 2012 5:47am
omg, I have a funny husband.

Okay, so you remember how Milo's friend has a stomach issue and he's puked in various locations in our house?

And that one of the times, he puked on Milo's sneakers and then said that it was a good thing that he hadn't puked on his OWN shoes, because his shoes were worth so much more money?

Well, he's coming over later this morning and Curtis just said that he needed to get some work done before the friend shows up and starts talking his ear off.

And then he went into his impression of this friend: "Um, Mister Duhn? I just shit on your couch. It's a good thing that I didn't shit on *my* couch because our couch is just a higher quality couch..." ...anyway, 15 minutes later, and I'm still bursting out in giggles every few seconds.

2013

Wednesday, January 2, 2013 5:36pm

Kiddo and I ate an early dinner at the mall and there was a family with two daughters sitting behind us. I'm going to guess the girls were, maybe 11 and 9.

And the older girl was telling about her day: "We were in the lunchroom and Melanie pulled a HUGE bottle of perfume from Victoria's Secret called 'Pure Seduction' and she sprayed us all with it and then for the rest of the day, I felt like I was seducing everyone!"

...which was adorable on its own. But what made it so much funnier was how incredibly hard her little sister started giggling when the big sister finished her sentence. It made my day. :)

Monday, January 21, 2013 3:16pm

My kid handles getting all of his privileges taken away with such good humor, you'd swear he enjoyed it or something. Seriously.

(He also handles getting zeros in Science class with such good humor, you'd think he enjoyed that too).

Monday, February 4, 2013 9:43pm

So me and my neighbor, Gary Acrossthestreet, were both out shoveling our driveways and he came over to shoot the breeze and he was going on and on about how, back when his daughter was at the middle school, he had to do battle with the district to get bus service because our houses are both at the very tippy edge of the village, and, since there are sidewalks the whole way, any children on our road were expected to be walkers (his daughter graduated from the high school recently).

So, he's talking about how crazy the traffic is outside of our house in the mornings, and what a zoo it is by the Tim Horton's, and it's just not a good place for kids to be walking at that time of day.

So yada yada yada. And then, thinking that I'd throw some more misery into his grumpy soup, I said, "Oh and then there's that MEAN crossing guard!"

And he looks at me and said, "Oh that's my father-in-law, Art! He's a great guy!"

Gaahhhhh! Small town life! I forgot that everyone's related to everyone else! :face palm:

Wednesday, March 27, 2013 9:27pm

For most of my life, I've been a magnet for *'complete strangers (always men) with a lot on their minds,'* and tonight the charmer who engaged me was a pimple-faced teenage cashier at Tops, who waaaaaay over-filled my grocery bags, and ranted about 'asshole managers,' and 'this piece of shit store,' and 'when I don't live in East Aurora any more, I'm totally never going to shop at this piece of shit store.'

There were also muttered soliloquies about asshole managers giving all the hours to the new hires "and that just ain't fair," and "I'm the exact thing the asshole managers hate: I've got a brain!" etc. etc.

I nodded sympathetically, like I always do, but on the inside, I was thinking (like I always do), 'Dude, you need a yoga class, meditation breathing, new age music, a gifted prostitute, something. You need something or your head's totally going to explode.'

Friday, April 5, 2013 4:07pm

I was driving down the road, giving a loud and enthusiastic performance of The Zombies' "She's Not There," and I looked over at Kiddo and thought, 'he has no idea how lucky he is to have a mother who likes to sing.' I wonder if he was thinking the same thing? ;) (well let me tell you bout the way she looks! The way she acts and the color of her hairrrrrrr!)

Monday, April 22, 2013 3:15pm

Whole family in the living room, Curtis and Milo are studying for a science test:

Curtis: "What is the difference between weathering and erosion?"

Milo: "(gives the correct answer)"

Shelly: "Right. So, weathering is what causes the paint on our house to flake off. Erosion is what's happening on our hill."

Curtis: "Yes. And Milo, that also answers the question, 'how weathering and erosion annoy your mother.'"

Friday, May 31, 2013 4:42pm

Kiddo and I are watching Step Brothers. I'm either the worst mother ever or the coolest. I suppose if I hear Kiddo say, "Got a nice V of hair going from my chest pubes down to my ball fro," I'll have no one to blame but myself.

Monday, May 27, 2013 9:42pm

One of the things I love about my kid:

Milo: "I'm really tired. I'm going to bed. Good night!"

Me: "Night Kiddo!"

Curtis: "Night Kiddo - at some point, I still want to hear your new song."

Milo: "Oh yeah."

(he goes upstairs, presumably to bed....and appears 20 seconds later with his guitar)

And now he's playing his song for us.

Monday, June 3, 2013 4:23pm

If it weren't for body language, I would be positive that my cat despises me. But no. She loves me. She can't help it that the tone of her meow sounds like, "leave me alone, I hate you!!"

Monday, June 10, 2013 3:31pm

My child came home from school, discovered me awake and looking at my phone in bed, started talking about his desire to spend this summer making an album. He got excited, and brought a few instruments into the bedroom so he could tap keys, play chords and whistle a few of the parts to the new song in his head for me.

Raising a child who's CONSUMED by something... It's charming and adorable and CONSTANT. That's pretty neat.

Monday, June 10, 2013 9:17pm

Literally true: My husband watches Apple keynote speeches like they're sporting events....and then he has us watch a highlight reel. Holy buckets.

Wednesday, June 12, 2013 12:44am

So I said, "Oh Chester! You BREATH is so NASTY!"

And Curtis said, in a silly deep voice, "I AM THE BREATH OF DEATH."

Which, of course, reminded me of this song.

Which, of course made me rewrite the lyrics to fit our dog today:

[Church song: "I Am the Bread of Life"]

I am the breath of death

I am made of chipmunk corpses

and miscellaneous wildlife poop

No one should inhale around me

unless he wants to vomit

And I will gross you out

And I will make you gag

And I will ma-ake you wish

you had no sense of smell!

Tuesday, July 2, 2013 2:20pm

I had a dream last night that Kiddo was little (3-4 or so), and he was leaning in as I traced my finger over his face and counted his freckles. We used to do that all the time, and I woke up smiling and a little sad.

Monday, July 8, 2013 8:14pm

Just drove past a teenage couple leaving the Kone King. The boy was pushing the girl, her milkshake, and her crutches in a Tops shopping cart. They were both laughing, but that poor girl was folded up like a pretzel. I can't imagine she was very comfortable. :)

Monday, July 8, 2013 10:54pm

Another post about how hilarious dog people are: So tonight, I was at the Tops in Orchard Park because I had $.40 off a gallon of gas. I had Doggy with me and he was hanging out the window watching me.

A woman pulls in, coming toward us and pulls up to the other side of my pump. She's got a tiny little dog in the back seat of her car and neither of them noticed my dog when they pulled up.

So she gets out of her car, starts the gassing process, and notices my dog. "Oh my goodness!" I hear from my side (I couldn't see her, the pump was too tall).

Then I hear her open the door to her car and the next thing I know, she's holding her dog a few feet away from my car so that our dogs _can look_ at each other. Her dog looked like a (very cute) mix between a chihuahua and a Jack Russel terrier, and it mostly looked nervous and wiggly.

My dog was doing everything to declare how friendly he is, -short of saying the actual words- and he was wiggling and whining and making a spectacle of himself.

Both dogs were getting pretty worked up and suddenly (this whole exchange only lasted a few seconds), a light bulb must have popped over the woman's head because she very abruptly said, "Oh! I'm making this worse, aren't I?" and quickly put her dog back in her car. I laughed and then my tank was full and I waved and drove away.

Dog people. They're (we're) just a little out there.

Tuesday, July 9, 2013 2:08am

"You know damn well that we're hungry."

Friday, July 12, 2013 9:59pm

Meditation for one fair summer evening: Go outside and stand perfectly still. Un-focus your eyes so you're just using your peripheral vision. And take it in as thousands (or maybe only dozens) of fireflies look for new friends along Cazenovia Creek tonight.

Thursday, July 18, 2013 2:06am

So earlier this evening, Kiddo and I were playing Scattergories and our letter was M and the clue was "Term of endearment."

So, we're going through our various answers and we get to that one and I said "My darling," and Kiddo said "Milliliter." He read it as "term of measurement."

...So Curtis called me 'Milliliter' from the other room just to add to the hilarity. :)

Wednesday, July 24, 2013 7:30am

How to be ever so helpful: Tap tap tap on your kid's bedroom door, hear that 'oh god I overslept' dread-gasp on the other side. Say "Kiddo, it's 7:15!"

And then, when you hear him say (his voice, dripping with severe annoyance), "My alarm clock is set for 7:20,"

THEN, say, "Oh! Well enjoy those last five minutes!"

DIFFERENCE MADE.

Tuesday, July 30, 2013 2:08pm

My husband's a stand-up comic today:

Me (being serious): "Somehow I'm on Anthony Weiner's mailing list..."

Curtis: "Did he send you a dick pic?"

Me: (lol) "NO! But the subject line was 'I'll let you decide,' and I was just thinking that it seems to me we've all pretty unanimously decided about this guy..."

Curtis: "Did you decide, 'Oh yes, yes, it's very impressive?'"

Me: (lol) "You're an idiot."

Monday, August 12, 2013 4:32pm

Milo's entertaining friend is over for a sleepover.

He walked in, left his shoes in the middle of the mudroom floor, dropped his underwear ON THE COFFEE TABLE (who needs a suitcase when all you're bringing is underwear?), strolled up the stairs, found my kid, and yelled "OH MY GOD IT'S A PEDOPHILE!"

Curtis wearily said, "Want to get a hotel room?" I begged "YES," and now we're both hunkered down with our earbuds blocking

53

out the noise. I managed to stay in the main living space for 13 minutes before I needed to remove myself to the bedroom.

Wednesday, August 14, 2013 6:52pm

Greatest Hits

So, at the beginning of the summer, Milo started playing music with two kids from East Aurora. One of the kids (the keyboard player who's obsessed with Billy Joel) is Milo's age and he knows him from the middle school talent show. The other kid (the drummer who appears to have no musical ability whatsoever) is two years younger and best friends with the Billy Joel kid. They're both very nice boys and they only stay for a couple of hours and then they go home, so it's all good.

Okay. So, the first time these two boys came to our house, the younger boy's grandparents dropped them off. And the grandparents seemed a little nervous about dropping their grandson off at a house where we didn't know him and he didn't know us. So, to put them at ease, I said, "Oh, they'll be fine! My husband and I are both home...there's no guns in the house, no drugs in the house...they'll be fine."

And the grandparents both smiled at me but seemed a little shocked. And it's stuck in my head that I may have said the wrong thing there, and considering that this is rural Western New York, I had a feeling that it was that I'd equated guns with drugs as being bad things to have around children.

But the grandparents said nothing, and I said nothing, and these kids have been over quite a few times with no problems, so I'd basically forgotten all about it.

Until today, when the young kid shows up carrying this big plastic rounded case, which was about the size of a keyboard, except that the top side was rounded like a folded taco. And I asked him if it was a keyboard (though that made no sense since the older boy is the keyboard player, but whatever), and the kid says, "Oh no, that's my new bow!"

"Oh! Are you a hunter?"

"Well, I'm allowed to, but mostly I just do target practice at my grandparent's house."

Yep. If there's ever a wrong thing to say to someone...I'm going to manage to say it! ::rolls eyes::

Monday, September 16, 2013 8:48pm

I'm so annoyed with myself. My mom invited me over for dinner and I went, and it was delicious and then Mom said that my dad was going to a special choir practice because the church is going to have an 'oldies from the '60s and '70s church music' concert in early October.

And I wanted to ask him to let me go too - I know all those songs! I love all those songs! And since it was just a once a week for a month commitment, it sounded like a perfect opportunity, tailor-made for me.

But then I got to thinking about how much I prefer that I'm unrecognizable, but that if I show up at St. Bernadette's with my dad, people will know who I am - and that I look the way I do, and no doubt they'll all be secretly thinking 'isn't it *so awesome* that Slutty Shelly got fat?' And on and on and on (like the song says: this old town never did really care that much for me).

And it was all ego laced with vanity and pride and old hurt feelings. And even though I knew these were *Shelly issues* and that the folks at church would, at the *very least* be kind to me (and more likely, they would be wonderful and welcoming and happy to see me), I still didn't say to my dad, "I want to go sing songs out of the Glory and Praise book with you!"

And then, before he left, my dad turned on Fox News and they were doing their 'Here's all the ways Obama is ruining everything that was clearly perfect until he came along' shtick, which added annoyance and anger and you-aren't-one-of-us-ness to my already icky feelings of ego and vanity and pride, so I just hung out with my mom (which was very nice!), did my best to filter out the television, and then let my dad walk out of the house without ever saying "I want to go too! I'll sing any part you want me to sing! You can stand me far away from the microphone if you want! You don't even have to give me a songbook - I know all the words because when I'm alone in my house or my car, I listen to those old songs, and I sing along! And I know that doesn't make any sense considering how I feel about religion in general and Catholicism in particular, but, whatever! I still want to go! Take me with you pleeeeeease!"

So anyway, now here I am, sulky, mad at myself, and wondering what they're singing right now. *sigh*

Barely managed mental illness is such a bitch.

[Comments]

- Lol! Yes! Although most people my own age don't know I'm home and wouldn't know me on the street. And I like it that way. I used to have a pretty uncanny ability to make straight girls loathe me. And I like being exempt from male attention, and I really like not seeing the gleeful, absolutely real expressions on my female former classmates' faces when they do discover who I am. So I mostly stay home, and I have an ultra-cute dog, who adds beautifully to my own invisibility, and I hang out with family and new people who don't know to be shocked by my appearance, and that usually works for me. It didn't tonight though.

- Hometowns are just hard. They're full of people who knew you as a child and a lot who only really know your parents' version of you. There are connections to the past EVERYWHERE, and when your past is as loaded with wrong choices as mine is... well, that shit gets complicated.

Friday, October 4, 2013 9:11pm

The folk choir at my parents' church sounded wonderful tonight! What's crazy is that they only did one song that I was expecting: the Sr. Janet Mead version of the Our Father, which is so much fun.

56

But nothing from the St. Louis Jesuits or Ray Repp, etc, etc. So, they should probably just do a few more concerts so they get the rest of the songs covered. :)

Saturday, October 12, 2013 9:25am

Kiddo: "Dad says I can't play [this videogame] around you, though, because it's so violent."

Me: "Oh good! Well as long as you're not exposing ME to violence, that makes it all okay!"

Thursday, October 31, 2013 7:11pm
Greatest Hits

Welllll crap. You know how sometimes, before you become a parent, you create all of these ideals and intentions for how you're going to parent, and then, when you actually -are- a parent, you feel you should probably stick to those ideals, even if, in practice, it totally sucks??

Well, tonight, before Kiddo left to go trick or treating with his girl-who's-just-a-friend-who-he's-in-love-with, Kiddo and I were eating our dinner and watching last night's South Park. Did you see it? There was a running tagline throughout. Can you remember it?

"She queefed in my face!"

Greaaaaaaaaat.

So Kiddo's getting ready for his night out and he imitates the Canadian accent of the guy who kept repeating it (over and over and OVER again), "She queefed in ma face!"

And I said "Oh god, Kiddo, you can NOT say that out loud, Ever! But particularly not in front of your girl-who's-just-a-friend-who-you're-in-love-with!"

And then Kiddo says "Oh, it's okay Mom, it's just another word for Fart."

So then, all those old ideals of 'If your kid asks you a question or displays ignorance, even if it's embarrassing, you have to tell them the truth in the most age-appropriate way,' kicked in.

And he's 14. So, age-appropriate means 'You've got to just tell him.'

So I took a deep, deeply uncomfortable breath and said, "Oh Kiddo. No it's not. I'm sorry. This is going to make both of us miserable for a minute." <another deep breath> "Okay, when a woman and a man are making love, particularly in certain positions where her legs are raised ... ." (and I did use all the words, I'm just dot-dot-dotting because, well, you know) "... --and it's not something she can control! It's just totally embarrassing, and it just happens sometimes!"

So, Kiddo made the face you'd expect the whole way through and then finished getting ready, and then I dropped him off to trick or treat with the girl he's in love with, and I think it's *fairly* certain that he won't use that word in front of her!

GAHHHHHHHHHHH.

Friday, November 1, 2013 2:58pm

Spare a kind thought for people who are hurting today. I had Doggy at the vet for his rabies shot and a nail trim, and everything went fine and the techs at the vet are so sweet and funny and Doggy's so cute.

But then, as I put Chester into the car, a married couple came out, and the woman had thin, wispy, just-starting-to-grow-back-from-cancer hair, and she was leaning heavily on her husband, and she was crying so hard she could hardly see in front of her. I can't even imagine how shattered she must be, losing a beloved pet and facing her own mortality at the same time.

Saturday, November 2, 2013 11:12pm

snicker I just remembered a snippet from our conference call with Curtis' parents earlier today. Gramma Sonie was asking

Kiddo about trick or treating, and she said, "did you two make out like bandits?" ...and there was perfectly shocked silence from Kiddo. ...The silence was actually funnier than an answer would have been!

Thursday, December 5, 2013 2:54am

"Mama? Kitty dropped your earplug on the floor?

And I picked it up because she's not supposed to have it?

So I should get a treat because I'm so good, right?

Right Mama?"

(Notice Mary. She's never been sorry for anything in her life).

Wednesday, December 25, 2013 12:50pm

Up until last night, I was *So Pleased* with myself for actually sticking to a smart and modest budget with regard to Christmas presents. But then I put the gifts under the tree and was like, 'Dang. That is a LAME number of presents.'

Kiddo is lovely and grateful and not greedy --this is definitely my issue, but when you've just got one kid, who's a teenager and doesn't need/want much, and you don't blow the budget for the first time in your life? The presents under the tree can _only_ look lame!

Tomorrow I'll be proud again. Today I seem to have fallen victim to the 'Amount Spent = How Much Love I Feel' mindset. :/

2014

Friday, January 3, 2014 8:44am

A dump truck filled with snow just went by the house. I love quirky little things like that, where, if you weren't from an area that gets huge amounts of snow, you wouldn't know that, when there's no good place to push the snow off to the side somewhere (say, Main Street in the village where there are few parking lots), that they have to load it into dump trucks and take it somewhere else. :)

Saturday, January 11, 2014 8:19pm
Greatest Hits

Well folks, it's been a long time since I've had a good, painfully embarrassing story to tell, and great news! The wait is over!!!

It all started earlier this evening at Delta Sonic car wash. For the uninitiated, Delta Sonic up-sells more than any other place on the planet: "How about the Super Kiss Plus?" "Can we offer you Rain-X and Body Gloss?" "Will you please donate $3 to the ASPCA?" And I was so good! "Nope!" "No thank you!" "Yeah, okay."

But then we got to the interior wash section, which was the real reason I was there. And the cute boy (those darn cute boys!) asked if there was anything special they should focus on. And, not sensing the trap, I said, "The back seat. I'm going to have kids in formal wear in there tonight and it's filthy."

"Oh!" he said. "Would you like us to shampoo the seats? It'll get all that ground-in dirt out, and it's only $10!"

"Yes!" I said, like the Dumbest. Person. Ever. Born. "That sounds like a Brilliant idea!"

So Kiddo and I hung out inside Delta Sonic and waited a half hour while they did the 10 minute interior wash - and, because I hadn't yet woken up to my mistake, I was feeling fantastic! Like they were giving my car extra attention and aren't I so lucky?!

And the clock is ticking away. We were due to pick up Milo's friend-who's-a-girl at 7:15, and it was 5:40, but I wasn't worried - he's a boy! They only take 3 minutes to get ready!

So. They finish with the car. And there is plastic wrap over the front seats. Because the seats - all of them - are DRENCHED. They've just been SHAMPOOED. And I just PAID TO HAVE THIS DONE. ON PURPOSE.

Driving home with the windows open did not help.

Draping the back seats with thick towels and spending 20 minutes giving those seats an enthusiastic lap dance did not help.

The seats were just as drenched as ever. Because they'd just been shampooed.

So finally, I had to break down and send the poor girl's mother a text asking her to drive. I told her what I'd done, mentioned my now-clammy butt, told her Curtis was asleep and I can't drive his standard transmission car, the whole shebangabang.

And she was lovely and said she'd be happy to drive, and, if I don't mind, maybe they can take some pictures of the kids at our house?

Oh, sweet mother of god.

I looked around at the house, with its charming inches of dust and dog hair, the counter LOADED with dirty dishes, the Christmas decorations in bags and boxes on the living room floor, the empty cardboard boxes from Amazon that are such a nice size that I can't possibly throw them out (I might need them!) - ALSO on the living room floor.

We had 30 minutes. So I start freaking out and screeching instructions at Milo, and I started unloading the dishwasher.

And, because I was being efficient and fast, I quite literally (but not purposefully) threw two dinner plates across the room where they shattered spectacularly.

So while I picked plate shards out of my bare feet and struggled to keep from going into a full panic attack, Curtis came flying out of the bedroom asking if everyone was okay.

And, instead of praising the gods that he was awake and telling him to call the girl's parents and tell them we could drive after all, I just started barking instructions at him too.

We somehow got the house -close enough- to not-disgusting, and we took some very cute pictures of Milo and his date, and they left and all was good.

And Curtis turned to me, laughing as they drove away, and said "You managed to say 'shit' AND take the lord's name in vain in the three minutes they were here."

(Did I mention the girl's mother is a motivational speaker for Catholic teens?)

The moral of the story: If a cute boy tries to up-sell you at Delta Sonic, no matter how good the offer sounds, SAY NO! With that said, the house looks nice and my car smells fantastic, so it wasn't a total disaster!

Sunday, February 9, 2014 3:42pm
Here's why my kid is funny: he's doing a poetry assignment and he said that the meaning of the poem "Do Not Go Gentle into that Good Night" is YOLO.

Saturday, February 15, 2014 4:18pm
You know what feature I hope future Kindles have? "What page you were on when you fell asleep with your thumb on the screen."

Tuesday, March 11, 2014 5:03pm
So it's gorgeous today, and Doggy and I were sitting on the steps watching the cars go by.

But in the winter, I usually put salt on those same steps, so when we came in, I said "Curtis, is my ass white?" (From the salt, you/he knows what I mean!)

and he said: "uhhhhh, as I recall, yes?"

Tuesday, March 18, 2014 6:21pm
Random thought as various children rush through the auditorium on their way to the back practice rooms before the Spring concert: 'Oh good. That boy's pants are too short too.'

Wednesday, March 19, 2014 3:19pm
So last night, in the middle of that eternal band/chorus concert, I had to get up and leave the auditorium because I got the giggles and couldn't stop.

The string orchestra was playing down at the base of the stage (basically the pit, only it's a wide-open area on the same level as the first row of chairs). And, to enhance the sense of intimacy, the lady director was sitting in a chair directing them.

And the song was slow, but her hand movements were waaaay faster than the song seemed to indicate. And she was hunched over, and I leaned over to Curtis and said, "wow, she's really getting a workout, isn't she?"

And Curtis didn't act like he'd heard me, and I was feeling a little miffed, because I wanted to goof off, and he wasn't playing along.

But then he leaned in, really, really close, and murmured, "I bet she gives a hell of a handjob."

WELL. That was the end of my composure. I had tears streaming down my face, my shoulders were convulsing, and finally, I had to leave the room.

Wednesday, April 23, 2014 5:43pm

Greatest Hits

There comes a time in every parent's life when they look at their child - the child who they love and adore more than anyone else on the planet - and they think, "Oh my god. Where did I go wrong?"

And it happens to everyone! Your parents felt that way about you at some time or another, your intimidating "perfect" friends have felt that way about their own kids before (not that they'd ever admit to it, of course). It's universal. We know this.

But still.

So as you know, we are a family of three long-haired people. Keeping drains moving is a task that requires attention. I've written about this. Recently.

Well, the shower has this awesome do-hickey thing that I bought at the grocery store for $2, and it has tiny little holes that keep all the hair from going down the drain. It's icky to clean out, but way better than cleaning out a drain.

So Kiddo was cleaning his hair out dutifully, but lately, he just up and stopped. So I initiated my usual punishment (outdoor dog-poop-scooping for 15 minutes for every infraction), and he was doing better about remembering.

But today, there was a bunch of hair in the drain again. So I told Kiddo that he needed to go clean his hair out of the drain and then go clean up dog poop, and he said "Uh-uh! I cleaned my hair out this morning!"

And I said, "Well, there's a bunch of hair in the drain, and it's not mine and it's not your father's..."

And he said, "No way. I cleaned out my hair, just like always, and I rinsed it down the sink."

Me: "Wait - you did WHAT?"

Kiddo: "I rinsed it down the sink!"

(Kiddo notes my probably very amusing facial expression)

Kiddo: "…Isn't that what I'm supposed to do?"

Me: "NOOOO! You put it in the garbage!!!!"

Kiddo: "Oh! Well, it went right down…"

Me: "GAAAAAAAHHHHHHHHHHHHHHH!!!!!!!!!!!"

New punishment: HE gets to clean out the nasty drains from now on.

Tuesday, May 20, 2014 10:31pm
Greatest Hits

#TheWorldWeLiveInToday :

So, as usual, I was the last straggler through the manned checkout line at Tops, and, as usual, the same teenage boy was there to check me out.

This time, however, I had Kiddo with me, and Kiddo was wearing his Pixies hoodie.

So the teenager, who has only ever grunted pleasantly at me, gets super animated, shooting devil horns, and "Dude! Pixies!" and whatnot.

So Milo goes up ahead of me so they don't have to shout past me while I'm loading my groceries on to the conveyor belt and the kid is like, "Dude, how old are you?"

And Milo's like, "15."

"Dude, 15?? Where do you go to school?"

"East Aurora High."

"Yeah, I graduated last year. You play guitar, man?"

"Yeah."

"You should try out for the talent show."

"Yeah, I played it."

And the kid frowns at Milo and says, "Wait. Who ARE you?"

"Milo Duhn."

And the kid starts cracking up and says, "Dude!! I'm friends with you on Facebook!!!"

Friday, June 20, 2014 6:41pm
Curtis just said that his dad informed him that both Curtis and Kiddo need to wear "real dress shoes" for the dinners on our cruise.

To which I repeated, for the millionth time, "We can't afford a free cruise. it's pathetic."

And Curtis nodded sagely and said, "we can't even afford to get within the proximity of money."

Monday, June 23, 2014 4:02pm
Milo is unloading the dishwasher and he's listening to a stand-up comic in his earbuds (Spotify is a little dangerous for when kids reach the stand-up comic phase. God only knows what corrupting crap he's exposing himself to). And every 30 seconds or so, he'll chuckle or "heh heh." But just a second ago, he burst out with a loud "HA HA HA HA!" Whatever it was, it tickled me too.

Thursday, June 26, 2014 1:05am
Rachel Maddow was just preparing us for bad news from the Supreme Court with regard to birth control.

I'm someone whose doctor advised her that a second pregnancy would likely be just as dreadful as the first one (two and a half pound babies? They're not cute with all those tubes stuck everywhere and machines breathing for them). So I don't get to have any whoopsie pregnancies. I need 100% reliable, no bullshit, no 'what shape is the moon tonight' or 'crap, I thought you bought condoms last week' birth control.

So I have an IUD. Which, if you don't have insurance (or haven't met your deductible yet, which is why I know my information is up to date), costs $850 up front - just for the device. That doesn't include the prescriptions you take ahead of time, and it doesn't include the doctor visit where they dilate your cervix and place it just so (and even with the heavy-duty pain and relaxation drugs, it still HURTS, and you need someone to drive you).

The idea that any employer would be arrogant enough to claim he knows better than his employees' doctors is so stupid, it's laughable. That this case has gone to the US Supreme Court - and that an insane "conscience ridden" boss (conscience ridden, my ASS) might win this case? It's unforgivable.

An IUD is a 99.99% reliable, completely reversible method of birth control. That means, I didn't need to get my tubes tied and my husband didn't need a vasectomy. --And we're as protected as people who had those permanent surgical procedures. If science had found a way to cure HELLP Syndrome, and we'd wanted to have another baby, that would have been an option for us.

I'm so mad about this. It wasn't so long ago that the birth control pill was invented. And Catholic fathers of married daughters thought they had the right to weigh in on their daughter's birth control choices. And how did those women react to their father's opinions? "Thank you for your concern, but you don't get to have a say in this private matter that is *MY* damn decision, *DADDY.*"

But somehow we think it's okay that our *bosses* should have that right??

I really hope Rachel's wrong. I really hope the Supreme Court shows Hobby Lobby the door. And, of course, I'd really love it if no self-respecting woman ever supported Hobby Lobby again. Your boss isn't your daddy. And even if he was, what you do with your cooter is none of his damn business.

Tuesday, July 1, 2014 12:16am

I think my favorite thing about Pinterest is when people post things like "Eat Right and Get Fit Now!," and then their very next pin is for Peanut Butter Oreo pie.

Saturday, July 12, 2014 11:38pm

3-week-old, random newspaper quote that is still cracking me up:

"He was literally a pillar in our community."

Tuesday, July 15, 2014 7:13am

I asked Curtis to cut my hair and take 2-3 inches off the length. Except, Curtis hasn't been to a barber in over 25 years.

I was pretty sure things weren't going well just based on how he seemed to be cutting too fast. But I held my breath and trusted. At some point, he said "Wow. Cutting hair's a lot different from cutting wrapping paper."

Anyway, the end result is a rather adorable, slightly longer than chin-length bob, and a husband who, 10 minutes after the incident, was still having a hard time not crying. I think I'll stick to cutting my own hair in the future. It's too traumatizing for Curtis. Now we know.

Tuesday, July 15, 2014 3:55pm

We got a mailer addressed to "Resident" today that was totally TAILOR MADE for my kid!!! A brand new All-Ages local venue/recording studio called The Music Room has open mics every Thursday from 7-11, AND it's just a few blocks from our house!!! Best News EVER!!

Tuesday, August 12, 2014 4:45am

I'm sitting in bed reading an article printed on paper. And I'm a little sleepy, so I scooted down in bed and turned off the light...

And was so surprised that I couldn't read my article anymore! Nothing spoils a reader quite like a light-up Kindle. ;)

Wednesday, August 27, 2014 2:06am

Oh! Oh! I have a MARVELOUSLY funny, TRUE story, courtesy of my grandmother, who shared it tonight at Game Nite:

So a man rings her doorbell, and she goes to answer.

He says: "You don't remember me, do you?"

And my grandmother says, "Well, you're familiar, but no, I don't know who you are."

"I'm Paul Such-and-so. We met at Some-other Such-and-so's wedding."

Gramma says, "Oh yes, of course!"

Paul says, "Yeah, I've been meaning to drop in and see you for a while, now. I drive past your house all the time, and I always think that I should stop in and check on you. But I'm always going here or there, and I've never had the chance. But finally, today, I had some time to come by and check in on you."

So my gramma says, "Well that's very nice of you! Thank you!"

And Paul says: "So, how old are you?"

Gramma says: "91."

Paul: "Oh. I'm 80. Well, it was nice to see you!"

And then he left.

Gramma took it in stride. She thinks that it must have been pretty dark at the wedding reception, and he must have thought she looked pretty good, but that he must have had a different opinion in the harsh light of day.

(and then Aunt Laurie started singing "Don't The Girls All Get Prettier At Closing Time," and everybody laughed our heads off)

Saturday, September 6, 2014 8:51pm
Life/ back to school edition:

Me (mom tone): Milo, don't leave your backpack in the middle of the floor.

Kiddo (grunting teenager tone): okeh.

(Short pause)

Kiddo (pleasant, funny, human tone): Wow! I haven't heard you say that in a long time!

Thursday, September 11, 2014 8:29pm
Today in the Wegmans parking lot, a gorgeous, regal woman with excellent posture, perfect flowing hair, a cart full of canvas-bagged groceries, and wearing gauzy dress that I coveted, stood four cars down from me with her car remote in her hand pointed at her car. Her expression, posture, and arm were basically like, "unlock, you fool!"

...and then a few seconds passed, and the car didn't unlock, and I watched as her eyes drifted to the vanity license plate (MRTAX), and then her entire demeanor changed, and her shoulders folded in on themselves, and she muttered "Oh jeez!" and skittered across the parking lot.

Her car wasn't in the next row or the next row over from that, so I don't know where the heck she ended up. I was so tempted to call out "I've done that, too!" or some other commiserating thing, but she didn't seem the type to find humor in everyday mistakes, so I let her be and went and did my own shopping.

Thursday, September 18, 2014 8:16pm

My day just went from 'Fine, thanks' to WONDERFUL! I picked Kiddo up from his band practice and we drove the entire way home with him singing melody and me singing harmony to "Daydream Believer" on the radio. It's been a long time since I could convince Kiddo to sing along with me in the car. It felt so good!

Thursday, October 9, 2014 4:23am

Curtis: "So you've got a birthday coming up. Do you want anything?"

Me: "Oh, as usual, I want everything and nothing."

Curtis: "Actually, I *can* give you one of those!"

Friday, November 14, 2014 5:26pm

I'm certain that, even my own parents, when they brought newborn-me home from the hospital, did not gaze upon my face with such constant loving wonder as my dog does.

If he could sing, I suspect my dog would break out in Joe Cocker's "You Are So Beautiful" at least once a day. I find I like this very much. :)

Wednesday, November 19, 2014 10:53pm

Milo: "I always look at other families' pictures, and they're always hiking or whatever, and we're nothing like that."

Me: "I'm sure if you looked at our pictures, it would look to other people like we have a really full life, too!"

Milo: "No. They'd see we have a dog and that we're always in front of the TV."

Me: "Oh."

Milo: "Wait-- did I just make you feel bad??"

72

When you're snowed in, there's no place to go to escape the blunt truth of a teenager.

WHEN are they re-opening the schools? :/

Thursday, November 20, 2014 2:44pm

I found a plow guy on one of the Facebook yard sale pages, and now my guys are trying to mark the edges of the driveway for him.

Friday, November 21, 2014 11:56am

One thing is certain. You KNOW all the local hippies and doomsday preppers are feeling *pretty* smug right about now! ...eating all their homemade breads and kitchen window lettuces and canned goods like they're the kings of the world...

Sunday, November 23, 2014 6:45pm

WOW, it is a whole other (way better!) world today! Crews have been hard at work, hauling massive truckloads of snow out of the village. There's on-street parking and even bike lanes! You can see the traffic circle, and, while its still slushy, and the side streets aren't perfect, it's not terrifying like it was. Now it just looks like we had a big snowstorm. It doesn't look like the apocalypse just happened. Hooray!!

Sunday, November 23, 2014 7:14pm

The line at Kone King is only slightly shorter than the line was at Tops. We're so hardcore here. ;)

Friday, December 26, 2014 3:44pm

I really hope he's not up there writing another 'I hate my mother' rock song. Those suckers hurt. And now he's got a stage to sing them on. That ought to be fun: "Okay, this next one is called, 'My Mother is Useless, Part 17. Hope you like it!"

2015

Wednesday, January 28, 2015 3:05pm

Me: are you going to be a dick all day or can you just be grateful that I'm driving you all the way to Guitar Center?

Kiddo: how about a little of both?

Wednesday, February 4, 2015 3:53pm

Also today, the end of the driveway has been absurdly narrow from the giant snowbanks, so I used the metal ice pick tool and widened it by A LOT. Now, hopefully, every time we leave the house, our car won't get felt up like a schoolgirl in a Japanese subway porn clip.

(and yes, I have been giggling at my cleverness ever since that sentence popped into my head. And yes, I DID hide this post from reputable folks!)

Saturday, April 4, 2015 2:32am

I had a really, really, really good winter. I felt strong and happy, worthy, kind of pretty even. Just good.

And then last night, I was singing on stage at open mic, and the song was in the wrong key for me, and just like a flip of a switch, I thought, "God, I'm so fucking ridiculous, what the fuck am I even doing up here?"

It happens every year. The snow melts, and I go back to being the version of myself that I can't stand. I thought this year might be better because I'd felt so remarkably great over the winter.

I'll probably delete this soon. I just needed to confess it out loud.

Saturday, May 2, 2015 5:57pm

My mother gave us this chair that she no longer wanted.

Mary says, "I love this chair! It doesn't smell like animals!"

Sunday, April 5, 2015 1:10pm

My long-deceased kitty, Mika, came to visit me in my dreams last night. Curtis and I were walking through our old neighborhood, and she was following us, like she always used to. It was so nice to see her again!

Saturday, May 23, 2015 1:01am

So Doggy and I took our walk much earlier than usual tonight. And our regular walk takes us past a couple of bars. Normally we don't encounter anyone, but tonight, 3 drunk frat-types stumbled out of 189 Public House, and one of them dropped his formerly unopened enormous can of beer. So beer is squirting every which way, and he grabs it up, cracks it open and shotguns it while his friends cheer him on.

I was standing about 10 feet away, wrestling the dog, who very much wanted to sample his first taste of beer.

Finally, the boy finished, and they all noticed me.

One of them says, "I'm sorry you had to see that, ma'am."

And I said, "You boys be careful getting home tonight."

And another of them said, "Oh yeah, we're walking!" And I said, I'm very glad to hear that."

...and I just went through that whole long setup to state that them calling me 'ma'am' and me calling them 'boys' felt like the *most right thing* in the world.

Wednesday, May 27, 2015 7:49pm

I got my hair cut tonight, and the girl was genuinely lovely and sweet. And we were talking about what to do with my hair, and I said, "I hated my last haircut. The girl cut the sides so short, and it just never looked right." And the girl's nodding, and *completely* without guile, she said, "Yeah. As soon as you walked in, I thought, 'I wonder if that's how she *likes* her hair!'"

My guess is that she'll be lying in bed tonight, thinking, "oh god. That probably wasn't a very nice thing to say out loud....." :)

Thursday, June 11, 2015 11:11pm

Dear always super friendly, capable, and lovely Tops employee: That was a huge bummer tonight, when you invited me to participate in your breath-takingly ugly bigotry. Look, I know I look just like you. But please don't assume I think like you.

I know I have bigotry in my heart - but unlike you, I consider it a failing and not something to be celebrated.

I hate that I know this about you now.

Friday, July 17, 2015 10:42pm

I kind of just killed it singing backup on Gimme Shelter. I'm feeling a little rock star-y right now.

Tuesday, July 21, 2015 10:35pm

Today's "Gee thanks, Captain Obvious!" advice comes from WebMD: "To avoid heat-related ankle swelling, try to avoid the heat."

Wednesday, August 5, 2015 8:19pm

Doggy and I went out and played ball because it was breezy and glorious this evening, and I noticed there was a mama deer with her two babies down by the creek. So I grabbed my Kindle and my lawn chair and set up camp to watch them and read and pet Doggy. It was so lovely!

At one point, the deer all perked up their heads in alarm and ran off, and I wondered what had spooked them. A few minutes later, I saw and heard two young lovers hiking along the creekside. The boy waded into the water fully clothed and crossed the creek to the place where the deer had been. The girl stripped down to her bikini, and followed in after him, scolding him and laughing and making a ton of noise.

The two continued past me, completely oblivious to mine and Doggy's presence at the top of the hill (he was silent for once), and it was all very sweet. A idyllic evening.

......Until the jagoffs down the road had to bring out their bangbang sticks and start shooting up the evening.

That's the problem with being, literally, the last house at the edge of the village. It's farmland just a little ways down the road, and I'm sure they don't think anything about getting in a little target practice. But noise carries, and I find it deeply annoying, and my dog finds the randomly-timed noises *completely terrifying.*

So now we're in the house, Chester's enjoying a little peanut butter slathered on an old bone, and the jagoffs are still shooting their guns. At least (I assume) they're not shooting at anything alive. *sigh.* It was a nice evening while it lasted. :/

Wednesday, August 26, 2015 10:08pm

Years and years ago, back when we still lived in NC, Curtis and I got a generic Sleep Number bed. And it's served us well, but we've had to replace the pump a few times, and there have been other, mostly fixable issues with this bed over the years.

Well, for the last year or more, Curtis's side won't hold air for more than a day or two (he's patched it before. But it's a lost cause by now), so the shop vac lives over on his side of the room, since he needs it to pump up the bed so frequently.

So tonight, we were lying on the bed, talking about my dental crisis, and how the timing just couldn't be worse, what with Milo's ear surgeries, and all the other crap that's been piling on for so long.

And so we're lying there, and Curtis said, "Damn, I'm sinking again."

And then there was this pause, and he said, "Wow, it's like my side of the bed is this perfect metaphor for our lives. It loses air, we pump it up, it loses air, we pump it up..."

Sometimes that's just all you can do, is keep pumping up the damn bed. -Then again, we have a bed to sleep on. We're fantastic. Our problems are just annoying. Really, really effing annoying.

Wednesday, September 2, 2015 8:54pm

You know, one good thing about impending house guests is that I finally just throw shit away. All the rest of the time, I look at all the crappy gee-gaws and do-dads floating around my house, and I'm always all mealy mouthed, and "Oh, but there's nothing wrong with that *fill in the blank piece of nothing*, I should just let it keep floating around because I bet someone wants/needs it." When the houseguests are closing in, I turn into Oprah: "YOU'RE going in the trash! And YOU'RE going in the trash! EVERY THING IS GOING IN TO THE TRA-ASSSHHH!"

Wednesday, November 11, 2015 12:10am

Curtis was going up the stairs to bed. I'm going to be downstairs for a while.

I said, "Will it bother you if I play the ukulele while you're sleeping?" And he said, "only if you're standing at the foot of the bed."

Friday, November 20, 2015 3:29pm

I was just sitting upstairs on the bed with my overly attentive cat (who only becomes overly attentive if she's cold or hungry), and I picked up my phone and said to Siri, "Tell Milo to feed the animals."

And before Siri had even computed the order to send, from downstairs, I heard the excited tappy-tappy sounds of my dog's nails as he dashed to the living room to tell Milo to feed the animals.

Monday, November 23, 2015 6:10pm

Did you ever notice that you never, ever fix the bathtub drain when you have clothes on?

Friday, December 11, 2015 2:10pm

Tonight, my car was completely encased in ice when Pink Floyd practice ended. I'd been standing still for 3.5 hours and had some energy to burn off, so rather than waiting for the defrogger to melt it, I went at my windows with the ice chipper and some muscle. I felt exactly like Edward Scissorhands with ice flying every which way. It was so much fun. :)

Monday, December 28, 2015 10:51pm

Do I have any Pink Floyd fans amongst my local friends? I'm going to be performing Dark Side of the Moon with some super-awesome musicians at the end of January (I'm doing the lady parts).

It's a benefit concert to help get the word out about The Music Room. Let me know if I can give you a flyer to hang at your place of business and see me for tickets.

I love these people. Come hear us play!

2016

Wednesday, January 6, 2016 2:12pm

If you had a special occasion coming up, would you pay to get your hair and makeup done? I have two sides at war in me right now about this show coming up. On one hand, I'll be the only female on stage and the only person not playing an instrument. I should look as beautiful as I can. On the other hand, I've spent almost all of my adult life consciously striving to be invisible. So, going out of my way to look nice (as opposed to just blending in), feels foreign and weird and icky, and how do I even know I wouldn't need to itch all that shit off my face within 15 minutes anyway?

I don't know. I don't know. I don't know. Someone tell me what to do. Also, I looked at a local website that offers both hair and makeup, and it said it would be about $100. For hair and makeup. To wear for one evening. Which is slightly less than what we spend on a week's worth of groceries.

And this show is special. It's really important to me. I haven't had a special occasion that I genuinely gave a shit about in over a decade. But look at my profile picture. That is honestly and truly what I look like every single day. I'd feel ridiculous all gussied up. Aaaaaaaaaagggggggggghhhhhhhh.

[Comments]

- Wow, I am so pleased with these answers! They really helped me solidify my feelings with the whole issue. It's not about the money, I guess. It's that I'm afraid I would spend all that money, and come out looking ridiculous. The hair's probably a no-brainer. I'm pretty sure that it's not my hair that's hopeless, it's just me. I think someone with an ounce of patience and some skills (or even just some hairspray?) could probably do something where my hair's near my face but not IN my face, and that might be nice.

82

- But makeup. ugh. I sweat when I'm nervous and everything makes me itch. These are all good and valid reasons to stay the hell away from makeup. And still. There will be times during that show when every eye in the house will be on me. I've been jokingly referring to my solo (Great Gig in the Sky) as "Early 80s, full bush, porn noises." They will absolutely be looking at me. So I think I probably should look more special than what I or a friend can do, you know?

- Thank you so much everybody! I love all of these answers - so varied, but all so useful! My big night is January 23, so I've got time to mull everything over. Felicia made the best point of all, which is, that when all this is over, I'll wonder why I was stressing about it. I mean, we are talking about a rock show in a tiny venue in a suburban plaza. It's not like I'm going to be playing Madison Square Garden or anything. BUT. There will be six (sometimes seven) of us on stage. Three of us are aged 43-55, and the other three are early 20s. I have an old-lady crush on all three of those glorious young men. (Is there anything on this earth prettier than a 20 year old? I say nope) So, standing next to the older guys, I feel like I fit right in - we all look our age and perfectly fine/whatever. But standing next to those pretty, pretty boys? I feel like a partially deflated, gray hot air balloon. And I know that all the hair, make up, and flowy clothes will not turn me into a completely different, decades-younger person. But I wouldn't mind a bit of a perk up, you know? I'm not looking for anyone to offer to take me home, but I'd like it if one or two people --who don't have to say it-- say, "Wow, you look really nice!"

- Anyway. Maybe I will take a trip over to Sephora. I would very much like to have a conversation with someone who knows what they're talking about. I have never in my life picked out a lipstick color that I liked on myself. A shade or two darker than my own lips is such good advice, thanks.

- Lol. I made an appointment for hair and makeup. I watched a couple YouTube videos on makeup, and decided that I'd be spending sooooooo much money on colors that might look stupid, and applicator brushes, and etc, etc. Just watching the videos was giving me palpitations. Also, I mostly watched videos on applying makeup to fat faces (ugh, sometimes I fucking loathe accurate search terms!), and I found myself falling into a pit of despair. So rather than go further down that path that makes me feel like I should never leave the house under any circumstances (a feeling I fight a lot, actually), I decided to close YouTube, call a salon, and hope for the best. My appointment's at 2:30. I have no idea how I'll keep myself looking nice until we go on at 9. Wrap myself in tissue paper?

- Also, I ordered new bras and they came yesterday. None of them fit right, but one of them was only off in the cup size. Other than that, it fit quite nicely. Even before I started stressing about hair and makeup, I was thinking that I absolutely HAD to get a new bra. I replaced all of my bras with pullover, sport-ish bras when my baby stopped nursing, and I haven't bought another one since. My baby. Who will turn 17 next month. --Again, people are going to be watching me moan into a microphone. Someone is probably going to glance at my chest, and it would be nice if they didn't think, "Huh. Don't most women usually have two separate breasts?"

- Singing-wise, I'm ready. I've got this. I'm going to be really good. Looks-wise, I'm doing what I can and saying extra prayers to St. Jude, the patron saint of hopeless causes.

Sunday, January 10, 2016 5:19pm

It's Duck-and-Cover Day here are the Duhn's! We've got snow squalls outside, and a child screeching cuss words every few seconds here on the inside!

I can't even TELL you how much I'm biting my tongue, but trust that my yap is zipped, and I'm not saying, "I told you so," since that would likely get me murdered.

He has this huge project due tomorrow. Huge. And he had all of Christmas break to do it, and his dad and I were like, "Kiddo, it's going to take you longer than you think it's going to!"

And he was all, "You don't know anything! I know what I'm doing! Stop trying to take away all my fun!" (okay, maybe he just said, 'I know what I'm doing' out loud, but the other two things were definitely implied).

(as soon as I put my earbuds in and he didn't have an audience, he did settle down. And Curtis has already disappeared upstairs. That seems very wise)

(oh boy. Now more cussing.)

Tuesday, January 19, 2016 2:50pm

Something to help me keep things in perspective (Overheard at Game Nite): "I don't know who Pink Floyd is and I don't know what he sings." LOL

Saturday, January 23, 2016 6:52pm

So, some of you know my glamour saga around this night - in that I don't have the faintest idea how to even DO glamour. So anyway. I hired out the hair and makeup tasks. I think I look pretty great, except when I get right up on the mirror, and then I'm like, 'Geeeeeez, I look old! Look at all those wrinkles!'

I told the lady I hadn't worn makeup other than mascara since my wedding day 17 years ago, and first she laughed nervously, and then she said, "we'll keep it really light."

Her version of light and mine are different, clearly, because, oh man, I am powdered within an inch of my life.

So anyway, I walked in the house after the appointment, and Curtis said, "WHOA," and I was like, "I look really old, don't I?" And bless him, he said, "No you look really hot."

So give that man a cookie, because if he'd agreed with me, I'd probably be barefaced and crying right about now.

Anyway. I'm wearing all clothes from my former life as an employed person, except that I got a new bra for the occasion-

-one made of satin and isn't a pullover (see above re: glamour). It is so awesome! Unfortunately, even with my shirt on, I'm a bit like a teenager getting to first base for the first time. I'll have to remember to not feel myself up when I leave the house. A satin-encased rack feels delightful! I recommend it! -Of course, it's also freaking tight as shit and I can't wait to take it off, but meh, I can deal for a night anyway.

So yes. I'm sure there will be pictures and videos to come. I'm too nervous to anything but pace, so wish me luck!

Sunday, January 24, 2016 1:47am

Alrighty! I'm home, home, home! So far, only one person has posted videos of me, and if you go to my wall, you can see them. I woke up yesterday morning with a head cold, and I spent the last two days eating zinc tablets and throat lozenges like they're candy and drinking SO MUCH water and tea. Fortunately, the cold stayed in my sinuses, so I sounded a little 'cold-y', but I had enough power to hit the notes.

The show was fantastic. Everybody played well. We all made little clunky mistakes here and there, but overall, we were great. I hope everybody feels they got their money's worth.

As the backup singer, I had lots of time on stage to be mindful of how lucky I am and how grateful I am to David Hallett for giving me this opportunity. I'm so glad I took those moments and really felt it - not just the nerves and the fear (of which there was so much!), but also the JOY and the LOVE and the FUN.

Now, I am going to go take off all this makeup, which looked very nice, and lasted the whole night. I don't care to apply more for a very, very long time), brush all the hairspray out of my hair, take some nighttime cold medicine, and sleeeeeeeeeeeeeeeeeeeeep.

Saturday, February 20, 2016 1:24pm

My mother-in-law just reminded me how, when Milo learned to ride a bike, we allowed her to bring him a celebratory can of Coke, because sodas were a very, very rare treat.

And just this morning, I was scolding Kiddo, telling him he's got to eat at home more often, because sustaining oneself on snacks from the 7-Eleven is gross and unhealthy.

I can't get over how perfectly this exemplifies the difference between 'my child is old enough to ride a bike,' and 'my child is old enough to drive a car.'

Friday, March 18, 2016 3:32pm

Whenever we get in the car after Open Mic and I've played, I always make Kiddo praise my performance. And, as you might expect, an overtired 17-year-old tends to not be as effusive as I'd prefer.

So anyway, I'm doing my usual fishing for compliments, and he's like, "Good! You were good!"

And I had also sung a silly song with one of the other grown-up regulars, and so I asked Milo, "And the one I did with Steve? Was that one okay?" And Milo said, "Literally, you sounded like a Mormon couple."

Feb 25, 2016 11:42:29pm

Greatest Hits

I just saw the craziest thing. So we live above a creek, on an eroding hill, about 20-30 feet up from the water, and we see a lot of geese, all the time.

So, I'm standing at the kitchen sink, and it was like I saw a meteor flying over in my peripheral vision. So, I looked up for real, determined that it was a Canada goose, and started laughing because he was flying so low, his feet had to have touched the roof of the house. BUT THEN, he flew straight into the brush-y trees that line the back of the property. And there's no leaves yet, so it was just like a net of sticks.

And he went ass over teakettle, his body bumper-carred around for a second or two, before gravity finally pulled him, headfirst (feet perfectly pointed up), down, out of my sight line.

And I was like, "Oh my god, he needs help!" So I threw on my Crocs and my winter coat (the winter coat being the universal symbol for 'I haven't put a bra on yet today'), and ran outside with the dog, who was very curious to see what all the fuss was about.

And I'm carefully wading through our mud-and-poop early-Spring yard, wondering what the heck I could even do for an injured goose who's crash landed on a hill too steep for my big ass to climb.

So the dog is already barking, because he's spotted five deer who had been peacefully enjoying their afternoon on the other side of the creek. And I get back to the spot where I last saw the goose, realize more fully just how steep that hill is, and I start hearing (but not seeing) crazy rustling below me. Finally, after about 5 seconds or so, the goose freed himself from the brush he was stuck in, and he flew down to the creek, where he started honking in the most perfect rage ever.

So, the deer have long since departed, the dog is still going bananas - now at the goose, and the goose is absolutely losing his shit at us from down in the water.

And finally, I dragged Puppy back inside, went upstairs to locate a bra (Kiddo was due home any minute. It would be traumatizing to see Mother freeballing around the house), and I have been grinning to myself ever since, formulating exactly what colorful words that poor goose must have been yelling at us. I think the goose must have been fine, but I bet that crash landing really HURT.

Saturday, April 16, 2016 11:23am

Kiddo was just blowing his nose in that way that people do when they feel like, if they just blow harder, maybe something will finally loosen up in there.

And so, he's like, "BLOOOWWWW! BLOOOOOOWWWWW!!! BLOOOOOOOOWWWWW!!!"

And the dog's ears were keeping time with Milo's blows, moving back farther and farther on his head.

It was like the perfect doggy communication of, "Oh wow, that noise is awful."

Tuesday, April 26, 2016 4:09pm

I only hate selfies because any time I try to take one, I always end up looking like I'm trying to act like this is the least awkward and bothersome Pap smear ever.

Tuesday, May 3, 2016 10:17pm

[Link to article about Delayed Sleep Phase Disorder]

Curtis texted this link to me. He was SO HAPPY!!

Me: Omg Curtis, people like us are really rare! And we found each other!"

Curtis: Well, we found each other at Eat N Park. In the middle of the night.

Monday, May 16, 2016 3:49pm

Miscommunication of the day:

Me: Kiddo? I found a plantar's wart on the bottom of my foot...

Kiddo: I AM NOT GOING TO GET THAT.

Me: No, but you might!

Kiddo: Why the fuck would I get a wart on the bottom of your foot???

Me: ????

Me: ....

Me: (laughing) Ohhhhhh, no! No! I'm telling you that I found a plantar's wart on the bottom of my foot, and they're contagious, so you need to check your feet and make sure that you don't have one!

Kiddo: (comically relieved) Ohhhhhh. Yeah, okay.

Wednesday, May 18, 2016 12:28am

Doggy and I were back home from our very short, late-night walk, and I was sitting on the steps feeling decrepit, and this young couple comes along. It was dark, so all I could tell was that she had very long, very boofy hair. And they're doing the we're-so-drunk-we-have-to-hold-each-other-up-but-that's-okay-cause-we're-in-love walk.

And they're drunk, so they're not modulating their voices appropriately, so Chester dashed to the corner of the yard to greet them and woof at them.

And the boy knew Chester. "Oh my god, I haven't seen you in years! Oh my god it's so good to see you! I'm sorry I can't play with you but I'm a grownup now!"

And the kid had actual, literal tears in his voice. So I'm thinking he must have been away at school, or maybe he's graduated now, feeling aimless, scared, restless...better go get drunk...oh my god, it's a dog from my childhood! I'm an old man now! No one told me nostalgia would hurt so much!

Anyway. It was charming and sweet and relatably pathetic.

Wednesday, May 25, 2016 3:49am
Greatest Hits

Okay, I'm finally at my computer, and I want to write this down now, before I forget. Also, I'm using real names and places, and it's a little snarky, so be cool:

Yesterday was the 120th birthday party for the long-dead former housekeeper of the Jolls House, which is now home to the Orchard Park Historical Society.

I lived in Orchard Park briefly: My parents bought their new-construction home in 1988. I went to Orchard Park High School for my Junior and Senior years. Then I went away to college at WVU and came home for two summers before taking up year-round residence in Morgantown, West Virginia.

But here's what you need to know about Orchard Park: Orchard Park is rich people. Somehow, even the (very few) people with no money are rich people, if you catch my drift.

My mom has belonged to the Orchard Park Historical Society for a long time. Twenty years, give or take. And she has held various positions within the organization. For years, she complained to me

91

that there wasn't enough publicity. That they even brought Santa in on a firetruck one year for a Christmas open house, and no one came because it hadn't been publicized well enough.

So I said, "Gosh, the publicist should make up a Facebook page. That's such an easy thing to do, and it could bring in so many eyeballs." Well. Lo and behold, there actually already WAS a Facebook page. It had a couple of poorly centered, church-basement-y pictures, and a long, obnoxious application to join the historical society. That was it.

So *I* said, "I could take over the Facebook page. I'll put up shareable 'flyers' when there's something to advertise, and I'll put up old pictures of Orchard Park other times. I'm sure there are tons of old pictures in the Jolls House!"

And Mom thought that was great, and the publicist contacted me and told me I should please take over all publicity duties, because she didn't want them anymore. And I was like, "Um, NO. I'm doing this as a favor to my mom. I genuinely, positively, and truly do not give a rip about the Orchard Park Historical Society. But I'm bad at saying "I love you," so instead I'll maintain the Historical Society's Facebook page, and hopefully my mom will get the message." (I suppose I didn't use those exact words)

Anyway, it all got straightened out, and I'm officially in charge of the Facebook page, though there are four admins, total.

At the end of last year, a new lady, Chris, joined the Historical Society. And Chris is a writer and a community-minded person, so she took over the job of publicist. I like her a lot. She's warm and lovely. And we've met a few times, and she's gotten me into the Jolls House to go poking through their pictures.

And Chris is ALWAYS asking me to join the Historical Society, and I'm ALWAYS telling her I'm not a joiner, and that I sincerely have no interest in the Historical Society. Yes. So Chris has been on me to post about this birthday party for more than a month now.

And I had said that I would post as the date got closer, and she agreed, but then would send me reminders a few days later. And every time, she would tell me how much she wanted me to attend, "so that everyone can tell you what a great job you're doing!"

I created a nice little ad for the party and posted it to the Facebook page, and then I posted another one that she had made the Friday before the party. But I never even acknowledged her requests that I attend this party. I was not going to go to a birthday party for a dead woman! I have no trouble entertaining myself! Yada yada yada.

But she kept on, and finally I emailed back, "Chris, you're RELENTLESS!!" And she replied, "LOL, you should talk to my kids! But please come! My self-esteem depends on people coming to this party!"

ARGH. Because now she's said the one thing that's going to get me to go: Essentially, "I'm insecure. I'm so afraid no one will come." Who can't sympathize with that?

So, ugh, FINE, I'll go to this dang party.

So I walk into a full house. Of course. The former publicist spots me and comes over to chat me up with some ideas, and then Chris sees me and comes over and gushes about how happy she is that I came.

So I stood there with them for a couple of minutes, and then a woman comes down the stairs, and says, "Are you Shelly? Sue wants to talk to you up in the office."

Sue is bossy and awesome, and I'm simultaneously terrified of her and a little in love with her. She's somewhere in her early 80s, but she's still sturdy, if that makes any sense. You know how most people into their 80s are starting to look breakable? There is nothing frail about this lady. She looks like she could probably still pitch a softball game.

So I go upstairs to the office, which is a very narrow room. My theory is that, when they created an upstairs bathroom, they just cut one of the bedrooms in half, and this office is the half they didn't need for the bathroom. It's NARROW. And on each side, there is a desk with piles of papers, and at least one filing cabinet. Even someone who doesn't get claustrophobic would totally feel like they were drowning in this office.

But Sue and another older dude (neither of whom seemed to get the memo that wealthy Orchard Park people are supposed to be underfed, by the way) were in there, and then Sue pulled me deep into the room, and I started literally sweating into my bra, because holy shitballs, that was close quarters.

And she's asking me questions and dictating instructions, and here's where the real conversation starts:

Sue: "Oh, you moved away and came back? Are you glad you came back?"

Me: "Every day. I love being home."

Sue: "Where did you live?"

Me: "Well, I went to school in West Virginia, and I ended up staying there seven years, and then my husband and I spent nine years in North Carolina."

Sue: "What Is WRONG with North Carolina these days??? Oh, they're just terrible!"

So I shrugged, and as carefully as I possibly could (not knowing what point she was trying to make, or how either of these people lean politically), I said, "Well, it wasn't like that when I was there. For one thing, we lived in the Research Triangle Park area, and people are bright there. Regardless of how they vote, the people are...are ...bright."

And Sue fixes me with one of those mischievous, *I see you, and we're totally allies* looks (thank God), and she turns to the man. "What do YOU think about all this?" And the man stands up from the desk, and he's probably 6'4, 250 at least, and he's READY for COMBAT.

And Sue's got a grin a mile wide, and she's READY for COMBAT.

And now I can feel the sweat starting on my upper lip.

Man: "You know how it is when you've got raccoons in your basement, and you don't care who gets them out, you just want them out? Well, we've got raccoons!"

Sue (yelling): "Of course I care who gets the raccoons out of my basement! What a stupid thing to say!"

Sue turns to me: "Are you for Hillary?"

Me: "Yes! Or…you know…Bernie… …"

She waves her hand at me like, 'Yeah. Bernie. That's cute.'

And the man starts in on Hillary: "She was in charge of keeping Bill's women quiet! All of his mistresses! She was the one who shut them up!"

And Sue completely ignores him, and she says to me, "Give me your address. I'll send you a sticker for your car."

So, the man leaves the room, Sue hands me a pen and paper, and I breathe a little easier. The big scary man is gone, leaving one less body in that tiny, roasting room.

Sue waits while I write out my address. She's saying things like, "Now make sure you put it on the inside of your car. You don't want anybody ripping it off."

And then she says, "I know where you live, you know."

Me: "You know which house is mine?"

Sue nods: "I drive past it when I go to The Iron Kettle. (The Iron Kettle being a restaurant out in the boonies that has excellent, cheap, no-nonsense food, and is usually filled with 3/4 or more senior citizens)."

Me: "Oh right!" (and, to myself, I'm thinking, 'is she telling me that she'll know if I don't put her sticker on my car???')

95

Sue: "Now about this transgender business. What do we do about it?"

Me: (incoherent nothing)

Sue: "How do you convince people that a transgender person isn't a rapist? Because they're not, you know."

Me: "Right. Well, I mean, you remind them who pedophiles actually are. Pedophiles nearly always identify as straight men, and they seek out positions of power, and they find ways to be trusted alone with children. They seduce children."

Sue likes my answer. "That's right! Now, will your mother want a Hillary sticker?"

Me: "Oh, Lord, no. She's an anti-choice Catholic."

Sue: "So she's for Trump?? How could any woman vote for Trump? He's a misogynist!"

Me: "Oh, I know. He called Rosie O'Donnell a fat-ass. I can't get over that! ...But I never, ever, ever talk politics with my mother. It works out better that way."

Sue: "Ugh. Well, regardless. Your mother is one of the nicest ladies I know. She's so accommodating. And she's just lovely."

Me: "Yes."

Sue: "You're a good kid. You're a kid to someone as old as me, you know. I like you. I'll get you that sticker."

I have been dismissed.

I go downstairs because earlier in the conversation, she had told me I need to get a phone number from the Historical Society president, a man I've met once before and instantly disliked. He's sitting in the front room with three women. I approach with my paper and pen.

Me: "Hi. Um, I was told to ask you for Mr. So-and-So's phone number?"

President: "Why?"

Me: "Um, well, I guess he's been going through all the pictures in the office, and he'll have some for me to put on the Facebook page?"

President: "I HATE Facebook."

Me: "Yes, you've told me that before."

President: "I'm very protective of this place, you know."

Me: "Yes. I would never post anything that would put the building at risk. Most of the pictures I've posted are old-timey ones of Orchard Park."

There was one lady next to the president, who was dressed to the nines in USA gear. Head-to-toe red, white and blue. Red, white and blue dangling star earrings.

She said, "Do you live in Orchard Park, dear?"

Me: "Actually, no, I'm in East Aurora."

USA Lady: "That's where the Made in America Store is! Every single item for sale in that store is 100% made by Americans! You must Goo --now write this down. You must Google Ricky Lee. R-I-C-K-Y. Ricky Lee. I saw him play at the Grand Re-Opening of the Made in America Store. He has this song called, 'Looking for America,' and it should be played in every school, church, and synagogue in the country. It's just--" (And I swear on my dog's life, this woman got choked up. The skin around her eyes and nose got red, the whole shebang) "--It comes from the heart. Ricky Lee. Google it on your computer."

President: "662-XXXX"

Me: "Oh! For Mr. So-and-So. Right."

97

President: "And get the word out to young people that we need new blood in here. I'm 80. I can't run this place forever. And tell them where we are. No one ever knows that we're right in the middle of the village. Can you tell them where we are?"

Me: "Of course! Sure!"

Then the mother of one of my high school friends came in and rescued me. I hugged her tight. It wasn't a 'Hey it's great to see you!' hug. It was more like an 'Oh thank the sweet baby Jesus, I'm rescued!' hug.

And the rest of the visit was pleasant, and the birthday cake was yummy, and then I left.

It's a whole 'nother world at the Historical Society.

May 23, 2016 3:22:25am

It was LATE when I got outside to throw balls for Doggy. So, I took some trash out, found a ball, threw it a single time, and then I heard...

...I had no idea what I was hearing. But Doggy and I both turned to the noise.

And out on the main road, three deer are, single file, running for their lives down the center of the road.

And behind them is a dark red sedan, who totally saw them and had no intention of hitting them, and he turned onto my road, and drove past me. I don't know if the driver saw me or not, but I pointed toward the deer and mouthed, "That was so cool!!" at him, just in case.

He probably did see me, since Doggy went apeshit when he saw the deer. Unless the driver's radio was loud, I'm sure he heard us.

I'm also sure our neighbors speak fondly of us to everyone they meet: "Oh, the Duhns? Yes, they're ideal neighbors. Quiet as mice all day long. ...less so in the middle of the night, though..."

Friday, May 27, 2016 9:51am

In-laws arriving in a few hours. Chester says, "But, Mommy, I thought we agreed that the mess doesn't bother us?"

Wednesday, June 1, 2016 8:30pm

Hickies McGee is strolling around the house looking like the Unibomber. Way to keep it on the down low for your grandparents, kid.

Wednesday, June 8, 2016 1:17am

Me to my husband: "I need to pull my hair back now because I have to make lunches. But first, I want to state that I'm having a good hair day and I want you to notice."

Husband: "Oh yeah, you look very nice!"

Me: "Thank you. Okay, that's all I needed."

Tuesday, June 14, 2016 3:51am

Gilly, our ancient betta fish, has been on hospice care for the last two weeks or so. I keep telling him it's okay to let go, but although he hasn't eaten anything in well over a week, he keeps hanging in there.

This is sad for two reasons: #1: I've never had a fish who was so obviously dying like this. With other fish, it was pretty much 'Alive-and-fine today, Dead tomorrow.' And #2: no one gets a betta fish for any reason other than someone buys one for your kid.

But after your kid reaches a certain age, there's absolutely no reason to get another one. I'm fairly certain that Milo hasn't thought to feed Gilly on his own in over a year. And I have no desire to have a fish. Fish are completely pointless as far as pets go, imo, so Gilly is it for us. This is our last fish. And he's dying a lengthy death.

I can't imagine that he'll still be with us tomorrow, but I also couldn't imagine that he'd still be with us today, so we'll see. Other than the breathing, he looks like a dead fish.

Wednesday, June 15, 2016 1:36pm

I'm too greedy to be a real Socialist, but good grief, Capitalism is absolutely terrible.

Friday, June 17, 2016 3:42am

Me to my husband who was playing Rocket League with his friends online: "Aww, Meatloaf collapsed on stage tonight."

Husband to his guys: "My wife says Meatloaf collapsed on stage. Damn, now I'm hungry. ... (Laughs)... Shell- Danny says he would do anything for food."

Me: "Yes. Me too. But I won't do that."

Husband: ...Danny says his wife won't either. Yeah, well, that's marriage for you."

Saturday, June 18, 2016 2:31pm

I generally try not to say anything about this candidate because I resent that I can't choose to ignore him like I do the Kardashians, the duck people, that family with all the kids, and anyone who's ever appeared on TLC.

I respect them all about the same. --they're all smart enough to get microphones and TV cameras pointed at them (which is not stupid), smart enough to get money for nothing, and smart enough to convince their dupes that wild shenanigans, piousness, and/or plump lips pass for a grand, enviable, worthwhile existence.

Saturday, June 18, 2016 11:23pm

Me to Curtis: "Do you remember that episode of Family Guy when Peter and Lois got really high and believed they were making amazing music, but really they were horrible? Do you ever wonder if biology has made it so that when we hear our kid, he's so unbelievably good, but other people are just hearing some mediocre kid?"

Curtis: "Definitely not."

Sunday, June 19, 2016 9:54pm

Tonight, we say goodbye to Gilly the fish. On this stupidly hot night, I was about to refill my water glass when I realized I had not seen Gilly in a few days. I gave a longer look at his tank, and, sure enough, he was lifeless in his rock castle.

So I gave him a proper send-off, over the hill, and, as I may have mentioned already, tonight is stupidly hot. So after I dumped him, I looked across the (very low) creek and noticed at least a dozen fireflies blinking their welcome to him.

Rest well, little fish. As far as fish go, you were completely fine and very pretty.

Friday, June 24, 2016 12:21am

Tonight's 'Oh right, young folks don't have the same frame of reference as me' moment: a sweet kid approached me after my open mic set, and said he really liked my first song. He asked if I'd written it.

It was Bob Seeger's Turn the Page.

Friday, July 1, 2016 1:00pm

Last night, I had a good open mic set, and I got two big boosts to my musical self-esteem. First, there was a group of kids in the back of the room, and when I started singing, I heard one of the kids say, "Shh! I want to listen!" And second, after my set was over, as one of the kids was going outside, she stopped and said (this is 100% true), "my heart feels warm when I hear you sing."

I think I'll tuck those compliments deep in my brain and carry them with me forever.

Saturday, July 2, 2016 10:27pm

Doggy really enjoys your patriotism.

Saturday, July 23, 2016 3:59am

My cat is sneezy. She'll get actual head colds every now and again, but mostly it's like she's got allergies. Anyway. We were just lying in bed snuggling... And she sneezed in my eye.

Friday, July 15, 2016 7:46am

How did I not know that Donald and Melania Trump have a 10-year-old child named Barron? And that she is 46?? And he's 70? Rich people are so gross.

Tuesday, August 16, 2016 1:47pm

Reason #36,784 why I am so freaking sick of summer: the relentless noise from the (completely necessary) window air conditioners makes conversations impossible. This was the exchange between me and Kiddo just now, but the characters are completely interchangeable. We've all been snappish and pissy all summer long:

Kiddo: #!@#%!!

Me: what's wrong?

Kiddo: Oh, this damn ,,,, never fails t,,,,,,

Me: Kiddo, I can't hear yo-

Kiddo: NEVER MIND!!!!

I'm so desperate for a 40-degree day, you don't even know.

Saturday, August 27, 2016 9:02pm

I thought my kid was smiling at me with great affection. It warmed my heart and filled me with great joy. Then I looked in front of me. And there was his girlfriend. Duh.

Friday, September 2, 2016 8:03pm

Chester made new friends just now.

Our yard is a wide rectangle. The front and back yards are shallow. The village-side yard is where we play ball.

And I could hear girls approaching from the non-village side. And I was pretty sure I was hearing one of them calling "Milo!"

But Doggy was running, and the voices were quiet enough that it was possible I was imagining things.

And then Doggy was running toward me, and then suddenly he wasn't, and then I heard, "MiloooooooOOOOOOOMYGODTHERE'SACORGI!!!!!!!"

And suddenly, I had three cute girls in my yard with their phones out, taking turns cuddling my dog and taking pictures of him.

It was hilarious. It was all, "No! Turn him my way, I didn't get a good one yet!" "Ohhhhhh, I love corgis!" "You are so cute!" "Stand still!"

They were here for *minutes* before one of them remembered where they were and asked if Milo was here (he's not).

Then the girls finally took Chester's hint, and threw the ball, and they all started gushing again, because they'd never seen a corgi run before, and it is unusually adorable. And they took turns throwing, and finally they decided to go off toward town.

And it was adorable. Now I'm going to check Instagram and see if my dog's famous.

Monday, September 5, 2016 6:06pm

Me: Do you know what tomorrow is? (It's our anniversary)

Curtis: I do. And would you like to do anything to celebrate September 6th?

Me: I'd really like to go out for a nice meal.....

Curtis: Do you know here you'd like to eat this nice meal?

Me: I was thinking The Roycroft, but I don't know if I'm really a Roycroft kind of girl...

Curtis: Soooo...like maybe Ted's Hotdogs instead?

Tuesday, October 11, 2016 9:39pm

I went outside at 7:35 to look at the harvest moon, and I got bit by so many mosquitoes that I had to come inside before I ever saw anything.

Seriously. I think people who claim to love being outside must all be lying. It sucks out there.

September 16, 2016 8:04:47pm.

[Youtube Video: What About Bob Dinner Scene]

Milo gets invited to his girlfriend's house for dinner, like All The Time. I'm sure at some point Milo must have mentioned to his girlfriend's mom that I hate (hate hate hate) cooking, and rarely do it. So she invites him over at least once a week, usually more.

So I just picked Kiddo up, and he described in great detail (as he always does), the amazing food he ate at their house. So I said, "You're always good about saying thank you, and communicating how much you like the food, right? Because cooks like to be appreciated."

And he laughed and said, "Oh yeah," with just a little too much emphasis. So now I'm pretty sure this is what it's like at his girlfriend's house when Milo's the dinner guest.

Milo just found Trisha! (not like she was lost, but still..)

1. Milo was a preemie baby. He was 11 weeks early. He weighed 2 pounds, 8 ounces. Trisha was one of his many presents, but we took her into the hospital because she was the smallest toy.

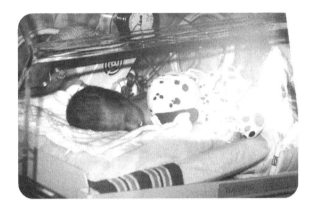

2. Here is Milo's 5th birthday party. Please ignore the cake. I had momentarily forgotten that I do not possess any artistic ability. Look behind the cake. Trisha is on the side table wearing her own party hat - a Duplo Lego. Milo put it on her, I didn't even notice Trisha had been in attendance until I looked at the pictures.

3. Reunited and it feels so good!

Saturday, October 1,, 2016 9:52pm

Milo: ugh, there were four of those black and red beetles in my room tonight! I don't want to sleep in there now!

Me: well, did you just leave them in there?

Milo: no, I scooped them up and put them on the windowsill in the laundry room.

Me: ...????....

Milo: well it was raining, I didn't want them to get wet. I'm not a monster!

Monday, Oct 3, 2016 10:30pm

If Trump had started out with an actually-modest loan of, say, $50,000 from his dad, he would most likely have a few perfectly fine subdivisions with his name on them, and be the guy at the country club that you told your kids to stay away from at all costs:

"He's unpredictable, kids. Janey, if he mentions your developing body, RUN AWAY. Jimmy, if he offers to get blow for you and your friends, RUN AWAY."

Monday, October 17, 2016 8:38pm

I was raped 24 years ago today, on October 17, 1992, and again on October 22, 1992. They were related incidents, but two different attackers. One was my ex-boyfriend, and the other was his best friend.

The anniversary itself really isn't that hard, but I was already shredded from the last week, and from Brock Turner before that.

Thank God I have a dog.

I'm fine, really. It's just a hard day in a hard week in a hard year. Everybody has to tread water sometimes. I'm treading.

[Comments]

- You guys are so wonderful. You know how sometimes you hear a song, and the details of that song feel like they fit your life in a weirdly apt way? Well, there were details around Brock Turner (not the drugged part, I was all-too-sober) that felt too close. And this last week, some of the things Trump said about his latest accusers have been... omg. Way too close.

- When I went to bed with my headache, before I fell asleep, I worried that I'd probably made everybody in my friends list uncomfortable, and that I should get up and delete the post. So I picked up my phone to delete, and there were already supportive and loving replies. And I can't even explain how much I needed that. I was teary, and humbled, and so grateful.

- I woke up to more loving words, and a handful of private messages from people saying, "Me too."

- I spent a lot of years in therapy, and it helped so much. I can still be triggered (obviously), but I can talk about it and hear about it, and it's okay. Sometimes, entire months can pass and I don't think about it-- which is huge, btw.

- If you're out there, and you're a 'Me too,' I hope you'll read the comments on this post and feel them yourself. Even decades later, sometimes it's just too much to shoulder alone.

Friday, October 21, 2016 1:35pm

I went over to Hook's Shoes, for a well-fitted pair of geriatric kicks.

The guy I had was so funny! He was this grandfatherly dude, and he LOVED my feet (appropriately, not in an icky way at all). So when I describe our conversation, I want you to read his voice like he's marveling at me.

Shoeman: Let's see what we've got here. Whoa! You've got a really wide foot!!

Me: I know, it's so hard to find shoes that fit right.

Shoeman (measuring): Look at that! 8E!!

Me: yeah.

Shoeman: Okay! So, do your feet cause you any pain?

Me: Yeah, I have plantar fasciitis, and a Morton's Neuroma. But that only bothers me when I wear my Crocs.

Shoeman: yeah?! What happens then?

Me: within about 30 seconds of putting them on, three of my toes go numb on my right foot.

Shoeman: no kidding!! Okay, lift your skirt a little for me so I can see your ankles better. ...Wow. Look at that pronation!!

Me: Yeah, my foot doctor said that I need to wear shoes any time that I'm standing or walking.

Shoeman: I'll say!!

Anyway, then he picked me out a fine pair of shoes, loaded them up with metatarsal and heel padding free of charge, and offered to send my Crocs to "the old circular file," (which I gratefully allowed). These new shoes feel wonderful.

Thursday, October 27, 2016 3:15pm

I just had a dream that I was at a graduation party that turned into a Trump victory party, and a man got in my face with such vicious glee that I ran out of the party without my shoes. Swear to God. No exaggeration.

Come on November 9th, get here fast. I'm desperate to stop feeling like every man who looks a certain way wants to put me in my place and will do it by force just for fun.

Saturday, November 5, 2016 3:26am

Reason #6,593 why I love my Kindle: I can set the font size anywhere I want. So I can pretend that I don't get that silly middle-ager eye strain.

...until I have to reset my Kindle, and it reverts back to the default font size, and then I get all pissy, and, "What the hell?? Nobody can read words this small! Jeeeeezzzz."

Saturday, November 5, 2016 4:58pm
Greatest Hits

Here's my fun little story for the day:

As you know, Milo got his license. As you also know, I don't like to leave my house. So the other day, I asked Milo to go over to Bulldogs Feed to get dry food for Doggy and Kitty. I took pictures of the packages so he'd know what to get. I told him to introduce himself to Chris and his wife Robin if he had any questions. I understood full-well that Milo would not be introducing himself to anybody.

So he came home, and he had gotten exactly the right items.

I said, "Perfect! Did you have any problems?"

Kiddo: No.

Me: Did you introduce yourself to Chris?

Kiddo: No.

Me: Did you need any help finding anything?

Kiddo: No.

Me: Well that's just wonderful! Thank you so much!

Kiddo: ....

Kiddo: Yeah. I got to the counter, and Chris said, "Do you know what you're doing?" And I said, "I think so..." and Chris said, "Because your mother always gets the 18 pound bag."

My kid can't go incognito anywhere in East Aurora.

Sunday, November 6, 2016 2:34pm
I'm holding tight to my ukulele, my dog, my guys, the beautiful leaves falling from the trees, and the desperate hope that love will always trump hate. Let it be so.

Monday, November 7, 2016 12:35pm

My cat, who loves me, was giving my face an extra enthusiastic scent-marking and drew her runny wet nose across the full length of my left eyebrow.

I'm a tad unsettled.

Tuesday, November 8, 2016 5:06pm

My intestines definitely could not handle another day of this.

Tuesday, November 8, 2016 5:32pm

I follow more black feminists this year, and their posts aren't nearly as loving toward the suffragette movement as white feminists are. And that's good for all of us, I think. First, we feel defensive, then we hear the words, then we stand together.

Tuesday, November 8, 2016 9:04pm

Seriously. I could throw up. I never should have turned on the TV.

Tuesday, November 8, 2016 11:03pm

I was about to say something about how we lived through GWB.... But then I remembered the hundreds of thousands of people we killed, tortured, and couldn't protect.

Yeah. I'm shitting bricks.

Wednesday, November 9, 2016 12:58am

Curtis was trying to talk Kiddo and me down from the ledge, and in the middle of all of it, he said, "I mean, it's going to be a humanitarian crisis....."

So yeah. Even calm, steady Curtis is on the ledge.

Wednesday, November 9, 2016 1:26am

The entire family is in the living room right now. Like, we can't bear to be away from each other. Like, this is.... omg

Wednesday, November 9, 2016 5:28am

It just really hit me, what a shitty, shitty day the nicest, weakest kids are going to have at school today.

Friday, November 11, 2016 5:15pm

I keep swearing I'm going to stop raging into the void, but I guess I ain't there yet.

Wednesday, November 23, 2016 10:34am

Greatest Hits

Weird, partly delightful, then somewhat triggering, 'new normal' morning.

I took Kiddo to school, went to Tops to order dinner rolls for Thanksgiving tomorrow, and then went to the ATM because I gave Kiddo my last $20 yesterday.

When I pulled in, another car was pulling away. I drove up and tried to put my card in, but the person ahead of me had forgotten her card in the machine.

I wasn't sure what to do. The bank wasn't open. So I took her card out, did my transaction with my own card, and took the lady's card with me.

I pulled away, and once I was around the building, I saw a single car parked in the lot, running. I was pretty sure it was the car that had been pulling away when I arrived.

There was a lady, older than me but not old, talking on her phone, and I thought she looked angry.

I pulled up to her, she put on a strained, customer-service/polite-to-strangers expression and rolled down her window.

I said, "Are you Susan (Lastname)? I held up her card. Her whole demeanor changed, and all of her emotions played across her face for a few seconds as she realized her mistake, realized I could have driven off with her credit card, realized that she wouldn't have known her card was missing for some amount of time, and all the other million thoughts any one of us would have had in that situation.

She put her phone down and got out of her car, and her eyes were sparkly with tears, and she looked completely overwhelmed. She sputtered for almost a whole minute: "You've got to be kidding me...I didn't...I did?..you found? Oh bless you! It's Thanksgiving and nothing is...(she gestured to her phone)... you know....never mind...oh, you're an angel!"

And she went on and on, blessing me, and then she reached into her wallet and handed me a $20, and, me being me, I reached for the money as I said, "Oh you don't have to do that!" I'm a dork. And I took the money.

Then I drove over to Elm Street Bakery and got myself one of their amazing breakfast sandwiches with my good deed money and came home feeling pretty normal and good.

And I opened Facebook, and there was a loving message from someone who called me courageous, and then there was a post at the top of my newsfeed from another friend, opening up about how she'd been sexually assaulted as a child, and that her attacker went to jail for it. She'd hinted before, but this time she said it. Because she woke up this morning and couldn't hold it inside anymore. Today, she was ready to join this awful November cacophony of "Me too."

And I think this will be my life (and all our lives) for a long time. Something normal and Happy Life-y will happen, and then something else will remind me that nothing will ever be the same again. That a veil got pulled back from my eyes, and nothing will ever put it back.

I'm not ready to call it a good thing yet, but maybe it was a necessary thing. Maybe I needed that veil pulled. Maybe bringing all that old helplessness and fury back to the surface will give me (and all my sisters) the strength to know how to fight back. Maybe this time I won't have to stay in the dark place for so long. Maybe this time, I won't have to devote so much energy to putting on a convincing portrayal of "Fine."

Because right now, I'm not fine.

And I know a lot of you don't get it. And may never get it. Why one current event led to this reaction. And that sucks, and it's really lonely.

And, dammit, there just has to be a reason why so many of us had to flash back to this specific pain again, all these years later. There has to be some way to channel all that pain together into something good, and powerful, and fucking righteous.

This is the new normal. It's pretty raw. It's a lot sadder. Sometimes it's okay. Sometimes it's even nice. But at least it's honest, so there's that.

Thursday, November 24, 2016 3:30am
Greatest Hits

We ordered this Amazing, OMG, school fundraiser chocolate mint pie. And it was delivered on Tuesday of Thanksgiving week; timed so that people with impulse control could take it to their holiday dinner parties and share it with many loved ones.

We, of course, cut into ours within seconds of its arrival at our house.

ANYWAY, so this evening, I was enjoying a piece of pie, and Chester was right up in my lap, begging me with his sad little eyes while I repeated, "It ain't gonna happen, Chester. Off," which he ignored.

And I took another bite and noticed that the airy mousse topping was giving me just a little indigestion, so I scraped some of it off and scraped it on my plate. I finished my piece of amazing fudgy mint pie and set the plate with the uneaten mousse on the end table.

Chester's shifty little landshark eyes never left that plate. But he was behaving.

Enter the cat.

Like many ample ladies, Mary sometimes misjudges exactly how far her backside sticks out.

So she daintily jumped up on the table, and sat down, asshole first, on the mousse.

It was clearly very surprising.

She leapt off the table with Chester in hot pursuit.

Now, I'm not a prude. I've seen some stuff. But you know what I never, ever wanted to see? A cross-species reenactment of 9 1/2 Weeks.

OMG, you guys.

Tuesday, December 13, 2016 3:19pm
Greatest Hits

We've been stressing a little because the dress code for Christmas dinner for our cruise is listed as "Evening Chic." And you know us. You could put all three of us in zillion dollar formal attire and no one would think, "Wow. Those people are so chic."

So anyway, Curtis' dad contacted the cruise line for clarification of what we can get away with wearing, and the cruise people said, anything from a tuxedo to a button-down shirt with no tie. Just no shorts or sneakers.

So I was relieved until Curtis reminded me that he and Kiddo both only own sneakers.

So then I got grumpy, and was like, "Well, they're BLACK sneakers, that ought to be good enough!"

And Curtis is laughing at me, and then I said, "I mean, you'll be a gracious and well-mannered diner, who the fuck cares what you put on your feet?"

And then Curtis said, "We're punks! Meahhhh!"

And then he's marching through the house, raising his fist, and shouting, "Cruise punks!!"

Anyway. I love my husband. He's the most wonderful kind of dork.

Cruise punks!! Meahhhhh!

Saturday, December 17, 2016 2:02am

I mean, I've lost most of my followers because of my disrespectful bitchery. And I do care. I hate it. ...Just not enough to stop screeching, apparently.

2017

Monday, January 09, 2017 1:05pm

Today's benediction: Should you ever need to set up a Go Fund Me, I hope you have family and friends rich enough to cover it.

Sunday, January 15, 2017 11:28pm

There was this super friendly, gregarious, quintessentially BUFFALO man at the laundrymat. Chatting away to me about this and that, spitting into the trashcan every few minutes. He said he should just go over to the Bar Bill and watch football while his clothes dry, and I said, "They're still playing football?" And he looked at me like I had to be from some other planet and said "Yeah. It's THE PLAYOFFS."

And then he said something about when the Super Bowl was, and I said, "Then you'll have to find some other sport to watch." And then he looked at me like I had to be from another planet in a different solar system, and said, "Well. They're already playing HOCKEY."

He was still very friendly. He stopped trying to talk sports with me, noted that I was folding men's jeans, and asked if I had a son.

"Yes!" I said, "He's a senior this year!"

"Is he going into the military? ..or ..college?"

"He got into UB and Fredonia, but he hasn't decided which one he wants yet."

"What's his major?"

"He has no idea."

"Well tell him not to major in anything stupid. Like English or something. Make sure he comes out with a SKILL. Welders make good money, plumbers, ...Hell, tell him to get his Class A, he can work anywhere!"

I nodded, yes, thank you...and zipped my lips. I figure if I admitted that I'd majored in English and Women's Studies, that might even be a greater sin than not knowing it was football playoffs time.

Saturday, January 21, 2017 3:38pm

I couldn't make it to the Buffalo march for a myriad of reasons (#1: Crowds). But so many people I know and respect made it to Buffalo, and Washington, and Tulsa, and Raleigh, and Charlotte, and Atlanta, and Denver, and NYC. I'm so proud of you, I'm so proud of you, I'm so proud of you. I'm so grateful you went. Today, finally, my newsfeed has made me cry for the best reasons.

Sunday, January 22, 2017 5:08pm

Oh, we voted, asshole. You'll always have a little footnote following you forever: Lost the popular vote by 3 million. And 4 million people around the world marched the day after your inauguration. Trust us, we fucking LOATHE you.

Wednesday, March 8, 2017 12:58pm

We tried and tried to save her. But finally, she met a wind that was just too strong.

Friday, March 10, 2017 4:10pm

sigh

Sunday, March 12, 2017 1:01pm

A few hours ago, a man in a pickup rang the doorbell and asked if he could take our wood. I told him what we've told all the others: someone has dibs on the huge piece but help yourself to anything else.

So he's been out, sawing away for hours. And every now and again, the sawing will stop for an extended period of time, and I'll look out, and he'll be talking to some other random man who'd like to take the wood.

I've watched them shake hands, I've watched them have in-depth conversations over that huge piece (I didn't know, but apparently everybody and their brother wants to haul away the huge piece), I've watched new friendships bloom.

Since neither my spouse nor I am neighborly or outdoorsy, it's been quite a show all day long. A little strange. I have no desire to form shallow bonds based on a mutual interest in firewood, but I feel like I should want to take part in a ritual like that, you know?

Lastly, the original guy (dark clothes) has got to be some crazy he-man or something. Because he keeps picking up these big pieces of wood with one hand and plunking them in his pickup like they weigh about as much as a winter boot. It's unnerving. I'd pick up one of those logs, freeze mid squat, and need to find an emergency chiropractor.

Saturday, April 1, 2017 12:10pm

That poor giraffe. Today was the first time that I woke up and *hoped* she'd had that baby when I wasn't looking. After watching her stare blankly at the wall all day yesterday, I suddenly find myself wishing this could all be over for her sake. It's cool, April! You've healed the nation, now have that baby and heal yourself!

Sunday, April 9, 2017 9:48pm

I'm not saying she's in labor, but omg, her belly is practically sideways right now.

Monday, April 10, 2017 7:41pm
[Youtube Video from Finland, 1979: Gregorius sings YMCA]

So, as you know, I like to play open mic at The Music Room. But here's the thing: I'm a lot (lot lot lot) older than the kids who play there.

And I play a decidedly uncool instrument--- and I don't even play it well.

But though all those things are true, I still love the opportunity to play. And I try to make sure that most of the songs I pick are songs the kids would either recognize, or at least find tolerable for the duration of my three-song set.

And I really, really want them to think I'm a little bit cool. Even just 'cool for an old lady' is fine.

But deep down, in the darkest murky depths of my heart, I'm just a little worried that when I play, this is what those lovely children are hearing.

Saturday, April 15, 2017 7:38am
HOOVES! HOOVES! HOOVES!!!!!!

Saturday, April 15, 2017 10:38am
I'm so glad humans have hands. And towels. /vomit

Wednesday, April 19, 2017 4:59pm
I/we feel constant, all-the-time alarm. It's why April the gestating giraffe was able to so fully inhabit our brains: The world is so awful, so constantly terrifying.

Our expectations of others' moral compasses is so soul-crushingly disappointing, that a silent livestream of a giraffe who might be in labor (for a *MONTH*, omg) was the cleansing spring rain our flame-engulfed brains needed.

I should be on the lookout for another silent live video. Maybe tropical fish this time...

Tuesday, April 25, 2017 6:23pm

No lie, the #1 thing I hate the most about having a late-teens kid, is I can't force him to wear a helmet when he skateboards anymore, and he's not old enough yet to know what mortality feels like (so he never chooses to put one on).

Monday, May 29, 2017 8:37pm

Greatest Hits

In order to graduate, every East Aurora student has to complete 30 hours of community service at some point during their high school career.

Think of all the summer and school breaks when kids can chip away at those hours.

My kid did it all during the months of April and May of this, his senior year (in addition to attending school and starting his new job at the co-op). He's been a little busy. And stressed.

Milo did most of his work at Lothlorian, which is a nearby farm that does horseback riding for kids with disabilities. He was a side-walker, and a barn cleaner, and he loved it. Milo's sweet-natured and patient, so he was very well suited to the task.

But the rules for community service were that you couldn't do it all in one place, so Milo also scrounged a few hours here and there at other places.

Yesterday, he was supposed to finish his last *four* hours by doing yard work at the Knox Farm mansion in the Secret Garden. But apparently there were Important People doing some sort of wedding planning seminar in the Secret Garden, and they were adamant that a crew of stressed out, last minute, Community Servicers could not share the same space.

So the kids did *three* hours of work in other places on the farm, most of which seemed like, "Um, I guess one of you could weed over there...." sorts of things. Which was a real bummer. I'm sure the garden club, or whoever put out the call for a crew of kids to work in the Secret Garden had to be livid. Anyway.

All 30 hours were supposed to be completed by last week, but the principal gave Milo and a few other stragglers an extension.

And he still needed one more hour. He had no idea what he was going to do.

But luck was on his side. One of his classmates sent out a Snapchat last night, asking if anybody still needed community service hours. They didn't have enough kids to read at the cemetery service this morning for Memorial Day.

So Milo, who has no religious or military affiliation (but who can be reverent and respectful), volunteered and was to read a short biography for a soldier whose last name was Frantz. He practiced the biography all last night.

He was a little stressed out, because, how do you pronounce that name? Like Franz? Or like France?

Anyway. I told him to get there early and to ask someone if they had any idea how to say the guy's name, because, under no circumstances would it be okay to mispronounce the name of a person being remembered.

So he did. He arrived a little early, found an old man in uniform, and quietly asked if he had any idea what the pronunciation was. And the man said, "Oh sure! I knew him!" Then the man, who surely had other things to do, walked Milo over to the buried serviceman's grave, told him a few stories about what he'd been like, and gave him the correct pronunciation (France).

I think that's so nice.

What are cemeteries to a teenager, but parks where you go to make out, fall in love, play guitar, tell ghost stories, and smoke? There's a nice big headstone in Oakwood cemetery, with the name Weed on it. It's probably one of the most photographed places in town.

So this was something different. Kiddo went to this ceremony, because reading this one paragraph to a crowd would finally mean he's cleared to graduate. And in the process, he met a man who, just by knowing the person buried under the grass, made it into something meaningful and special.

So yeah. Service. Even when it's something as little as helping a kid understand that those words he's about to read off his phone screen don't come anywhere close to describing a young man who'd lived, it's always appreciated.

And I'm glad Milo had to do these 30 hours. I'm not convinced that he would have gotten so much out of it if he'd just chipped away at it over four years. Doing it all in a short period of time, and having to mix it up with different tasks for different people was probably great. And he learned an excellent lesson: instead of always saying "Thank you for your service," it's every bit as important to say, "How can I be of service?"

Tuesday, May 30, 2017 4:54pm

You can want police officers to be safe on the job, *AND* fully expect police officers and police departments to be held responsible when they kill a civilian who wasn't threatening them.

They're not conflicting assertions. They're not.

Saturday, June 3, 2017 5:22am

Y'all. I just can't even with Lefties suddenly pulling out the well-worn, "Whatever happened to free speech??" schtick with regard to Kathy Griffin.

I will be happy to explain it to you with the exact same clarity that you were able to express when it was the other side under fire for saying stupid, offensive shit:

125

You are free to say nearly anything. No matter what you say (as long as you are not expressly threatening another person), the police will not show up at your house and take away your freedom. You can say it. You can say the N word, and you can dump ketchup on a mannequin's head that looks a little like Trump, you can, you can, you can.

What you are not free from, is the consequences of your actions. If you lose friends, or fans, or your job, that's not the same thing as losing your freedom. That's just being a damn grownup, and facing the consequences, even when they suck, and even when you think the punishment was too harsh.

And you know this. So, stop playing dumb. Seriously. Cut it out.

Saturday, June 3, 2017 10:53am
I was getting my hair cut, and the girl was talking about all the concerts she's going to at Darien Lake this year. And I said, "I haven't been to a concert at Darien Lake since Lilith Fair." And she said, "What's that?" And then I cried for my lost youth.

Thursday, June 8, 2017 5:56pm
Y'all?

I'm hiding this?

From my grandmother?

Because it would hurt her feelings?

*

*

*

*

Elm Street Bakery has the best molasses cookies I've ever eaten in my life.

Tuesday, June 13, 2017 4:07am

All I've done today is cry. I'm supposed to be making a compilation of old Kiddo videos for his graduation party, but literally all I've done is boo hoo hoo for, like, nine hours.

I remember when we were moving from NC to come back home. --a move that was 100% my idea--, and we got to moving day, and I had, like, four boxes lovingly and immaculately packed.

I feel like I'm preparing for this party in exactly the same way: My house looks like a bomb went off, but, dang, that closet no one goes in sure looks beautiful!

Wednesday, June 28, 2017 1:20pm

I almost forgot!!

I would like to take this moment to publicly (to my limited user list anyway) apologize for asserting that Elm Street Bakery makes better molasses cookies than my grandmother.

I was wrong.

Elm Street's molasses cookie is excellent, but it's just a bit lighter and sweeter than Gramma's. Gramma's cookies are darker and a bit denser than ESB. Both are soft and satisfying and dusted with sugar.

But Gramma's are just enough more flavorful that I thought I should make clear that I was wrong, that I know I was wrong, that I understand the depths of my wrongness, and also, how sorry I am for having misled my friends.

Monday, July 10, 2017 7:10pm

Greatest Hits

I've been (stupidly) reading 45's tweets again, with all of his fucked-up word choices. Referring to the "beautiful new healthcare bill" like it's a person. So I came up with this. I may have too much time on my hands.

[THE BEAUTIFUL NEW HEALTHCARE BILL an erotic musing]

The old healthcare bill admittedly still had heart. It was still warm and loving with the children. It treated his parents with kindness, even though he could barely tolerate five minutes of their bitching.

But he couldn't pretend that he was attracted to the old healthcare bill anymore. It's breasts, which had ballooned spectacularly during pregnancy were now saggy and deflated. It's ass, once a firm handle for his powerful thrusts, was now fleshy and dimpled.

The old healthcare bill hadn't bleached its rosebud in years.

And he despaired that the old healthcare bill didn't even bother with basic hedge-trimming unless it was going to be wearing a swimsuit. And honestly, did anyone really want to see the old healthcare bill in its swimsuit?

Yes. He was ashamed of the old healthcare bill.

But the new healthcare bill? He hadn't seen under the new healthcare bill's sexy layers yet. Oh, but his imagination was rich. In his mind's eye, it was barely legal, and not fully formed. It hadn't been beaten down by the ugliness and harsh realities of the world yet.

It was naive, giggled prettily at his jokes, and was impressed by his wealth and paternalism. Where the old healthcare bill regarded him as being far too impressed with himself, the new healthcare bill would praise his wisdom and business acumen. The new healthcare bill would be aroused by a ride in his fancy car.

Oh sure, in the dark recesses of his mind, he knew he should be loyal to the old healthcare bill. It worked hard and remembered to do all the chores that he couldn't bother himself with.

But he fell asleep every night, thinking of the new healthcare bill. Riding him. Bucking against him. Its ecstatic (and surely un-faked) cries loud enough for the neighbors to hear.

As he drifted off, he imagined his neighbors' faces. While he basked in sexual afterglow, they'd huddle together in misery. His satisfaction, their disappointment. As it should be.

Thursday, July 13, 2017 5:08pm

If you send a teen to Tops....

Wednesday, July 19, 2017 5:52am

The saddest story ever:

I was drinking the most marvelous mint chocolate chip shake, made with the last of the ice cream.

A chocolate chip was stuck to the side of my glass.

I tilted the glass and stuck my tongue inside to get that chip.

And dumped half the shake down my bra.

Monday, July 31, 2017 4:56am

The scene: I'm switching the laundry, Curtis is wearing his headphones and playing Rocket League on the Playstation.

Me: Dammit Curtis, you put those heavy jeans that take so long to dry in with the regular laundry again.

Curtis: I CAN TELL YOURE USING WORDS, BUT IVE GOT MY PODCAST ON A LITTLE LOUD.

Me: Oh, I'm just bitching at you, it's probably for the best if you can't hear me.

Curtis: AGAIN, THAT SOUNDED LIKE WORDS, BUT I CAN'T PAUSE MY SHOW UNTIL THIS ROUND IS OVER...

Thursday, August 3, 2017 9:27am

I'm sitting at my desk, which is right next to the window looking out at Mill Road. And eight young track-team boys -probably all 9th graders, went running past the house. They were all tall string beans, but they didn't have their man-shoulders yet. So, 13 or 14 years old is probably right.

And they're all running like they've been doing this forever. They're running like they're enjoying themselves.

They go by, I go back to this daggone task (which I did FINALLY get right, no thanks to GD Windows 10), and I forget all about them.

Until about 3 minutes later, when another kid, same size - skinny, tall, probably a freshman, goes clomping by. And every footfall was forced and miserable, and you just KNOW that his mom probably told him he had to join an extra-curricular this year, and since he's tall and skinny, but not athletic enough to play a team sport, he should "try cross country/track! Then you're just competing against yourself!"

He *was* running. He hadn't quit, so points to him. But that child was NOT enjoying himself.

130

Thursday, August 10, 2017 4:16pm

Greatest Hits

From the Everything Changes files

I nearly always have Kiddo unload and reload the dishwasher because bending and holding that position bothers my back the most. -And he ONLY does the dishes. He doesn't wipe counters, or put recycling away, or take out the trash, or do any of the other things that most of us would include under the umbrella of 'doing the dishes.'

But yesterday, my back felt fairly strong. I was moving just fine. So in the afternoon, I unloaded and reloaded the dishwasher, scrubbed the sink, swept the floor, took out the trash, and had the kitchen looking pretty great.

And then, because yesterday was some kind of gifty miracle day, I unloaded and reloaded and ran the dishwasher again a few hours later, and then unloaded it one more time before bed. Like, I stood and marveled at my cupboards. I don't think I've ever seen them with every single glass, plate, and dish clean and put away.

And then this 'morning' (3pm), I came downstairs, and the kitchen *was still clean.* -There was one fork in the sink, but the counters were still perfect. Not a single dirty glass, dirty plate, empty can, wadded up paper towel, Mighty Taco wrapper, Tim Horton's cup, or unwiped spill anywhere. Not a single crumb.

And my first reaction was euphoric, "Omg, this is what it feels like!!!" Because I've never in the last 18 years woken up to my kitchen looking the way I left it. (I keep stupid hours, so someone has always been in the kitchen by the time I get up)

But then came the grief: pretty soon it'll be like this all the time. Today the kitchen is still clean because Kiddo and Curtis both needed to get up and get to work early. But soon? Soon this'll just be how it is: the kitchen won't get that gross; the tabletops will stay visible, and if there's crap on them, it'll just be my crap, and it'll get picked up with some regularity. There are a few places where Curtis leaves papers, socks, and cords, but he doesn't leave a swirling vortex of detritus everywhere he goes. Swirling vortexes of detritus only happen with kids.

Like, it's one of the things I've been looking forward to: that someday, I'll pick up a mess, and a new mess won't immediately get dumped in that clean spot. And maybe, just maybe, my house might reach a point where I can keep up with cleaning because it never gets overwhelming.

But there's a trade: do you want a visible kitchen table, or do you want the kid, who will dump every bit of his crap on it?

(I know, I know, there are some weird unicorn families where the kids live there -and- pick up their shit. We've never been that family. Everrrrrrrr)

Anyway. I like my cleared off kitchen counters. I like the kid better.

Monday, August 14, 2017 2:34pm

Here's what I wish 45 would say to the Charlottesville idiots:

"Hey marchers! Stop carrying my campaign signs amidst all your Nazi and Confederate shit! You want to flash your dumbass little sieg heils? Whatever. You're nothing new or interesting. If you break the law, we'll throw your ass in jail.

But you have *GOT* to stop putting words in my mouth. I am bad enough all on my own. My soul is tarred enough with my own sins. I sure as hell don't need to be associated with your Blood and Soil bullshit.

I'm bad, but geez, I'm not *Nazi* bad! Maybe stop making it look like I am, you little assboils!"

(And I'm not convinced that he isn't Nazi bad, but I wouldn't mind hearing him promise us that he's just a standard issue, non-violent, Thanksgiving-uncle racist, and not someone who thinks it's time America had itself another bloodbath, you know?)

Wednesday, August 16, 2017 10:04pm

One of Kiddo's upcoming roommates sent an email to say that he'll be bringing a full-length mirror and an iron and ironing board, so no one else will need to bring those items.

Milo read that out loud to Curtis and me. And then all three of us cracked up.

And then I said, "Oh, but I bet a kid like that would smell great!" And Curtis sternly reminded me that it wouldn't be appropriate to sniff our son's roommates.

Monday, August 21, 2017 5:56pm

1. Not smart enough to protect eyesight

2. Not smart enough to know he'd have his picture taken being not smart enough to protect eyesight

3. Dear toxic masculinity: your poster child is an idiot.

Monday, August 21, 2017 9:03pm

I wanted him to be led out with bandages on his eyes so badly! Even if he'd whipped them off right away and yelled "Gotcha!" I'd have laughed.

Tuesday, August 22, 2017 2:58pm

Putting my desk next to the window is one of my happiest choices in years. It's rainy, rainy, rainy today, and I'm watching the rushing rain roll on down the road. I keep cracking the window so I can smell the rain even though it's still humid and I can hear my dad's voice in my head, saying, "You're air-conditioning the outdoors!!"

Thursday, August 24, 2017 3:36pm

Greatest Hits

We took two cars to school today. One stayed at school.

Kiddo drove the vibe, I rode in the passenger seat, and Curtis followed in his car.

Me: Me neither

"...and someday I'll have kids, and I don't know how to raise kids...."

Me: Kids are easy. Don't be an asshole to them and they won't be an asshole right back.

And I jabbered on, ticking off wisdom like a laundry list. And I said, "One thing that always happens when kids go away to college, is their parents will start to seem smaller. Less worldly. Because your world gets so much bigger, and you learn so many things and meet so many people. We'll start to seem ..quaint."

And Kiddo didn't say much to that. But when I shared it with Curtis, he stopped crying long enough to laugh, "You think he ever thought we were worldly??"

Anyway. Today sucks. Tomorrow, we'll see.

Friday, August 25, 2017 10:28am

Kiddo did all of his unpacking on his own. --I actually think he was happy about that. He's an adult ready to adult.

So last night, he sent us a picture of his dorm room. I'd prefer that he strap a Go-Pro to his head so we can see all the things he sees, but, alas, that's not how it works.

So last night, he sent us a picture of his dorm room. I'd prefer that he strap a Go-Pro to his head so we can see all the things he sees, but alas, that's not how it works.

This morning, he texted and said his bed is comfortable. He's light on details, but what he does tell us is enough that we know he's safe and happy.

Curtis just gave the dog a giant gourmet dog treat from the farmer's market. One of the ones that I break into a zillion pieces over the course of many days.

When he came back into the room, I said, "Did you really just give him that whole treat??"

And he said, "Yeah. The house feels weird, and we need comfort."

The house definitely feels weird. And huge.

Friday, September 1, 2017 3:59pm

Curtis, looking in the fridge: Mm, that chicken looks good.

(I always keep shredded rotisserie chicken in there. Easy tacos.)

Me: Do you like chicken legs?

Curtis: I do!

Me: I always keep them separate, because Kiddo likes them. But Kiddo doesn't live here anymore.

Curtis: <<CRYING>>

Me: <<CRYING>>, but what I mean is, Kiddo's not here, so you can eat them!

Curtis: It's like leaving a chair for Elijah. 'We'll keep the chicken legs separate, just in case Kiddo comes home!'

Monday, September 4, 2017 6:52pm

Milo always ate entire watermelons. Like, I'd buy a whole, big round watermelon, and he'd cut it in half and eat 1/2 today and half tomorrow. Or the whole thing today.

So, for years, I've been like, "When Kiddo's out of the house, I'm going to buy those adorable cups of cut up melon, because I just want a little, and I hate food prep.

So today was The Day!! I was in Tops, I had a hankering for a little bit of watermelon, and walk over to the cut-up fruits case, and "EIGHT THIRTY-TWO???"

I put down the cup of cut up watermelon and bought a few slices instead. That was $1.54. Still not a great price, but close enough.

Eight thirty-two. Who am I? The QUEEN??

Wednesday, September 6, 2017 1:11am

I was pregnant on our wedding day. Kiddo was a baby on our first anniversary.

So, this is our first anniversary by ourselves, just Curtis and me (and a couple animals), in our house.

So, it's special. And weird. And totally new. And totally the same. I don't know if we'll do anything special today (the 6th), or if we'll wait for the weekend. But I feel like we should mark this year a little differently. Maybe walk a labyrinth or something. This year is a massive transition. The biggest transition since getting married and becoming parents. We should acknowledge it together. Move forward, hand in hand, eyes open, into the next stage.

Happy 19th to us.

Saturday, September 9, 2017 5:04pm

So I was just out of the shower, laying on the bed with the fan blowing, feeling content in my soul. And the door wasn't closed tight, so the cat came strolling in and hopped up with me. And I was petting her, and loving her, and sadly thinking that she might not still be with us this time next year (her life-long health problems are becoming more pronounced, and the regular old-age stuff isn't going great either). She's got another vet appointment next week, for a huge multitude of reasons, and yeah.

I was thinking with some regret about all the times I've agreed with Chester that she's a bad cat, and, yeah, she's pretty bad, but she's also very sweet and snuggly, and she can't help it that it's in her DNA to trip me every single time I walk into the kitchen. And I was petting her and she was mashing her face against my hand and against my face, and loving me right back...

And then I got the half-second warning: One single, barely noticeably different exhale. Just enough time to close my eyes, but not enough time to get away or even flinch.

She let out one of her patented mega sneezes, and a Silly String of snot went straight into my squeaky clean hair, and that was the end of lovey-time. "FUCKING GODDAMMIT MARY!!!!!!!"

And I jumped of the bed and stormed down the hall, shouting, "I'M SORRY I YELLED, I KNOW YOU CAN'T HELP IT!" and then I re-washed my hair, and apologized some more to the cat. And, seriously. Her days may be numbered, but, holy cats, she's going to be herself right up until the very end.

Friday, September 15, 2017 11:12am
We had a very encouraging vet appointment for Mary today. The vet said she is absolutely not going to Heaven.

...which we already knew, but still. So happy that she got a hopeful prognosis.

Friday, September 22, 2017 10:09pm
100% Reasonable: Give a few hours of Day One, 'OMG-I-think-I'm-dying' period cramps to anyone who says contraceptives are just for sluts.

Sunday, September 10, 2017 6:07pm

Walked the labyrinth just now! Very romantic. Loved every second. Don't ask about the uneven ground, thorns, allergies, and bugs crawling on us.

[Comments]

- The drive on Rt. 240 is exceptionally pretty. One of the prettiest drives in Western New York, I think. Only a smattering of trees have started to change, but the goldenrod is EVERYWHERE. Such a pretty day for a drive.

- Labyrinths are deceptively huge, and this one didn't have a bench in the middle, and my back reeeeeally didn't like walking on uneven ground, and I was huffing and cussing, and Curtis was behind me blowing his nose (allergies) and cracking up. So finally we get to the middle, we're both covered in scratches, and, speaking only for myself, feeling as unromantic as one can. And I looked around and was like, "No one's going to care if we exit the right way, or if we just step over the weeds and walk out of here."

- And Curtis was like, "Well, I mean, we shouldn't hurt ourselves doing this..."

- And I was like, "I just want to be done. I want to go take selfies and call it good." And he shrugged and said that was fine. So that's what we did.

- So then, as we were driving home, I said, "Thank you so much for just rolling with it. And Curtis said, "Yeah. That's just husbanding."

- So, in theory, it was a great idea: romantic, free, ceremonial. In practice..... yeah, the ceremonial Mongolian Buffet was a bit more our speed.

Wednesday, September 13, 2017 10:55pm

One for Curtis's 'Honey, I was not at all inappropriate, but I still feel like I should tell you' file:

Curtis runs the Buffalo iPhone App Developers Meetup twice a month. They meet at Buffalo Game Space, which is multi-use and open to any groups with a reservation.

Last night, he and all the other Buffalo iPhone app developers left the room their Meetup was in and had to walk through a larger room. Where a nude figure-drawing class was taking place.

Best. Meetup. Ever.

Sunday, October 15, 2017 7:53pm

As you know, I bitch about this house all the time. I fantasize about bulldozing it and starting over from scratch constantly.

But there is one thing I've always liked about this house, and that's that it's long and skinny. It worked perfectly for our family: Curtis and I could be together, watching TV downstairs at the front of the house, and Kiddo could be upstairs at the back of the house, singing himself hoarse without bothering us.

And sometimes (often), when we (or I alone) would be in the living room when Kiddo was singing upstairs, we'd turn the TV off and listen to our talented kid. It's been one of the greatest joys of my life, being an ear-witness to the birth of a really good songwriter. And, when I'm missing Kiddo, I'm often missing his guitar too.

Okay. Put that detail to the side. Now I have a different story to tell: My mom buys all of her grandchildren new shoes at the beginning of every school year, whether they're in school or not, up until age 18. Every kid, every year.

So back in 2011, Mom would have had Milo, Brooke, Jenna, and Donald. And they were all walking through McKinley Mall with new their new shoes. And Mom needed something at JC Penney, so on their way down that long hallway to Penneys, they had to pass Barnes and Noble.

And Milo spotted the new, hardcover Demetri Martin book on a display in the doorway.

And, as I've been told, he went from amiable-kid-who's-just-happy-to-be-out-with-his-gramma-and-cousins to CHILD WHO WANTS --NAY, NEEDS!-- SOMETHING in an instant.

And Gramma Sally never (rarely) says no.

And Milo's such an easy kid who never asks for anything.

And it's just a book.

Of course, she has to keep it fair, so Milo's getting a $20 book, which means all the other kids are going to spend $20 in Barnes and Noble too. ..And they already got shoes…

Anyway, my mom was a very generous, great sport. But it was a lot of money all in one trip. And when I went to pick Kiddo up and she told me, I was so embarrassed, and I offered to pay for the book, and of course she said no. And I know I overreacted, because money's weird, and hardcover books are such an extravagance. But finally, I let it go, and I brought Kiddo, and his book, and his bagged box of old shoes home.

And he was cracking up in the backseat the whole way home. Like, cackling and giggling and just laughing his little head off.

So here is where I tie this whole long post together: That night, we sent Kiddo (who, at 11 years old, was still a child with a specific bedtime) up to bed. And Curtis and I sat downstairs, and we turned the TV off and listened to Kiddo as he laughed in bed for hours. And we didn't scold him for being awake until midnight, because the sound of your kid as he is tickled, over, and over, and over again, *by a book!* is a delightful sound indeed.

So I was super happy to see this show up today in Kiddo's Snapchat. I wonder if 18-year-old Milo will love Demetri Martin as much as 11-year-old Milo did.

Oct 05, 2017 2:47:33am

Reasons why Shelly is going straight to hell, #48,903: the mental image of that 76-year-old woman getting hit by a flying bounce house with kids inside made me laugh out loud.

Thursday, October 19, 2017 7:47am

Greatest Hits

I guess it's not very often that I'm out with the dog at 7:04am. But I was out with the dog at 7:04am today.

And I got the shocking visual gift of seeing my neighbor air-drying past his window, like, three times!! (I don't know my neighbors. It's a rental. I've waved to them, but I don't know their names or what they look like up close)

So the first time, I caught the side view, and thought, 'No way. My eyes are playing tricks on me.' So I stood there like Lloyd Dobler without the boombox or trench coat (but with just that much subtlety), and stared at his window, and got to see his bare butt two more times! (Alas, not the front. That would have been inappropriate.)

Anyway, finally he crossed the room again, this time wearing pants, blah, whatever, so then I got back to actually playing with the dog. And I was thinking about how kind the universe is, to bless me with a wholly random and unasked-for view of a young man's asscrack, and the world suddenly felt so full of possibility...

But then Kiddo's old bus went by the house, and the driver waved at me, and I waved back, and just like that, the world went back to being fine and pleasant, but where everybody wears clothes and the bus doesn't stop to pick up my son at my house anymore.

Tuesday, October 31, 2017 4:07pm

I spent last night and today cleaning a gross spill in the pantry, and then reorganizing it.

Curtis just walked in the door, came to a stop in front of my shelf and said, "If this shelf was the only thing people knew about us, they'd point at us as examples of people who really have their shit together."

Tuesday, November 21, 2017 11:48pm

(I was reading a post on Facebook that a friend had posted)

Me to Kiddo, who's home for Thanksgiving break: "Wow, Will M. just plays all the instruments, huh?"

Me: "I mean, I'm really impressed that he ever picked up a guitar."

Me: "You know. Because of how incredible his dad is."

Me: "Don't you think so?

Me: "Kiddo?"

(I finally look away from the iPad and notice that Kiddo has his headphones on and hasn't heard a word I've said.)

Me: *"I have missed this so much!!!!"*

Monday, December 4, 2017 3:17pm

Me (making an appointment to get a blood test for Mary): "Yeah, she's still not eating much, and not keeping much down, so I really don't have any expectations, but my husband says we have to 'stop dealing with hypotheticals and make our decisions based on facts."

Receptionist, laughing: "Omg, I think we're married to the same man."

Wednesday, December 6, 2017 8:05pm

My kid is such an incredible artist. To make yourself vulnerable and tap into something real and raw - particularly to communicated pain rather than anger - it matters.

I think about this all the time. That Milo doesn't just sing in front of people who already love him. And he doesn't have one batch of songs he only shares with his peers, and a safer batch for everyone else.

How hard must that be? How brave?

That's an artist.

I'm so proud.

Wednesday, December 13, 2017 3:12pm

I was in Tops this morning and there was this old camo'd dude with a hard, scowling face and a white, Duck Dynasty beard in line at the lottery counter.

I walked past him and about 15 feet later, I encountered a mother, trying to navigate her cart through the ridiculous obstacle course of shoppers and stupidly placed Christmas displays.

And the mother was tense. Trying really hard to get through the mess. Because her toddler is in the front of the cart, reaching toward the man. Reaching, pointing, and yelling, "Santa! I want Santa! Mommy, Santaaaaaa!!!!!"

Saturday, December 16, 2017 9:02am

This morning, I woke up in a miserable mood. My back hurt, I have a headache. I was pissed off from the second I came into consciousness.

I came downstairs, and the whole time as I started the coffee, and started the laundry, and fixed myself a sandwich, I was having a big, imaginary fight with Curtis. Lots of anger and sarcasm. I was totally winning, and I felt RIGHTEOUS!

Then I came in and turned on the tv and ate my sandwich and drank my coffee. When I got up to switch the laundry, I noticed that it's snowing pretty hard, and I thought how I really hoped that Curtis and Milo still get to go to see Star Wars today, and I'm so happy Curtis has his kid to go see science fiction movies with. And then I was thinking that I hadn't heard Curtis coughing upstairs in a while, and I'm so glad he's finally getting some sleep, and, gosh, I wish I could fix his sleep problem because I know how much he suffers...

And, I mean, I assume everybody's mind wanders all day long and you never really think about it. But for whatever reason, probably because the thoughts were so perfectly opposite, I realized that, at least for me, *Before Food* = Let me list all the ways my husband pisses me off. *After Food* = Omg you guys, can I just tell you how great my husband is?

I feel like, any time I want to confront him about anything, I should eat a few crackers first and verify that I'm not just hungry.

Friday, December 22, 2017 11:05am

Question for the day: How did you find out that Santa wasn't real?

I was young -kindergarten or first grade. I'd begun to hear rumblings on the bus about the realness of Santa, but I wasn't ready to really contemplate either way.

So one day, I was enjoying some alone time in our blue Ford Econoline van (when I was hiding out in the van, no one would find me and put me to work or give me shit for being lazy and reading while the sun was out).

And Mom had left her stack of women's magazines in there (she drove us all over creation and spent a ton of time waiting for us to emerge from wherever).

And I picked up Mom's Good Housekeeping, opened up to Dr. Joyce Brother's column (I also enjoyed Erma Bombeck, and Emily Post's Etiquette for Every Day), and read the question, "At what age should I tell my children there's no such thing as Santa Claus, the Easter Bunny, or the Tooth Fairy?"

And that was it. One fell swoop.

And like the sneaky, distrustful child I was, I decided to hold that secret deep, deep, deep in my black little heart, because if my parents ever found out that I knew, surely I'd stop receiving presents, or candy, or quarters under my pillow, and there was NO WAY I was ever going to let that happen.

Thursday, December 28, 2017 3:57pm

A few years ago, my grandmother was in Kohl's, and she had this whole mess of coupons, and she picked out a bunch of items. And she had it in her brain that, with all those coupons, her order was going to be nearly free. She was *shocked* when they rang her up and said it would be $100+.

That's EXACTLY what just happened to me at the eye doctor. "We have insurance! It's free! Right? WHAT??? $366???? Oh lord. Lord, lord, lord, lord, lord."

Friday, December 29, 2017 5:17pm

I had such a nice time hanging out with human peers today! But I was nervous, so I forgot to shut up and let other people speak.

2018

Monday, February 12, 2018 10:11am

Curtis has spent the weekend going from the pantry to the fridge to the freezer and sighing because there's nothing to eat.

So now I have him laying down on the couch and walking around the grocery store in his mind, because he never gives me any ideas, and how can I buy what he wants if he never tells me what he wants?? (We've done this before. The last time, he managed to state that he likes anything that's "cheesy and Mexican-y")

Finally, he declared that he would probably feel satisfied with "that mushroom steak business" his mother makes (which, in fairness, just might be the best tasting thing I've ever put in my mouth)

...mushroom steak business which requires 75,000 stupid-ass steps and produces no leftovers.

DUDE. YOU KNOW WHO YOU MARRIED, RIGHT???

Wednesday, March 28, 2018 2:42am

Yeah, I'm biased, but Milo Duhn's album, *Incongruity* (coming out this Saturday!), is the coming of age/breakup album the world needs right now.

(Even with all the cussing in all the songs. Omg, there is so much cussing!)

Still. The world needs this album right now. It's a sincere expression of anguish and pain, and there's so much beauty and introspection and wisdom.

The writing is superb. The voice is excellent. The guitar is spectacular. The production is as good as anything I've ever heard.

And the last song? Even more than the others, that last song will rip your heart straight out. OMG. That's the one I keep coming back to. I can't wait for more people to hear it so I can gush with someone other than just Curtis.

Monday, April 2, 2018 1:28pm

We've got brand new neighbors in the apartment next door (their U Haul just left). From where I was sitting, they looked like two youngish kids, both skinny, and dressed in jeans and hoodies, and neither was obviously male or female. I saw them go walking down the hill toward the creek, and I say this with absolute seriousness: if I'd have been showered and wearing clean clothes, I would have chased after them with a bag and told them to bring up any squeaky Kong balls they find while they're down there.

So yes. It was only my own grossness that saved them from me on *Day One* of their 'new adult apartment adventure' hollering: "Kids! Kids! You look about my son's age. Would you mind risking your necks on the hill and bringing up some balls?"

And now I have to sit with the knowledge. I'm THAT lady. The one who sees any random young person and instantly assumes they'd be happy to do me a favor.

Friday, April 6, 2018 3:21pm

Greatest Hits

I was just at the post office. I've needed to go for almost a full week now, and I've either put it off or didn't have the car, and anyway, I HAD to go. Blargh. And this whole week (this whole SEASON), I have had terrible, staggering headaches, and today is particularly bad. But. I'm upright and the car is here, so I HAD to go.

So. I get there, and there are two people at the counter being waited on. Both have whole sets of forms spread out in front of them. And there's a lady with twin toddlers ahead of me.

OMG, these babies. O.M.G. They were just as precious as precious could be. They were probably about three years old. They were dressed identically except one twin had a yellow hoodie with a giraffe head stitched on the hood, and the other had a pink hoodie with a horse head stitched on the hood. They had wavy brown hair up in ponytails, and they both had the kind of eyes that are just a little squinty so they always look like they're laughing. They were like expensive porcelain figurines come to life.

You would swear Heaven had sent down a couple of little angels to bless you while you stand in line at the post office.

And these glorious, sweet little babies started singing. "If you're happy and you know it spin around! If you're happy and you know it spin around! If you're happy and you know it ma meh nama nama nama, if you're happy and you know spin around!"

And, oh my, it was just stars-in-your-eyes precious. And so they did it again. And then they did it again. And then they did it again. And one of the tellers had to go in the back for 10,000 years. And the babies did it again. And they did it again. And then the other customer at the counter's whole family came in to see what was taking so long. And they were just as charmed by these babies as I was. So they did it again. And they did it again. And they did it again.

And there was one of those rope-line kind of barricades, and the little girls were juuuuuuuuust barely still short enough to walk under it, so they each had a hand on the pole, and they danced around the little rope-line May-pole, singing, "If you're happy and you know it spin around! If you're happy and you know it spin around! If you're happy and you know it ma meh nama nama nama, If you're happy and you know spin around!"

And then they did it some more. And again. And again.

Honest to God, by about 15 minutes in, my migraine had expanded to explosion-level, and I was holding on to the desk with my eyes closed and was breathing through my mouth. It was probably the closest I've come to puking in public since I was pregnant.

149

Anyway, those two customers who clearly needed to both write their life stories at the exact same time on a Friday afternoon FINALLY finished. The mommy mailed her one thing, I mailed my one thing, the 10 people behind us mailed their things, I'm sure.

I got out to my car, and the mom was parked next to me and she was loading her babies in. They were chattering about how cute my dog is. I praised them for being *so good* for that *long wait*. And now I'm home. And my head still feels like there's a grenade waiting to go off inside it, but my stomach's fine. And those little girls *were* so good.

But omg. I think they sang that song 40 quadrillion times while we stood there.

Saturday, April 14, 2018 2:40am
Kiddo said there were people singing along with his songs tonight at his show. He was so haaaaaaaaappy!

Tuesday, April 17, 2018 4:44pm
Our tax guy was going to stop in at the house to drop off some papers, so I went outside to shovel off the stoop.

And I put one foot outside the house and fell straight off the stoop.

So one leg is banged up, one leg shoots screaming cramps up the back of my knee and thigh when I bend it, and I'd like it if someone would put me in a medically induced coma, please.

Wednesday, April 18, 2018 11:37am
Mary has been weirdly attached to me since I fell. Like, she won't leave me alone. Normally, she might come hang out for an hour or two, and sometimes she might sleep at the end of the bed overnight. But since yesterday, she wants to be ON me. It's unbelievably annoying and also very endearing.

Curtis says she's waiting for me to be edible.

Har har har

Wednesday, May 9, 2018 9:03am

Was just standing in the self-checkout at Target, and there's a mommy and a 4(ish) year old kiddo. And he is grummmmmmmmpy. So he's being a bit of a jerk, insisting that he needs a thing, and the mom is hanging in there, and being kind, but also not giving in.

And then she says, "next time, bring your money and you can have the thing. But today, you're SOL."

And there's dead silence for like 5 seconds.

And then the kid gets madder and yells, "THAT DOESNT EVEN SPELL ANYTHING!!"

Let's all cross our fingers for the mom that her kiddo will have a good nap today and wake up sweeter.

Saturday, May 12, 2018 9:27pm

White House reporter: Does the president support John McCain?

Sarah Sanders: The president supports all Americans.

LOL - She #AllLivesMatter 'd John McCain. KLASSY.

Monday, June 18, 2018 8:25pm

One night, when Kiddo was an infant, I left him at home with Curtis and went to Walmart by myself.

I was standing in the shampoo aisle.

One aisle over, a baby started to cry, hard, like something had hurt it. I heard the baby's mother cooing and trying to comfort him, but the baby was very upset, and took a little while to settle down.

As soon as I heard that baby start to cry in pain like that, I let down. One minute, I'm deciding which shampoo I want, and the next, my whole front is tingling, and I have two giant, spreading wet spots on my shirt that I can't hide.

That's the memory that sparked for me when I heard the audio of those children being forcefully kidnapped by the American government.

So maybe that'll clear things up for you too. Like, your shitty, shitty, shitty, indefensible "politics" might cause you to try to justify what we're doing. But maybe, if you've ever breastfed a baby, and had an uncontrollable, biological, motherly reaction for someone else's child, maybe you'll pick up your phone, and call your representatives, and tell them that all the financial windfalls given to you by this crooked-ass, earth-destroying batch of monsters aren't worth it if it means we have to kidnap and torture children to get it done.

Tuesday, June 19, 2018 1:15am

Yep. Soooooooooooo, I just fell in the shower.

I'm FINE!

I took the shower curtain down with me, and sort of sat down hard on the side of the tub. So I think I'll have a pretty impressive ass bruise, but other than that, I think I'm good.

and yeah, I fall a lot. That's not cool.

152

But part of me is marveling a little that it hasn't happened sooner. Our tub is SLIPPERY.

I'd like to give two shout-outs. First to the awesome grab-bar that's installed on the side of the tub. It didn't prevent the fall, but once I was down, I was able to grab it so I didn't fall the rest of the way out of the tub.

And lastly, to my glorious husband. Our house is LOUD right now. It's a heatwave, and there are presently four window AC units and three fans running. But somehow, over all that racket, he still heard me come crashing down, and came running. Then we freaked out a little together over how much worse it could have been.

SIGH. Never a dull moment. I need a helmet.

Wednesday, June 20, 2018 2:07am
Give money. Then give more money. Then give more money. Try sleep at night. Then give more money. Then give more.

Saturday, June 23, 2018 3:51pm
I have a friend who, all through the elections, was placating and "We have to try to see their side," and "Not all white people," and "All Lives Matter,"

..and ever since the Republican leadership started jailing babies, she cusses with rage more than I do.

And it does my dead little heart good.

Wednesday, June 27, 2018 8:01am
I wonder what feels worse? Putting handcuffs on passive, praying and singing clergy-people, or taking screaming children away from sobbing mothers? I wonder if LEOs feel anything at all anymore? Other than all the winning, that is..

Thursday, June 28, 2018 11:06am

Good news at the vet! The doc told me to double Chester's glucosamine intake and give it 2x a day instead of once (so one dose twice a day), but other than that, no need to worry.

Doggy's been favoring one back leg off and on for about a month, and it wasn't getting worse, but it also wasn't getting better, and enough time had passed that it was time to ask someone who knows things.

Anyway, the doc got right up in there, got SUPER PERSONAL, and Doggy just hung out and didn't react with any pain. So, up the glucosamine and call if anything changes.

YAAAYYYYYYY!!!!!

Wednesday, July 11, 2018 10:02am

Our neighbors have a sweet-natured dog named Tiger, who they inherited about a year or so ago after a death in the family left Tiger homeless. And even though I only really see Tiger from my own driveway, I feel such affection and sadness or him, because he's a BIG DOGGY, but they have a tiny yard, so all of his exercise has to come from walks, which is great, but then sometimes, he'll be outside when I'm throwing balls for Chester.

And Tiger will sit, devastated, in their driveway, his ears shaped like upside-down triangles of anguish and longing. I don't know what kind of a dog he is, but he's very sleek and he looks like he could run about as fast as a car. So you KNOW he'd love to chase balls (they probably take him to the dog park to play, too. He doesn't have the body of a dog who lays around all day. But still. I try not to play with my dog when he's outside because the tortured disappointment in Tiger's body language is too much to bear).

ANYWAY. I had a point that's long since stopped being relevant, but whatever.

Tiger and Chester have the exact same bark when they're ready come inside. It's like the doggy equivalent of a throat clear or the little honk you give at a red light when the car in front of you has spaced out and didn't notice it's green now. It's like "(woof!)".

And the neighbors are as good as we are. We hear the "(woof!)" and we let them in.

Well, Tiger was just "(woof)"-ing for like 3 minutes. Never concerned or upset, just intermittently "(woof!)"-ing.

And it made me laugh, because I figure whoever let Tiger out was probably stuck in the bathroom, hollering through the walls, "Hang on, I need a minute!" "(woof!)" "You're fine! Just wait a second, I'm in the bathroom!" "(woof!)" "Tiger, I'm telling you, I'm coming, but I'm not done yet! Just hang out a sec!" "(woof!)" "Yesssssss, I hearrrrrr you, can you just be patient??"

At least that's what it's like at our house when my dog hasn't been let in after the first "(woof!)"

Wednesday, July 11, 2018 12:47pm
Jeepers, I sure hope someone's putting together a lip sync battle for ICE agents, so that, rather than seeing them all as monsters and sadists, we white folks can feel reassured that, deep down, they're all really just fun-loving goofballs.

Tuesday, July 17, 2018 2:09pm
Okay! Well, we're home from the vet specialist, and the news about Chester is both very good and very unsatisfying.

Good news first: The doctor at Orchard Park Veterinary Hospital was EXCELLENT. He felt up every nook and cranny of the dog's spine, legs, and feet. Oooo, Doggy hated it! He tolerated it, but it took Curtis and me both to hold him still.

Then he had Curtis put him on the floor, and we followed behind as Curtis walked Chester down a long hall, then out a side door, then down the whole back length of the building. The doctor saw how Chester bunny rabbits around, he saw his feet slip a bunch, he

155

saw Chester stumble a bunch, he watched him poop and pee. He pretty much saw everything that we see.

And validation from someone like that feels good. Like, we're not making it up, the doctor agrees that we really are seeing something wrong with our dog, but also, the doctor's not freaking out, so maybe we don't need to freak out.

Okay. So then came the unsatisfying part where he said that these symptoms could mean anything. That this specific batch of symptoms present for a whole host of different problems. And, that yes, DM is certainly a possibility, but without extensive further testing, he wouldn't say more than "It could be Degenerative Myelopathy. But also maybe not."

He gave us a long list of tests they should run. And it was a really long list.

A really pricey, long list.

For tests, not treatments.

Okay, so then came the point where I was extra, extra, extra glad Curtis was there. He asks the right questions in the room (and doesn't think of them two hours after the appointment's over like I do). He asked, "If we put off the testing, say for six months, is there anything that could be wrong with him now that will make us wish we'd done the tests six months ago?"

And the doctor said no.

He said he was going to send a letter to our regular vet, of different treatments we could try for now (first being NSAIDs, then Cortisone, etc. Pretty standard stuff) and see if we see any improvements. He said we should feel free to have a genetic test done to see how likely it is that Chester's a carrier of DM (one of his littermates was tested a few years ago and showed to be 'at risk.' Which doesn't mean anything definitive for Chester, other than family history).

But it wasn't a recommendation. It was an "If it'll make you feel better to know, go ahead and have the genetic test done."

So anyway. I told the doc that I've been limiting Chester's activity, and he told me that, as long as Chester wants to play, that we should play. He said I'm not hurting him by letting him run in the yard, even if he tips over a lot. (Within reason, of course)

So we left the vet without much of a game plan: Back to our regular vet to start with anti-inflammatories, and hold off on testing until his symptoms worsen, and make a decision then. And give Chester a nice life in the meantime.

I still got a lot of comfort from the visit. I feel like, whatever's coming, we've got some time. And I don't need to be scared every single time Chester's leg slips or feel like I've just killed my dog every time I throw a ball in the yard, and the front of his body stops where he wants it to stop, and the back of his body keeps going.

Anyway. Time is good.

Saturday, July 28, 2018 8:41pm

Funny, the things that spark memories from when you were little-little-little.

Kiddo just burped into the microphone (I know. He's 19. I think they grow out that stuff sometime. Around age 75 or so), and I remembered when *I* was a little kiddo, and I used to like to go down into our basement, where the equipment from my dad's band was often set up. And I'd sing into the (turned off) microphones and imagine I was big enough to sing on a stage. But the microphones all smelled like beer. So I always, ALWAYS, licked them. I liked how the texture felt on my tongue, and I loved how they tasted.

So yeah. Let this be a lesson: no matter how much parents try to shield their kids from germs, invariably their kids will find the weirdest possible ways to build a strong immune system.

Thursday, August 2, 2018 4:59pm

I just want to let you know that it's August 2nd and Tops has Halloween candy out at the front of the store, and it's on sale.

I am absolutely going to express my outrage just as soon as I'm done with this handful of mini Twix..

Friday, August 10, 2018 3:32am

[Headline: new-data-makes-it-clear-nonvoters-handed-trump-the-presidency]

You might think you aren't voting. But by staying home, you're just letting your grandparents choose your representatives.

—And your grandparents are almost certainly lovely people! But they can be lovely and still be atrocious judges of truth and character. Clearly.

Show up. If you don't like your choices, throw your hat in the ring. We need new blood showing up and giving a shit.

Saturday, August 25, 2018 6:52am

I was so happy at 10pm last night, because I felt sleepy, and I thought about how nice it would be to try to get on a day schedule again, so I did a couple quick little chores, and took Doggy outside. I asked Curtis if he'd do bedtime for the animals in a few hours, and then I went to bed.

And I read my book, and it was so perfect. I was falling asleep two paragraphs in, and I let my Kindle gently fall from my fingers and went off to sleep.

...and woke up, like, maaaaybe 30 minutes later because the AC wasn't turned up high enough and the room was hot.

So I got up and cranked the AC. Then I went and peed, since I'm in my 40s and I can ALWAYS pee, and then I went back to bed.

And I laid there and thought about thinky things, and decided I might as well read my book, because I'm not falling asleep, and the book seems like it'll be a good one. So I picked up my Kindle and read. For two hours.

And finally, I came back into my body and was like, 'omg, this is so stupid, I'm less tired than I was, I should go downstairs and hang out with the dog.'

So I came down, and there was just one dim lamp on, and I saw that Curtis was conked out on the couch, so I didn't turn on any more lights. So I whisper-asked Doggy if he wanted to wake up and come out of his crate. He said yes, and then we snuggled up in the chair together. I went back to reading my book, and Doggy sighed deeply, happy to get to go back to sleep while being petted.

And this house is pretty decrepit, and it's really messy, and it's weirdly empty because Kiddo went back to school and took his things with him. But sitting in my chair, in the mostly-dark, with Doggy sleeping next to me, and Curtis sleeping on the couch, and Kitty sleeping next to him... it was just one of those perfect peace moments, where nothing could get inside this bubble of silence and calm.

And now we're all awake. Curtis woke up VERY chatty, and my sleep schedule is clearly going to continue to be idiotic for a little while, and this was not how I'd hoped my night was going to go. This way was better.

Wednesday, August 29, 2018 4:55pm
A reminder: your son is more likely to be the VICTIM of sexual assault than be falsely accused of sexual assault.

So I know, it's real hard to give a shit about liberated sluts having to endure their turn under an entitled sweaty alpha male with an erection that ain't going to take care of itself.

So picture your son instead. Fighting and *losing*.

159

Then wring your hands about his poor, poor rapist's future.

Sunday, September 16, 2018 3:55pm

Motto of the Trump administration: "Oh, your PTSD hasn't flared up in a while? LOL, let's fix that, Honey."

Thursday, September 20, 2018 2:15pm

I feel so incredibly awful for Dr. Ford. There were millions upon millions of people who opposed Kavanaugh just based on his religious supremacy and views on presidential powers.

But now that Dr. Ford's come forward, she's carrying the weight and hope, and arguably the mental health of every single survivor who's already been decimated by the last two years.

I'm simultaneously feeling like we are simply asking too much of one human and feeling like she just HAS to at least try to save us all.

Sunday, September 23, 2018 2:02am

I saw the 587 millionth "Leftists are hypocrites because Juanita Broaderick," and #1 I do believe Juanita Broaderick. And #2 Democrats have been paying for Bill Clinton's sins ever since he showed up, and he is the literal reason why the Democratic Party finally gets rid of its creeps.

Shitty men come in all political stripes, and nobody's good enough about ditching their creeps in a timely enough manner. But Democrats are better. —Not perfect. But better. And with every woman we elevate, our party will get better still.

Sunday, September 23, 2018 8:21pm

Fratbros everywhere: "Wait, putting our dicks in unconscious people's faces is sexual assault now? So, what, we're ALL both criminals AND victims??"

Everybody else: "How the fuck are you dreadful people allowed to run the world?"

Greatest Hits

If you knew me when I was a kid, maybe don't read this.

Two stories, one about 7th grade, one about 10th grade (neither has violence):

(I got drunk two times when I was in seventh grade. I can't remember which event came first, so I'm going to tell this story as "The first time I got drunk," but it's possible that it was actually the second.)

The first time I got drunk, I was in seventh grade. My friend's older sister had a party, and it was probably intended to be small-ish, but most of the kids from the high school showed up. She lived on a dead-end road, in front of train tracks, near a pond. As the party got huge, most of the kids went down to the pond since it was a known party spot.

I don't know what everybody else drank, but my friend and I had alcohol from her parents' liquor cabinet. I think. The memory of the hows and the whys is very fuzzy.

Here's what I do remember: I remember that I was at the pond and there were kids everywhere. The next thing I remember is laying on the stones next to the train tracks and looking up at my classmate's penis. Right there. In my face.

He was a kid I'd known since kindergarten. He was every bit as much of a child as I was. And his penis was right there in my face. And swear to god, he said, "You kiss it."

And what did I know? I always wanted to be older and cooler than I was, but at that moment, I was still a chubby, barely pubescent, totally ignorant seventh grader.

So I kissed it. You know, like you'd kiss your grandma.

161

smooch

It was warm and it smelled like pee.

And then I don't remember anything. I know I woke up fully clothed and still drunk. It was getting dark, but you could still see. I know I wandered back toward my friend's house, and a kid I didn't know asked me if I'd seen Shelly Mason. And I said "why?" and he said, "Because her parents are here and they're pissed."

And then, the part that everybody will remember, is that the next day, my mom asked me what was on my jacket. And I had no idea. And she said, "It looks like someone blew their nose on it." And then I or one of my friends put two and two together and realized that my classmate must have jizzed on my jacket after I fell asleep/passed out.

Nobody. None of us. Me included. Nobody at any point said or thought that something *wrong* had happened. All we knew was that the kid who sometimes farts loudly in class tried to get me to kiss his penis and then had ejaculated on my corduroy school jacket. There was no violence, no fear, no scary masked boogeyman jumping out of the bushes. So, therefore, since we had no other bigger truths to draw on, it was a hilarious joke.

"The nose joke" was pretty famous, at least among the girls. I don't know if any of the boys knew, because, like I said, at that point, I was a chubby, barely pubescent nobody. Nobody would have high-fived my classmate for jizzing on seventh grade Shelly's jacket.

I think. I don't actually know.

***

Now fast forward three years. Tenth grade. In my school district at that time, "Junior high" was 7th-9th grade, and "High school" was 10th-12th. So kids my own age knew me, but I was brand new to the older kids. And now I was very pretty. I won't tell you about all the destructive and self-loathing methods I used to lose weight, because you've all probably done all the same things to be thin, and maybe still do them.

So I was thin, and beautiful(ish), and I'd managed to get quite a reputation for myself. -Plenty of that reputation was earned the old-fashioned way, God knows, I was no angel. But conservatively, I'd still guess that about 85% of the rumors about me had no basis in fact. I was a Very Catholic kid with an eagle-eyed mother, and I was grounded All.The.Time. So, much as I may have wanted to cultivate a more worldly persona, in 10th grade, it was mostly out of my reach.

So one day, I was on the afterschool/extra curricular bus, waiting to go home. The bus was parked outside the school, still loading. I was plunked down near the front, alone, in my seat, reading a book. And I heard someone say my name from the back of the bus.

And then someone responded. "You slept with Shelly Mason??"

And the original voice: "Yeah. A couple weeks ago."

So I got up and turned around. It was a senior jock. Probably one of the most popular kids at school. Very tall. Good looking, but in an instantly dislikable way. Total dick.

And I said, "You slept with Shelly Mason?"

And he barely glanced at me. I was pretty, but not popular enough to earn full eye-contact from the 1%.

He shrugged dismissively. "Yeah."

So I said, loudly, "*I'm* Shelly Mason."

And then he scowled and sat down. It was one of the new busses, with tall seat-backs, so if anything else happened in the back of the bus with his friends, I didn't see or hear it.

So that's twice. Two actual, actually happened, events from my own life that I got to think about this week because of Brett Kavanaugh. They're not "recovered memories," because I never forgot them. Nobody had to hypnotize me to help me remember them. They're just there. All the time. A boy put his penis in my face when I was drunk, and another boy (probably zillions of them, I was pretty

163

notorious) claimed to have had sex with me when he'd never even met me.

When we say to believe women, it's because we RECOGNIZE this shit from our own lives. We know exactly what it feels like to know a Brett Kavanaugh. We've met DOZENS of Brett Kavanaughs. And Brett Kavanaugh is not a good guy.

Oh sure, I'm sure he's got a great Heaven-earned redemption story that he tells himself, of a wild youth made good because of all his good deeds. Maybe some small ghosty part of him held his newborn daughter and thought, "If anyone sticks his dick in her face, I'll kill him." But he certainly never went back and apologized to the girls that he, himself, wronged.

Maybe he told a priest and decided that was good enough.

Or maybe he never thought they were sins in the first place. Maybe they're only sins when somebody else is committing them. Since the story he apparently tells himself is, "I'm a good Christian man, The end."

But we see you. WE SEE YOU. And whether it's given to you or not, you do NOT have the right to decide what happens to women's bodies. Your god might think you're super awesome. But we who are not the voice in your head think you're the same asshole you always were.

PS. Your wife sees you too.

Sunday, September 30, 2018 10:25pm

Even before I knew Kavanaugh was a legacy student, I got so pissed when he said that it was just his own hard work that got him into Yale. Like, how can a rich kid, who went to a fancy private prep school, have so little self-awareness at all the enormous boosts he was given?

My grandparents set aside money for my (and my brothers' and cousins') college. It wasn't a dumptruck-full of money, but it paid for state schools and rent and a reliable car. We all worked part time jobs, and we all had to earn our admission and grades fair and square.

But please. Like I could ever pretend like having my college paid for didn't pole-vault me over the vast majority of my peers?? Like I could, with a straight face, suggest that it was just pluck, ambition, and intellectual brilliance that allowed me to earn my degree? Riiiight.

Thursday, October 4, 2018 3:37pm

Plain Gramma died today.

I went in to see her yesterday, and she wasn't lucid or even really awake, but every time somebody leaned close to greet her or speak to her, she puckered her lips to give a kiss.

She loved everybody and everybody loved her right back.

She was exceptional.

Saturday, October 6, 2018 4:30am

Me: "Okay, Puppy, before we go outside, let me shine this flashlight at the yard real quick and make sure there aren't any deer for you to bark at since it's so late..."

(Turns on flashlight)

(Every deer in East Aurora is on my lawn and all raise their startled heads.)

Me: "Okay, Puppy, let's just give it a little minute. I need to open and close the garage door a few times for no apparent reason, that totally isn't intended to clear the yard for us or anything. Nothing to see here..."

Thanks so much for all the birthday wishes, everybody! I had a lovely day, and I'm using my birthday money to get a new night guard for my teeth, and we're hiring someone to build safe new steps with a handrail going into the house. So, wooooo, party!

I actually have a *not-money-related* birthday wish, since you're here. It's a two-parter:

1. Verify that you're registered to vote. In New York, the last day to register is this Friday, October 12th.

And 2. If you're a parent, I want you to tell your children why you're voting.

Everybody always talks about how young people don't vote. And they don't. I think a lot of the blame for that falls on parents. For one thing, zillions of parents don't vote, either. So, we have generations of citizens who don't vote, and can't even tell you why, other than some lame, dishonest, antiquated, lazy, 'they're all crooks' assertion.

But we do have one generation of citizens who always votes. *And because they all show up, they get to make the rules. That's how the system works.*

You know what they're worried about over on FOX News? Hordes of Mexicans moving to your hometown, the gay agenda to make your kids queer, they're coming for your guns, sluts using abortion to kill healthy newborns, the war on Christianity, the war on white men, boys in the girl's bathroom, and girls making false rape allegations against men who turned them down for a date.

The generation that watches FOX News votes. They show up. Every single election.

So, Moms and Dads, get your shit together. Make sure you're registered, and then tell your kids 2-3 specific reasons why you're going to vote this year, even though it's not a presidential election year.

I am voting because I think family detention is literally, actually, criminally evil.

I am voting because I believe that constantly blocking regulations that will help life on the planet continue is short-sighted, willfully apocalyptic, and only benefits the wealthy.

I am voting because I believe healthcare should be a guaranteed right to every American of every age, color, religion, employment status, and class.

And I am voting because I am a citizen, and I am a patriot, and this is a society.

I think that giving lunatics, monsters, sociopaths, and idiots the keys to government offices makes us all lunatics, monsters, sociopaths, and idiots. We have to do better.

So tell your kids. Every time there's an election, tell your kids why you're voting. Make them see that *who makes the rules* affects them every day of their lives:

Who's in charge of the school board affects what books they learn from, whether or not they get fact-based sex ed, and whether they hear a bigger picture than just "in 1492, Columbus sailed the ocean blue."

Who's in charge at the local sheriff's office affects whether they and their peers can be terrorized by law enforcement.

Who's in charge at governor's office affects whether guns are *pretty easy* to get or *insanely easy* to get.

Who's in charge in congress affects whether the president has anyone stopping him from giving in to his dumbest and cruelest impulses.

Register to vote. Tell your kids. Let them see your "I Voted" sticker on November 6th. Make them care about who makes the rules.

Thanks everybody!

Monday, October 15, 2018 3:20pm

Does anybody else get super triggered every time the president says that yet another dude has "strongly denied" any wrongdoing?

Friday, October 19, 2018 8:50pm

My kiddo's got his new merch design!! I'm so excited for him! I've spent the last 20+ years of my life washing band T-shirts that my husband and son purchased from young musicians in bars. And now I'll be washing a shirt with my own child's name on it!

I. Am. Living. The. Dream.

(Seriously, though, I think this is ultra-cool. I'm so proud of my kid.)

Saturday, October 27, 2018 3:37am

You want to bring back civility? It's so simple: Stop being an asshole, stop celebrating assholes, stop being nostalgic for asshole behavior that was tolerated in the good old days, stop giving power to assholes, stop putting assholes in front of television cameras and radio microphones, stop getting your talking points from assholes.... there's a pattern here.

Tuesday, October 30, 2018 8:23pm

I've been thinking about breastfeeding mothers a lot for months now, ever since the story broke about the breastfeeding infant who the US government kidnapped from its mother in the name of national security.

I've been thinking about how young and vulnerable new mothers are. New parents are usually/often also new adults. It's a scary, vulnerable time. Learning how to be a mom takes so much time, and when your babies are babies, most of the learning process is just learning how to be there with your body and your voice and your heartbeat and your reassurance.

168

Young parents are on my mind all the time. Especially the ones on foot, carrying their little ones, trying so desperately just to find a safe place.

I like rules too. Let's make rules that prioritize the safety of vulnerable humans.

Tuesday, October 30, 2018 11:56pm
Trump's claim that calling himself a Nationalist 'means he loves the country,' makes exactly as much sense as stating that extroverts' love for large gatherings makes them Socialists.

#youknewdamnwellwhatthatwordmeans #jackass

Saturday, November 10, 2018 7:10am
Literally every time I walk into my kitchen and it's daylight, I look out the window for East Aurora's albino deer. Even in the summer, there are breaks in the leaves, and I can see bits of the creek where she lived.

I probably only saw her 4-5 times total, but it was such a thrill to see her that I have truly looked for her every single time I've stood at my kitchen sink.

So just now, it's coming on daylight, and we had the tiniest bit of snow overnight, and I was looking for movement by the creek, and then I remembered: last night, a woman in one of the East Aurora groups that I belong to posted that the albino deer died back in September, likely of natural causes (She was quite old. Like, 12, I think?). The woman, as she put it, "saw her remains."

And that is so sad. East Aurora is such a special little village, but that deer gave us a bit of magic too.

Another woman said that the town of West Falls (a few miles thataway) has an albino deer now, so I'm really happy for them. Because every deer sighting feels lucky (well, when you're not in a moving vehicle anyway), but seeing a stark white deer off in the

169

distance...it's like seeing a unicorn. You can't even believe your eyes.

So yes. Rest in peace little deer. Nobody could agree on your name, whether you were Star or Starlight or Twilight or Whitey, but everybody who saw you felt touched by magic. And I know I'll keep looking for you every time I stand at my sink.

Sunday, November 11, 2018 5:07am

As a fat person with mental health issues who absolutely hates to travel, I can sympathize with the president for needing to 'take a day' upon his arrival in Paris. Long airplane rides make my ankles look and feel like they're filled with wet sand, and my ear pressure's never right for weeks, and the suitcases, and the homesickness, and even the pillows you bring with you feel all wrong, and you can't use your own toilet, and no other shower's water pressure is strong enough, and nobody ever just leaves you alone in silence to look at Facebook and eat your ice cream in peace.

I totally get it.

...but then, I shouldn't be president either...

Wednesday, December 5, 2018 4:03pm

The game that never gets old:

"Oh my heavens, this kitty is so starving!" ... (Mary chirps in agreement) ...

"This poor kitty! She's the hungriest kitty that ever lived! We better feed this poor starvin kitty cat!" ... (steps over dog) ... "Yeah, Sorry Doggy, but doggies don't get hungry! It's just science!"

... (grinds up Kitty's pill and mixes it with food, then uses a steak knife to cut the food even smaller, because she's a picky little thing) ...

170

"Oh my heavens. Well. This looks pretty special." ... (mix mix mix, put the silverware in the sink) ... "Oooookay! iiiiiiiiit's Mary's turn! Oh my goodness! Enjoy Mary's turn!"

(Turns around to meet the desperate face of the dog.)

Me: "Wait. Are you saying doggies DO get hungry???"

Dog: "BARK! BARK! BARK!"

Monday, December 10, 2018 10:57pm

Without exception, when I receive an email forward that encourages you to send it to "all the men who need a good laugh, and all the women who can handle it," I think, Seriously, WTF is it about me that made you think I'd WANT to handle it??

Wednesday, December 12, 2018 1:13am

It's fine to "say" that a pet is for your child, but understand that little kids have absolutely no concept of what an enormous responsibility a pet (specifically a dog) is.

So, in name, it's your child's pet. And hold your kid accountable.

But also get ready for YOU to be the one the pet comes to when it's hungry, bored, or needs to poop or snuggle. That needs to be cool with you, or your whole family's going to be miserable and resentful of that precious critter.

Saturday, December 15, 2018 2:48am

I mean, I know I'm spectacularly cynical, but this was so pitch perfect: Take a young Russian girl (Maria Butina), one who's "impressed" with older, "worldly" men. She can't wear too much makeup, or dye her hair, or have fake boobs, or look like a sorority sister at Florida State, or look like the president of the Celibacy Club (or "look" like a prostitute).

She can't be too hot, because then her stooges might not believe she's actually into them. She has to look wholesome. But still really pretty. INNOCENT. An unsoiled ingenue.

..then give her a gun fixation. Like, she HAS to know the difference between an assault weapon and a semi-automatic. She HAS to be thrilled by firepower. Like, aroused by that shit. Without even seeming to know WHY those big powerful erupting cocks make her breathe heavy and her clothes feel too tight.

And then set her loose on the Republican leadership.

I swear, it's like Putin's people watched Weird Science and then just applied the lessons they learned.

Tuesday, December 25, 2018 1:55am
I have a massive case of quaking hiccups, and I keep waiting for Curtis to wake up and be like, "WILL YOU CUT IT OUT!?!"

Friday, December 28, 2018 12:50pm
Every time somebody sends me a friend request, my first instinct is always to think, 'Oh man, they're going to regret this, aren't they....'

2019

Thursday, January 31, 2019 5:45pm

The president tweeted "The Democrats are the party of late term abortion..."

Yes, you jackass, that's exactly what we are. The Democrats recognize the need for, and humanity *required*, to step away from a grieving family and let them make devastating medical decisions without any commentary at all, other than, "I am so sorry for your loss."

Seriously, dude, eff right off with that cruel horseshit. Nobody wakes up in their seventh month, after feeling every kick and flutter, and thinks, 'Huh. These stretch marks are so ugly. And I'd rather have new things for myself. And the names I picked out were dumb anyway. I think I'll fly across the country, find a doctor who will have no reservations at all about terminating a healthy, near-term pregnancy (because you know they totally exist, lol), spend thousands of dollars out of pocket, and maybe treat myself to some fro-yo on my way home."

I know you like your "Everybody in the Dem party LLLLLLoves murder" fantasy, but seriously, grow up. Grow a brain. Grow a heart. Listen to *anybody* who's needed a later abortion. Apologize for being such a dick. And then sit the hell down.

Monday, February 4, 2019 7:36am

I was on the phone with my in-laws last night (They called Curtis first, he didn't answer. They called Milo next, he didn't answer. They called me, I answered. That makes me the good child), and my FIL mentioned a neighbor who had recently died of cancer, but that he had used marijuana for quite a while and had great results. And FIL got to thinking that maybe I should try marijuana for my migraines.

And I sputtered nervously a bit and finally said that I'd made a great study of marijuana when I was in college, and that it didn't do a thing for my migraines, but that it was awesome for my depression.

And then it was their turn to sputter nervously.

And once again, Shelly found herself plunked back into the role of NOT the good child.

sigh

Tuesday, February 12, 2019 12:19pm

I took Doggy in to the vet last week because I felt like he was acting weaker again (after holding steady for a few months). The vet was great.

She said that he's starting to lose some muscle mass in his back legs, and that's a very bad thing. She said that once muscle mass is gone, it's gone. So she wants Chester to do "a little physical therapy" to help him keep the muscle mass he has left.

We're supposed to do five sit/stands, twice a day.

So you have 5 bits of kibble. Have him sit, and then from sitting, have him get up and walk to you. The goal is that he has to use his back legs to push himself up.

Except he's so DESPERATE to get the kibble that he just starts doing ANYTHING, begging for that bit of kibble.

The first try is always fine.

"Okay Chester, sit!"

He sits.

Then I say, "Okay, come to me."

It's perfect. He gets his kibble.

Next time. "Okay Chester, sit!"

You can so perfectly see his little brain freeze and break a little.

He lays down?

No?

He gets up.

He woofs.

Me: "No, Chester. Sit!"

He lays down.

'Right Mama? This one?'

Me: "No Doggy, that one's down. I want Chester to sit!"

And then begins the frustrated, but civilized and conversational woofing. 'No, but I did it! I want the treat!'

He lays back down. He gets back up. 'No, but that's it!! Mama!!! I did it! Give me the treat! What? WHAT DO YOU WANT, I SIT!'

Me: "Nope. You know this, Doggy! Let's try again. Okay Chester, sit!"

He hovers his little butt over the floor and hesitates. Again, you can see his brain is really trying. And his brain is saying, 'No, that's not sit.'

Meanwhile, I'm getting excited. "Yes! That one! Chester, sit!"

Then he gets confused. Then he thinks about it some more. Then he sits.

'This one?'

I try to remember not to celebrate (because then I ruin his concentration and we have to start over), and put my hand out like "Stop." I back up a few feet. "Stay...stay...stay... Okay Chester, come!"

And that part he's got. Walking toward the food? Yes, he can do that one just fine, thanks.

We do this twice a day. It's been almost a week, and it's still exactly the same: One perfect Sit, and then a whole lot of conversation and trying again.

It's like the doggy equivalent to math homework. But so much funnier.

Thursday, February 14, 2019 4:38pm
Mary just sneezed while looking out the window.

Tuesday, March 5, 2019 2:02pm
My Instacart driver today was a pretty young mommy, and she had a toddler in the backseat of her ancient SUV. I never actually saw the baby, I just saw these little dancing, kicking boots.

So anyway, that's your happy picture for the day: there's fresh snow on the ground, and Curtis snowblowed so we could get a delivery. While Mama's boots crunch crunch crunch across the driveway, Baby's boots kick kick kick in the backseat.

So very sweet.

Friday, March 8, 2019 5:17pm
One of my friends posted an article where a pastor had said that you shouldn't masturbate, because masturbation makes you gay.

And one of his friends commented, "Well in that case, just call me Liberace."

And I laughed so hard the dog woke up and brought me a ball because laughter means playtime.

176

Sunday, March 31, 2019 7:35pm

I love my cat. I do. But, omg, I am *so over* her 2-3x/day events where she's compelled to come tell me she feels a sneeze coming on.

I don't know what past sin I'm paying for, but, holy crap, it must have been a doozy. Because no one who doesn't somehow deserve it should have to wipe *this much* cat snot off their body.

Monday, April 1, 2019 5:08pm

Biden might be fine. He might have the best ideas. I suppose that's possible.

But FFS, if your defense of him is that it's better to nuzzle unsuspecting, non-consenting women than to handle them like bowling balls.... well sure, sure, yes, that's true.

But maybe could we try setting the bar just a little bit higher than that? Men know just fine how to act around other humans, and we know this because they don't pull this shit with other men. They don't give each other back-rubs in professional settings, and they don't surreptitiously rub their cocks against them when boarding planes and busses.

No, they reserve that shit for women, and then they act shocked! Just *shocked!* and *hurt!* when women tell them to back the fuck off.

You know perfectly well that people close to Biden have been telling him for years that he oversteps his boundaries with women, and that he should cut it out, regardless of whether it's a sexual come-on or not.

But he's always gotten away with it because everyone insists he's just folksy and aw shucks, and that it's totally not because he's a powerful man who thinks the rules shouldn't have to apply to him.

I'm not saying he needs to bow out. I personally have no use for Joe Biden, but I certainly have no problem with him getting up on the debate stage and making his case. But, holy shit, giving him a pass on his creepy, handsy behavior just because he's on our side is so very self-hating and fucked up.

We have better options.

Saturday, April 20, 2019 6:08pm
Greatest Hits

A couple of mentions on Facebook of this being the 20th anniversary of Columbine.

I thought I'd written about this before, but it didn't show up in my Memories today, so maybe not.

So yeah, no surprise here, but here's a post that uses a historical event and makes it all about me and my kiddo

Milo was born on February 18th, 1999. But he wasn't due until May 3rd. He spent the first 70 days of his life in a see-through plastic box in the NICU. You know the story.

For the first few weeks, I didn't want to go in to see him. It seemed like every time I touched him (or later, held him), that his heart rate would plummet, and an alarm would go off and a nurse would come running and she'd brush her hand lightly but quickly across his back and he'd come back around and the alarms would stop, and I'd start crying.

Seriously, think about that for a minute. I'd never been a parent before. My own body was taking an eternity to heal. I'd read an organic, earth-mother-y, What-to-Expect-type book during my pregnancy that asserted that women who have miscarriages were probably ambivalent about their pregnancies.

So I remember drowning in this astounding despair: clearly my own feelings about my pregnancy were more ambivalent than I'd thought, since I'd nearly killed us both by getting this disease. (Kiddo was well into elementary school before a therapist finally got through to me what *unforgivable bullshit* that book was).

Anyway. So I had my own physical and mental issues that I couldn't get away from, and at the same time, I had a baby, living in a plastic box at the hospital, who was terrifyingly fragile, and who set off alarms with awful frequency.

And he was in the NICU for more than two months.

But as those two months went by, he did slowly begin to even out. The alarms brought nurses running with less frequency, he could be out of the box for slightly longer periods of time. Being at the hospital began to feel normal. It felt like 'just the way it is' that I had to scrub my hands and arms with anti-microbial soap for three minutes before being admitted to the room where they kept the babies in plastic boxes. It was comforting that there were always health professionals standing only a few feet away, ready to intervene. It was normal to go visit my baby.

Then, on April 20th, 1999, on my way into the hospital, I heard on the radio that there had been a terrible shooting at a high school in Colorado, and early reports were that a lot of people had died.

This is shameful, but I remember feeling very comforted that my baby was safe and sound in his plastic box at the hospital.

So I got my parking pass, parked in the hospital garage, walked through the hospital lobby, rode the elevator, scrubbed my hands and arms for three minutes, and waved to the receptionist, who pushed a button and opened the door. I walked to the spot where my baby's isolette had been parked since February 18th, and the isolette was gone. A smiling, *beaming* nurse was standing there waiting for me.

"Guess who's finally ready to be in a crib?"

She pointed at the opposite corner of the room, where the open-air cribs were. And there was Milo, in a crib, not attached to any wires at all.

And I felt fear. I kept my mouth shut even though my brain was screaming.

179

(((IF HIS HEART STOPS, YOU WON'T EVEN KNOW!!!)))

But she was smiling, she was so happy for me, so I remember trying to reflect her happiness, and being certain that I was failing.

She walked me over to him, and she said, "I have even better news. As long as he" (-I think she said 'keeps his bilirubin levels normal' but I can't really remember), "he can go home in about a week!!"

And I probably didn't actually see black spots in front of my eyes, but that's how bad the terror was. Like, "No no no no no no no no, it's not safe! Nothing is safe! You have to put him back in the box and hook him back up to all the machines, and he has to stay there forever!!"

But the nurse was so happy, and she was probably doing that thing nurses do, where they push extra hard to make you react the right way, because it's likely completely normal for parents to feel like *Death is lurking everywhere* when their baby has spent his entire life in a plastic box and hooked up to machines. I probably would have felt the same swallowed-whole terror even if a whole high school *hadn't* been shot up that same day.

And so, for me, school shootings always take me back to that day in the hospital. When I saw Milo laying in a normal, open-air baby crib *for the first time ever,* and I wanted to grab any machine I could find and hook him up to it, and then angrily point my finger in that lovely, smiling nurse's face and say, *"No.* You keep him *here.* Where it's *safe.*" Anyway. That's my story.

Wednesday, May 1, 2019 6:26am
Over the years, I've been the recipient of a shit-ton of unsolicited advice. Seriously, people can't help it.

Advice about my weight

Advice about my migraines

Advice about my periods

Advice about my kid's ears

Advice about my depression

Advice about all the jobs I should be working, and books I should be writing, and how much more I should be leaving my house.

Holy hell, the list goes on and on.

And I know all that stuff comes from a place of love! I know it. But there have been times, times when I was particularly hurting and vulnerable, when all that advice felt predatory. It felt manipulative. And I did not want to thank the person for their loving pushes, I wanted to tell them to go fuck right the fuck off.

What's the point of all this? Fight the urge. Fight the urge to push essential oils, or sacred marijuana, or Mexican chicken doctors, or garlic under the bed, or Vaporub on the feet. Nobody's interested in the fascinating article you just read about the miracle diet that magically takes away your crushing debt or whatever.

I know you want to help.

I know I look like I need help. And other vulnerable look like they need help.

But *particularly for the most vulnerable*, please, skip the Dr. Google, pop-up menu medical advice, and do something kinder, something that will be welcomed: Text a cute picture of your dog. Text a heart emoji. Text something funny.

Don't ask them to explain to you why going vegan isn't going to happen, even if it did take away your ex-husband's cousin's diabetes. Don't try to sell them your religion. Don't tell them that if they just fight harder, or pray harder, or stick this holy water-infused sprig of lavender up in their lady parts, that they'll cure themselves.

Sometimes all that help feels cruel.

Let me repeat that:

Sometimes all that well intentioned and loving advice feels cruel.

I'm not going to explain who or what sent me over the edge this time. Just know that I'm as fine as I ever am, and that this post can be applied to every sick person you know.

Also, thank you. I love you too.

Monday, May 6, 2019 6:09pm

Since Doggy started having aches and pains, he's not nearly as snuggly as he used to be. It's sad, but completely understandable.

But last night, he asked me to pick him up and put him on the ottoman, and then he tucked himself between me and the chair, and zonked out for more than an hour, waking up only if I took my hand off him.

Best hour of the week.

Thursday, May 9, 2019 11:35pm

For all of my reproductive years, I had the right to make my own decisions. I have my own functioning brain, and my own moral compass, and, frankly, I think mine is far superior to those belonging to the whorish, power-mad, money-drunk assholes leading the GOP.

...of course, I pretty much think grizzly bears are smarter and more moral than those c-words, but you already knew that.

But yeah. No one's going to thank you for handing over your daughters' and granddaughters' basic human rights over to their boyfriends, husbands, rapists, church leaders, congressmen, and fathers. And I certainly hope all the young people coming of age now will learn the lesson that my generation clearly didn't: When you don't vote for good things, you get very, very bad things.

Thursday, May 9, 2019 11:46pm

Thoughts while holding the cat: Hmm..... did that sneeze go in the direction of my water bottl—never mind. That one definitely got it.

Wednesday, May 22, 2019 4:55am
Greatest Hits

The following post is long and not particularly funny. It's more of a public service announcement, I suppose.

Also, with the exception of a few cousins, this is hidden from my relatives.

And now for something completely different, here's the story of how I learned that, yes, you absolutely *can* get high by eating a pot brownie.

So, last night (Monday night), around 10 or 11pm, Kiddo came home with pot brownies. And he offered me one.

I've always very firmly but graciously said no to Kiddo any time he's offered to let me smoke with him, but eating a brownie? That felt different...

(I had a voice injury years ago, and my doctors blamed it on chronic tonsillitis, and also on smoking during my high school and college years. I had already quit all smoking before I got pregnant. And when I was in my 30s, I finally got my tonsils out. With time and voice lessons, my voice slowly came back. Although, it still gets tired and scratchy super-fast.)

Anyway, honestly and truly, I didn't think you could *really* get high by eating something. 1.) I'm a big lady, and 2.) it's a brownie. It's been mixed with food and baked in the oven, and I was sure that scientifically speaking, mixing and baking likely remove a lot of potency, right?

Right?

So I ate the brownie. It tasted like the brownie mix itself was probably past the expiry date, and also like they'd been baked a few days before. So, still perfectly edible, but the sort of thing where, if you're me, you pause and think about your poor food intake decisions, and then still finish eating it. There was a pleasant weedy aftertaste.

I sat in my chair and waited for 10 or 15 minutes. Nothing. Whatever, that's fine. It was late, and I still needed to cook up a sausage rice dish (we just call it Sausage Business. It has crumbled sausage, brown rice, Ro-Tel, black beans, corn, onions, peppers, and cheddar cheese. It's everybody's favorite), and also do some laundry.

I got up, I cooked the meal. It took about an hour. I completely forgot that I'd eaten the brownie. It was a total non-event.

I scooped some sausage business into a bowl, texted Kiddo that food was ready if he wanted any, and went and sat down in my chair.

Kiddo came down eager, smiling, and bloodshot. "How do you feel? Are you feeling it?"

I shrugged a little smugly at him. "Nope. Nothing." (Smug, because, you know, 'kids these days aren't nearly as tough as we were back in MY day...')

He's like, "Wow, really? I mean, it takes an hour to feel it... Anyway, I am!"

I paused, because it was strange that he hadn't mentioned how long it takes to feel anything before, but whatever. I'd eaten my brownie well over an hour ago, and nothing.

I turned on a YouTube and started eating my sausage business. Kiddo began fixing himself a plate.

And then time stopped for 1000 years, and when I came back, Kiddo had his food and was going upstairs.

It dawned on me that I was OMG-SO-STONED, and I was relieved that Kiddo was going upstairs. I suddenly remembered that I look down on people who get intoxicated with their adult kids. So it was good that I could be high by myself where I could feel whatever I was going to feel in private.

Like, back in college, I got high *All The Time*. I think I smoked every day of sophomore year. And I remember it made me feel wonderful. This was before I was diagnosed with chronic major-minor depression (so obviously before I started on anti-depressants), and back then, the only time that my brain would shut up and leave me alone was when I was high.

So when I ate that brownie, my only thought was, *wouldn't it be nice if I could feel that silent, safe, and cozy feeling again.*

This felt NOTHING like that. Like, I don't have a font big enough to write the word NOTHING large enough that it would accurately convey how NOTHING LIKE THE OLD DAYS this was.

Ikeptcheckingout.Likegone.Like,IkeptfeelinglikeIwaseitherdying or disappearing.

I decided to turn on some music, because I thought that would help me stay rooted in time. It did help a little.

I kept forgetting to eat my sausage, and I was afraid I'd drop my bowl, so I put it down on the table next to me.

Doggy wanted some, and he wouldn't stop staring at me, but I thought that might be a good thing because I was starting to feel like I needed someone to pay attention to me, and if a bowl of sausage business kept the dog at my side, that was fine.

I kept checking out. It was unpleasant and scary. Doggy walked over to the door and stared at me like he needed to go out. I thought fresh air might help clear my head. Somehow, I managed to stand up and walk over to let him out. Then I managed to carry my bowl of sausage business to the kitchen.

I sat down on the mudroom chair (where we put our shoes on) and checked out. When I came back, Doggy was barking to come in. I could still hear the music in the living room. It was the same song that had been playing when I got up.

We went back to my purple chair, and I sat down and checked out. From really, really far away, -like, from the whole other side of the world, I heard the dog woof at me.

He woofed at me again.

I checked back in, and thought about all the parents who've taken opioids and overdosed in front of their kids, and no one ever mentions it, but probably tons of people overdose in front of their dogs, too. I thought about what a shitty thing I was doing to my dog. To let him be scared like that.

But *I* was scared. Like, every minute that went by, I got more frightened. The precious few synapses of my brain that occasionally re-fired, reminded me of all those funny stories of lame moms and dads who get too high and call 911.

In recent years, my depression has lessened somewhat, but anxiety has become a huge problem for me. And I have all of these practices, mostly centered around opening up the heart-rate checker on my watch and seeing that the number is fine, and taking deep breaths and repeating to myself that I'm not dying.

So I opened up the heart rate checker, and the number was higher than usual, but it wasn't a scary number, so I just did my usual anxiety practices and repeated to myself that I wasn't dying, and told myself I didn't need to call 911.

Except that I kept checking out. And in those rare seconds when I was back, I felt so dim. So maybe I was dying. Maybe I needed help. Maybe I shouldn't be alone. Maybe I was asking too much of the dog.

So I started texting Curtis, who was 35 minutes away at work, and Milo, who was upstairs but who is notorious for not seeing texts from his mother.

By some miracle, Milo came downstairs. I made eye contact with him, and I thought, "This is the most irresponsible thing I've done in his whole life."

And that's when I started crying. Not sobs, not ugly crying, just steady tears falling off my face. I'm pretty sure there were tears for the next two hours straight.

I was soooooooo embarrassed. And soooooooooo sorry. And Kiddo was absolutely lovely. He kept saying how funny this would feel tomorrow, and how he was absolutely positive that I wasn't dying. He offered to play cards with me or maybe Scattergories, and I thought that sounded really nice... except that I kept checking out, and so it was like he'd ask if I wanted to play cards, and then 10,000 years would go by and then he'd suggest Scattergories. Neither happened, but it was a nice idea.

He talked and talked at me. Offhand, I can't think of what-all he said, but I remember thinking, "He's really good at this. He's a very comforting presence. I should tell him how proud I am of him." But I couldn't hold on to a thought long enough to say it.

I had Kiddo watch the locator on my iPhone to tell me where Curtis was, and I remember, after three million years had passed, telling him to LOOK AGAIN because there is no way it should take three million years to get from North Tonawanda to East Aurora. Curtis was almost at Transit Road. Six million years after that, I asked again, and he was coming down Bowen.

And at that point, I still don't think I was quite all the way high yet.

Eventually, Curtis walked in. He looked grim and stressed and disappointed in me (He might not have been any of those things, but I was pretty well locked in a cycle of check out/die, check back in/apologize for being the biggest asshole ever born on this earth, so anything short of sweet, smiley singsonging was going to feel like grave disappointment).

Curtis sat on the ottoman and held my hand or petted my leg, and talked for a little while. I remember imagining that maybe I was unconscious and that Curtis was actually yelling at me to wake up, and then when I'd check back in and he was still talking to me, I wondered which one was real. Was Curtis really calmly talking to me or was he yelling at me to wake up?

Kiddo sat on the chair next to me and talked to Curtis. I think they talked about bands they like. That sucked. I couldn't grasp on to anything real.

Then Curtis had Kiddo get his guitar, and he told him to play his songs 'like they were lullabies,' and that was nicer, but it still didn't keep me rooted in time as well as when Kiddo would talk directly to me and ask questions and then repeat them until I answered. But both of them stayed right there with me. And I remember thinking how GOOD they both were to be there, and I did not deserve this kindness.

My voice didn't work. I remember thinking how absolutely stupid it was that my voice sounded so wrecked when I hadn't smoked anything. Sometimes I could surface enough to try to tell them something, but I have no idea if words were coming out or not.

I remember trying to communicate to them that when I got high as a kid, I always felt safe and quiet, but that this was so different, it was like someone had done one of those karate moves on me where my feet get swept out from under me and I'd landed on my back.

Anyway. Sometime after 3AM, I started to feel like I was checking out less often, and like I was back in my body for longer periods of time. I didn't doubt if this was reality so much.

Milo finally asked if I'd mind if he went to bed, and then a little while after that, Curtis went up to bed too.

I decided that I wasn't ready to sleep. I wanted to stay awake and be grateful for my realness for a while longer.

Around 7:30am, I went to bed. I woke up at 2pm. I was dizzy AF when I got out of bed, and I had a headache that was the pain equivalent of speakers blaring at full volume.

I got some coffee. I puttered around. The cobwebs slowly cleared, and I'd say by 7 or 8PM, I felt all the way normal again.

I used to imagine that some day, when pot became legal and if Curtis didn't mind and my doctor said it was okay, I'd like to stop taking anti-depressants and just be a stoner.

After last night…yeah. I'm sticking with anti-depressants, thanks.

Sunday, May 26, 2019 8:11pm

Curtis, raiding the garage for miscellaneous crap to create a makeshift ramp for Doggy: "See, this is why Marie Kondo is just *wrong.*"

Also, nope. Put me in the 'get a dumpster and throw everything from the basement, attic, and garage into it' camp.

Wednesday, May 29, 2019 6:52pm

It makes me straight-up bananas that Mueller only speaks in lawyerspeak, and that since half of the country only has the attention span for bumperstickerspeak, they interpret his words exactly opposite of how he said them.

For the record, it's mostly Mueller I'm pissed off at at this point.

Talk to us like we're four, dude. Like we're four, and we're dancing around because we have to pee *right now,* so you better use little words and say them fast, because we're only barely listening.

Maybe put some flashy flag graphics in the background instead of the flat government logo. Find a beautiful woman in a low-cut shirt to stand next to you and gut a fish or something to keep us from looking away from the tv.

Friday, June 7, 2019 8:11am

What happens when you go to bed before everybody else:

The house is left unlocked, the garage door is left wide open, and that chair that you (re-)hurt your back moving last week is now back in the middle of the room.

...But one of my other friends had to iron her high school kid's tuxedo and drive it to him this morning after he failed to tell her about a school-day concert, so as annoyed as I am, I don't win the coveted "Most Pissed Off Mother" award for Friday, June 7, 2019.

Tuesday, June 11, 2019 11:38am

When you're in public and subjected to popular radio music and, once again, find yourself wondering 'what the actual hell???'

..when he tastes tequila, he finds out how bad he needs ya.

I know, I know. Lyrics are hard. I can't write them.

But apparently, neither can that guy.

Friday, June 28, 2019 2:21pm

Greatest Hits

In the field of candidates, I was leaning pretty heavily toward Warren being my favorite. She's brilliant, and prepared, and ready, and she's got that Gramma energy that gets more done by 9am than the rest of us managed in all of 2018.

But after last night? I think Harris is the magic bullet. Because she's brilliant and prepared, *and* she's sexually attractive.

So. You've got a deeply stupid man in Trump. He's the original fuck-up son. He's the son who definitely never saw respect or affection reflected back in either of his parents' eyes.

He's the son who had his own deeply stupid sons and can't stand either one of them, because even though he can pretend that he, himself, isn't deeply stupid, he can't pretend that they aren't deeply stupid.

But he's got a certain charisma that works on some people, and he's got family money (it's new money, but who cares), and that works on nearly everybody.

190

And he's deeply stupid, so the people surrounding him are either deeply stupid themselves, or, much more likely, they're smart people, bending him to their will while keeping him flattered and preening.

And, oh, he likes women. Not fat women, not old women, not sixes or sevens or eights, and not women whose dads loved them. He likes them very young, very hot, self-loathing, and desperately insecure. Ideally from a foreign country where the women act like women.

He wants the kind of woman who sees him and is IMPRESSED by him.

He wants a woman who knows, from the moment he corners her and finds out for himself if she's wearing a tampon, that he's the man, and if she'll shut up and receive him, she'll be compensated. (And if she won't shut up and take his fingers and his pay-off, it doesn't matter, because, as he'd say, "she's a lying fat whore and *I* have no doubt about it, and *you* don't have any doubt about it either.")

Now imagine the men who put *that guy* into office. They're the ones who think men and women are on opposing teams, and, despite literally all evidence to the contrary, think the women are winning.

From their perspective, 45 beat Hillary fair and square (you guys need to SHUT UP about the three million fewer votes and the Russian interference!!), because, sure, she was smarter, and, yeah, totally a better human, but who would want to fuck that? Hell, her own husband doesn't want her! And that VOICE, amiright?? Like a freezing cold lake dumped down your pants!

Now here's Kamala. She's old, sure. Five years older than his highness's third wife.

In her fifties, ew.

But she's got a great, musical voice. And those suits can't disguise that smokin body. And she's just brown enough to be exotic, but not so brown as to be, like, brown-brown. She's got good, flowy hair. And there's no denying how sexy she is when she pins someone down with tough questions.

Kamala.

Hillary with sex appeal.

Hillary without the bullshit troglodyte husband.

The men who put 45 in office will have to watch their deeply stupid hero, not only lose a debate to a smart woman (happened before, no prob), but also flirt and fail with a hot chick.

She's the one.

Friday, July 5, 2019 7:33pm

Yep, my dog was just outside when some "great patriot" set off three loud bangs simultaneously. I hope they lost a whole hand. Fuckers. Whoever started the whole, "Everything Real Americans do should be deafening" practice was a titanic shitstain.

(My dog is fine. Thank god his instincts pushed him to our door and not out into the road or over the cliff)

Saturday, July 6, 2019 11:15pm
Greatest Hits

Doggy's been getting slowly but progressively worse. His back legs still support him pretty so-so once he's up, but he's really not great.

And he has accidents in the house. Only 2-3 a week, and then only when I'm being inattentive and not letting him outside within a few seconds of him loitering by the side door.

So I noticed him loitering tonight, and I jumped up. "Okay, let's go out the front door!" And he fast-walked to the front door, and we went outside, and it turns out it was some neighboring town's fireworks extravaganza.

I've had music/tv on loud for days to mask the scary noises, and these were far enough away that I didn't know they were happening until we were outside.

So Doggy walked to the top of the ramp, realized those were definitely scary noises, and hightailed it back to the house.

sigh Okay.

So we're back inside, and I wait a few minutes and he's loitering a lot, and he's sniffing here and there, looking for a place to go, and I go to the side door, all celebrate-y, and "Lets go outside!"

And I open the door, and the poppity-bang-bang festivities are still going on, so Doggy stands at the open door, and just, NOPE.

Okay. Close the door. Walk away from the door. We are on borrowed time here. And cleaning up piss and shit is such a miserable, gross experience, and I've already spent a whole week feeling furious at all the "festive" explosions. Adding a paper towel full of pungent warm shit to the evening would not be good.

Anyway, a few seconds go by. I throw open the door again. It's mercifully silent. I manage to cheerlead him down the ramp.

And the noise starts up again. Like I said, it's off in the distance, so he's not terrified, but he's also very much wanting to go back in the house.

I take a very deep breath and use my strongest, loudest, no-microphone-needed voice, and begin singing a Nanci Griffith song. "I'VE BEEN WALKIN, IN MY SLEEP. COUNTIN TROUBLES, STEAD OF COUNTIN SHEEP."

And it works. He starts wandering around in the grass. I stay within a few feet of him at all times.

"WHERE THE YEARS WENT, I CAN'T SAY! I JUST TURNED AROUND, AND THEY'RE GONE AWAY"

(This is the Duhn Family go-to comfort song. I've sung it at every fireworks and thunderstorm for the last 10 years. Curtis sang it to me during my c-section with Kiddo. We both sang it to Baby Kiddo so many times, it's surprising the lyrics weren't his first words.)

Doggy pees. Miracle of miracles. I'm begging him to go poop, but now the BOOM BOOM BOOM portion of the fireworks show has started, and he's kept it together as long as he's going to.

I go back in the house and cheerlead him up the steps (he still *wants* to use the steps, but he can only do it a few times a day and then his little legs just can't boost him up anymore. It took a minute, but he got in.

We wander with concern through the house together. I know he still needs to poop. I'm actually amazed that it hasn't started falling out of him by now like it tends to do sometimes.

We pace for a minute, two minutes. Surely the fireworks are over by now.

We walk to the front door. He needs some convincing, but finally concedes. It's quiet, praise dog.

He pauses at the top of the ramp, then finally starts down it. His body reminds me of a Fisher Price train. It's like he's made up of an engine, a middle car, and a caboose, and they all wobble separately.

He gets to the bottom and lays down a truly impressive load. The relief I feel that I don't need to clean that off my floor is almost overwhelming.

And now we're back inside. And he's snoozy on the floor, and I'm emotional because —I so hope I'm wrong— this is probably our last 4th of July with him. He's still got a little gas in the tank, but it's not much.

And I'm just feeling sad.

Wednesday, July 10, 2019 12:23pm

This post is about our mailman and how much he loves my dog.

Chester used to spend nearly unlimited time outside. If he wanted to be out there for long stretches, sniffing or snoozing or rolling, that was fine. I always stayed in the house in earshot if he barked, but I let him decide how long he wanted to be out there.

And I still let him decide, but the lengths of time that he spends outside have changed pretty radically in the last year. Chester's still bored in the house, but he really doesn't want to be outside for long, particularly if no one's out there with him.

So that's fine. He goes in and out all day long, just for short little minute-or-two bursts.

But before this year, it was pretty common that he'd be conked out on the driveway when the mailman came, and they'd have themselves a little lovefest out there. Our mailman is a sweet, older-than-me guy, very warm and chatty. And since he loves Chester, any conversation I've ever had with him has been about dogs, either mine or his. He is a *dog guy*.

But of course, he hasn't seen much of my dog at all lately, because Chester spends so little time outside.

Well, today was special. Chester had gone outside a minute or two before, and when I heard him bark, I assumed he wanted to come back in.

But when I went to the door, he was with the mailman, having a joyful reunion.

So I stepped outside to say hi.

The mailman said, with real worry, "For a minute, I thought maybe something was wrong with his leg..."

And I said, "Yeah, he's got a degenerative disease, he doesn't get around as well as he used to."

And my sweet mailman got so emotional, he could barely talk. It took him a good 30 seconds to say, "oh, I hate to hear that. They're such a part of the family, you know?"

So we had ourselves a little cry, and then I called Chester to come inside, and we said goodbye to the mailman, and he walked off.

I'm getting a hard, sad lesson in "the grief that comes before."

Wednesday, July 17, 2019 10:59pm

I actually..... I just saw the video of the "Send her back" chant. I'm actually a little heartened by it.

In it, 45's got his usual crowd of Clairol Age Defy #10 Evangelical white ladies behind him. And when their husbands start ramping up the "Send her back" garbage, all those nice white ladies, who really do have black friends, who really do teach black children, who really do treat black sick people, who really do want to raise children who aren't assholes.... all those nice white ladies looked at the camera and looked either ashamed or scared.

As if they know perfectly well that only garbage humans would threaten a former child refugee-now fairly elected American congressperson. As if they know damn well that Ihan Omar didn't say anything more surprising or controversial than any other representative says. As if, whatever their feelings about "the squad's" ideas, none of them think the squads deserve an arena of frothing, rageful wall-punchers threatening them.

We may never convince those nice white ladies to abandon the Republican Party. I know they've got fetuses to save, and you go to war with the army you have, not the one you want.

But I still saw shame. And maybe we can at least convince some of those women, who really don't like being associated with clear and obvious racist hatred, to find something else to do on Election Day 2020.

It's a nice thought anyway.

Sunday, July 21, 2019 8:40pm

Curtis is so good. He pulled the empty wagon for a few minutes, and let Doggy walk and sniff and poop, and then, when Doggy showed signs of fatigue, he scooped him up and put him in the wagon. A nice "quality of life" stretch of time for a sweet puppy who's had fewer and fewer of those lately.

Tuesday, July 23, 2019 7:24am

Headline: New York State becomes first state to outlaw cat declawing.

Tiny bubble of hope forms inside me: Omg, that's so smart!! That's how you begin to fix a country that hates each other!! You find one issue —any single issue! — that we can all agree on! And since we've proven beyond a shadow of a doubt that we will never agree who deserves human rights, how about if we legislate something around pets? Americans love their pets!

Clicks on comments section: "WELL, ACTUALLY...."

Tiny bubble pops.

Saturday, July 27, 2019 7:24am

Someday the aggrieved will learn the difference between 'under attack' and 'insufferable.'

Sunday, July 28, 2019 2:31am

I'd rather hear about your depression than your death.

Friday, August 2, 2019 7:35am

Dog poop everywhere.

He'd been so reliable for the last few weeks! But yeah.

We've stopped putting him in the crate at night because he has such an impossible time getting in and out of it. And this morning,

I made the grave, GRAVE mistake of staying upstairs to shower and gather up laundry (instead of just peeing and brushing my teeth like usual), and I came downstairs, ready to take advantage of the cool morning and get some laundry done, and instead I was greeted by an entire shit minefield (and a very sorry dog).

On a happier note, after I cleaned it up, I was sitting on the ottoman with the fan pointed at me, feeling despair at how much my back hurts and being certain that my house will smell like dogshit long after the dog is gone, when I noticed that my next-door neighbors got a kitten! It was in the window and VERY EXCITEDLY watching some squirrels out in the yard.

So yeah. Circle of life and all that. One neighbor spends her morning cleaning her dying dog's shit, the other neighbor is learning firsthand just how much of a ruckus an excited kitten can make at 6:30am when there are squirrels outside.

(I don't know what we'll do. He's been reliable during the day because I'm always there, and I'm happy to let him out 2-3-4 times an hour. But I have to sleep sometimes. And so does everybody else. And getting his legs over the lip of his crate really is a stumbling, painful hardship. ...And he's seemed brighter lately, and less like a dying dog, so... Hell. I don't know what to do. Just keep the paper towels and the mop handy, I guess.)

Friday, August 2, 2019 5:50pm

Everybody's got a story about a doozy of a mistake they made on the job.

Well, completely unintentionally, Curtis bought a real PT Cruiser last week while learning the company computer system at his new job.

(They were able to undo the mistake and will now "put safeguards in place" to stop employees from purchasing actual vehicles.)

Let us all be glad that his bosses thought it was hilarious.

Sunday, August 4, 2019 6:58pm

The first time I heard the term "Stochastic Terrorism" was when Bill O'Reilly got George Tiller killed.

Monday, August 5, 2019 4:21pm

Chester is having a good (and bored) day today, so we're playing the game that he made up when he was a puppy: He finds pens on the floor and brings them to me, and I give him treats. We had played a few rounds already, and he was starting to fall a lot, so I ended the game shortly after this one. Now he's zonked out in the corner. Sweet baby.

Tuesday, August 20, 2019 4:53am

Greatest Hits

If he doesn't go on his own in the next few hours, I think we'll need to take Doggy and say our goodbyes when the vet opens.

The first half of yesterday was pretty normal, but in the afternoon, he started falling a lot, and he needed help standing up after a short nap.

I haven't been sleeping more than a few hours at a time, and I was (am) so very tired. Curtis was home, so around 7pm, I asked if he'd mind hanging out with Chester and I'd go upstairs and sleep awhile.

When I came back down at 11:30, everything was different. I can't explain exactly how, but Doggy was walking different, and his face was so different. He didn't have his usual eager, ready-for-anything expression. He looked, frankly, terrible. He had, what I think they call a Thousand Yard Stare.

I've had the conversation a few times lately, and people always say, "He'll tell you when he's ready to go." I didn't believe them until last night at 11:30.

Curtis took Doggy out in the wagon last evening while I was asleep. He let him out to wander around a bit at that mini-park near the traffic circle in town. But Doggy got tired so quickly, so after he pooped and explored for a couple minutes, Curtis loaded him back into the wagon.

When I came downstairs, Curtis was researching wheel-carts for dogs. He had all of this hope that all Chester needed was a set of wheels and he'd bounce right back.

But I started crying and couldn't stop, and then Curtis started crying too, because I think he could see what I was seeing.

I texted the kids to come down and be with us, and they did, and we all cried together. Doggy laid on the floor and let everybody pet him.

Finally, they all went to bed, and Doggy and I are down here. His breathing is weird and labored, he keeps needing to go outside, and when he comes back in, I need to clean his backside as much as he'll let me. It's a little bloody and a little oily, and it's clear to me that his guts are bothering him so much more than everything else.

He's laying where I can see him, and his breathing is not okay. He's working hard. I keep telling him that he's been the very best doggy anybody could ever ask for, and it's okay, and I love him so much.

I keep hoping that we'll go to the vet and this will have been the death version of Braxton-Hicks contractions, and they'll give him some Imodium and a shot of B-12 and he'll be good for a while longer. But I think that's magical thinking.

So I'm here, and I'm crying, and I'm looking at all the pens sticking out of the furniture that Doggy didn't retrieve. I keep thinking, we should have said goodbye to him yesterday. But yesterday, he was still bringing us the pens. Yesterday, he was weak, but he still wanted to be here. And we just couldn't have known.

Wednesday, August 21, 2019 3:25am

Thank you so much for all of your likes and comments and texts and calls today. They trickled in all day long and were the perfect doses of comfort. I know I say it every time, but social media is best on the important days. Here's a couple pictures that Billie took before we left for the vet (Billie is Milo's partner who lives with us now).

I forget literally everything that I don't write down, so as I think of things I want to remember about this time, I'm going to put them on Facebook. You can read them or not. They're mostly just here for me, and they're in no particular order. I like when they pop up in Facebook Memories.

I can't remember if I read it in a book or a fortune cookie, but today I remembered the line about *'every year we pass the anniversary of our birth and the anniversary of our death. Only one of those dates is known to us.'* I thought it was neat and sad, that on two of Chester's death anniversary dates, I'd felt compelled to take his picture because he was being so especially cute. Spooky. Sad.

I fixed myself a turkey sandwich and baby carrots with bleu cheese for lunch today. It's my usual lunch. I probably eat it 5-6 days a week. Chester always gets the crust corners and he always gets the last carrot. Today, I finished my carrots and I threw the crust corners in the trash. It felt awful.

Chester was always a thirsty doggy, but for the last month or so, he just couldn't get satisfied. He drank and drank and drank. And tonight, I noticed that his bowl was less than half full and scolded myself for not noticing that sooner. And then I remembered.

Last week, I found Chester on his blue bed under the table, where he often napped during the day, and where he started sleeping every night after his crate got too difficult to get in to. But half of his body was on the floor, and his back half was still on his bed, and he was stuck, just waiting for somebody to come find him. I have my own troubles with mobility, and fishing him out from under there was difficult and awkward and I was so upset, wondering if he'd been stuck for the whole four hours I'd been upstairs. So I decided that I'd move his blue bed into the living room. I figured that he'd continue to sleep near the stairs (waiting for us to come back down), and that, if he decided to sleep on his blue bed, it would only be when I was downstairs and could help him get up when he needed it.

He never used the blue bed again. But Mary sure likes it.

I've always kept dumb insomnia hours, so whenever I went to bed at a time that wasn't the same as Chester's bedtime, I'd point upstairs, and I'd say, "Mama's so snoozy. I'm going to bed. You go be with Daddy." And he'd do the dog version of nodding and he'd go find Curtis.

Today I needed some sleep, and everybody else was already upstairs, and Kitty was asleep on Chester's blue bed. And even though I've never worried about her being alone before, today it felt wrong to leave her down here. So I said, "Hey Kitty?" And she woke right up. I pointed upstairs and I said, "Mama's so snoozy. You want to come upstairs with me?" And hand to God, she got up and followed me upstairs, and slept with me for a few hours.

Milo posted on Twitter about Chester today, and one of his friends said, "Chester finally got to go upstairs." It made me cry extra hard, but I loved it. I did my best to only ever be upstairs if I was sleeping or showering (and I can prove that by how absolutely filthy the upstairs is compared to the downstairs), because Chester would wait at the bottom of the stairs with the most pitiful face. He didn't mind it when everybody was sleeping, but if he could hear us moving around upstairs, he was the saddest boy ever.

It's cool enough to have the windows open tonight. I'm sitting at my computer, next to the open window, and a breeze just blew the smell of dog poop from out on the porch. It reminds me of last night. How I couldn't tell if he was staring at me because he needed me to help him stand, or if he was just staring at me because he loved me and he was usually looking at me. The shape of his face had changed so much, I couldn't tell if his eyes were pleading or soft. They just looked dark. So, I helped him up every hour, and lured him outside with treats, and he needed to go and go and go each time.

All night, he laid on the floor, his breathing too weird and jumpy and shallow, and I honestly and truly thought he'd die by morning. I folded laundry and played my ukulele and sang for him one last time. Finally, around 8am, just as the vet was opening and I was trying to plan what to say when I called, I got up and heated some pizza in the microwave.

I brought it into the living room and started eating it. And that hilarious dog. I watched the blankness in his eyes completely dissipate, and the old alertness and hope and hunger come back. He slithered like a snake for a few seconds, then he found something to push off from, and it took a lot of attempts and effort, but then he was sitting next to the ottoman, eager for pizza crust. For more reasons that one, I've always thought that dog was my patronus, lol. I, too, will be on my death bed someday, and I'll be like, "Wait. Do I smell pizza?"

At the vet today, they gave him a bowl filled with cut up hotdogs, cheez whiz, and biscuits. He gobbled the whole thing. I always used to joke that when Doggy went to the vet to get his nails done, it was always the 'best day ever!' because they kept him still by just feeding him treat after treat after treat after treat. So 'best day ever' was on my tongue when I saw the bowl of hot dogs and cheez whiz, but then I remembered why I was crying so hard, and then just cried harder.

We all stayed for the end, even Billie. We all petted him, and told him how much we love him, and what a good boy he is, and it was peaceful and devastating.

There's loud thunder in the distance that's getting closer. Chester would have hated it. Kitty's already under the couch and she's got a much higher tolerance for scary noises.

I went around closing windows. And when I got to the porch door, I was planning to walk outside and watch the storm roll in. But I couldn't bring myself to go out there. The porch was uniquely Chester's space, and only because of the ramp. So, it was newly Chester's space.

And the thunder was really loud, and I felt scared even though I used to love watching storms. Not tonight, I guess.

I closed the house and turned on music just like I have every storm for the last 10 years.

I just thought that he's been in the other room for too long and I'd better go check on him. And then I remembered.

This really sucks.

Wednesday, August 21, 2019 1:31pm

I'm at that horribly guilty stage of grief: thinking of all the things we can do now that we don't have our little anxiety machine policing every move.

The other night, as Doggy was laying on the floor staring at me, I thought, "Oh my god. I can make hummus again!" (he haaaaaated the food processor)

We loved him so much that it was worth it to tiptoe around his mental health needs, which grew more with every passing year (another reason why I've always felt special kinship with him. I'm sure we fed off each other's crazy).

But now I'm starting to feel some layers of freedom coming back, and I'm feeling relief followed by crushing guilt. I guess it's okay to have swinging emotions. I think it's normal. But it feels terrible.

Sunday, August 25, 2019 1:41pm

There is a youngish, decently attractive man outside, doing landscaping work across the street, and his female coworker is a smoking hot, all legs, super-model type, who is working every bit as hard as he is.

And he is really blowing it with the pickup attempts.

He can't seem to stop literally imitating Rain Man: "Gotta get the cones out." (their truck is parked on the road) "Gotta get the cones out. Gotta get the cones out. Gotta go to Kmart. Gotta watch Judge Wapner. Uh Oh. Uh oh."

Omg. I'm so embarrassed sitting in my living room, hearing all of this.

Monday, August 26, 2019 7:24pm

I've been too much of a coward to go out and tell the mailman about Chester.

Like, he's the mailman, you know? He's not my friend or my peer. He's just somebody who gets paid to walk up my driveway and deliver the mail every day.

I was asleep this morning and Curtis was awake. And the mailman rang the bell to deliver something from Amazon, and Curtis answered.

I asked Curtis if he told the mailman about Chester, and he (looked at me like I was bananas and) said no.

And I said, "I bet he knows anyway."

There's no poop in the driveway or on the ramp or on the porch (and there was ALWAYS so much poop at the end), and no doggy to bark at the doorbell or even to bark at the little bleep that the mailman's scanner made.

So I feel a little ashamed for hiding. Because that's what I've been doing. I should go out there tomorrow with a tissue box, and tell my sweet old mailman that Chester passed away, and we should have a cry together in my driveway.

I have no idea what my mailman's name is, but I do know he loved my dog.

We got a sympathy card from the vet today. It was so loving and sad, and the secretary wrote "We're so sorry for your loss. We loved Chester too." And I sat at my table and cried my eyes out. Because they were there that day, you know? The appointment was at 11:40am. They were about to go to lunch, but they waited. All the office staff was behind the desk. They were all crying too.

This week is different. I still feel around with my toes for the dog before I stand up (after he couldn't tolerate being picked up anymore, he usually camped out between my chair and ottoman. So, my toes got in the habit of feeling around for him). And I still expect him to bark at scary noises on the tv. I got my first Instacart order the other day, and I made a mad dash for the door so I could block Doggy off from the driver and the groceries. Oh right. I don't need to do that anymore.

But this week, it's all less of a shock. It's just sad. Sad sad sad.

Hug your doggeroos today on this National Doggy Day. Tell them they're so good and you're so happy they're yours.

Friday, August 30, 2019 7:06pm
Doggy's home. Up on the shelf next to Mika Kitty. He'll get his real urn in late October. I'm sad sad sad. But I hated having him away from me, so there's comfort here, too.

Sunday, September 1, 2019 11:40pm

I feel like political differences are perfectly encapsulated in the comments section of a local news story where another car accident has happened at a known dangerous intersection:

"This intersection is so dangerous! Why can't we get a red-light here?! It would save lives!"

"Well, if everybody would just follow the rules, these accidents wouldn't happen! Just put down your phone, close your legs, and pray in school, and nothing bad will ever happen to you! It's common sense, people!"

Tuesday, September 3, 2019 11:16am

Finally got to have that cry in the driveway with my mailman. His dog is also very ill and he said he'd hoped Chester would wait for him and they could go to Heaven together.

He also said, "I hope you don't mind; I've always said he was *my* Welsh corgi because he was on my route."

Wednesday, September 4, 2019 12:21am

I'm watching cat introduction videos because Billie brought their kitty, Matilda to live with us, and she's bored just living in the bedroom.

I think we'll need to get some kind of fence thing to separate them. Let Matilda have the upstairs hallway until the kitties get more accustomed to each other. They met briefly tonight, and there was hissing, but no violence. It's a start.

She's a cuuuuute kitty! FLUFFY!

Thursday, October 10, 2019 2:25pm

I was conked out in the chair and I could hear rustling and giggling in the other room, and then these sweet knuckleheads appeared and sang to me.

The cats, in particular, were really into it.

Wednesday, October 23, 2019 4:26pm

A man with a heavy southern accent saying the word 'dipshit' is one of life's great aural pleasures.

Sunday, September 8, 2019 10:46am

The Left: There are really easy things you can do to offset climate change in small ways: when you buy a new car, choose one with the best gas mileage. Keep your car's tires inflated, use LED lights in your house, eat less meat or no meat. Of course, as individuals, there's only so much we can do. Regulations against polluters are the most important to our health and to the health of the planet.

FOX News, who definitely is the voice of common sense or something: puts straws in a steak and declares, I'M NOT TRIGGERED YOU'RE TRIGGERED!

Wednesday, November 13, 2019 9:42pm

Yesterday, Milo came in from snow blowing and he was sad because this is our first deep snow without Chester to run through.

Sunday, November 17, 2019 12:22am

I started watching the TV show House tonight. I used to watch it when it was a new show, but it's been well over a decade since I've seen it. It's still a great show.

But, as always, when I watch something from the beforetimes through the present-day lens, I often find myself wondering if/how that thing contributed to 45 being in office.

So Dr. House is an unrepentant asshole. But, underneath it all, there's a decency and an unrelenting need to get the answer/do the right thing.

I wonder if some portion of the electorate thinks that all unrepentant assholes are good humans when it matters, because Dr. House was both excellent AND and asshole?

Hell if I know. I would love to live in a world where I'm not constantly asking myself that question though.

Tuesday, November 26, 2019 6:02am

Last night, I dreamed that I picked Doggy up and snuggled his little body to me. He was warm and stinky.

Greatest Hits

I AM ONLY VENTING. ABOUT MY KID. PLEASE REPLY WITH HEAD PATS, THERE THERES, AND ABSOLUTELY POSITIVELY NO ADVICE

Also, there's cussing.

There are two reasons why I never cook: 1. I can't tolerate standing in front of a heat source, and 2. Pots and pans are weird shapes, and they don't fit in the dishwasher in a pleasing way.

So if I'm cooking, it's because I am in the sort of headspace that can take on both: being hot, and dealing with pots and pans. On a great week, this might happen twice. Most weeks it's barely once, and when the bees in my brain are really really angry, three weeks might pass before I can bear to use the stove.

#3 on the list of reasons why I never cook, is that I have to scrub the pots and pans before they go into the dishwasher. I require that my pots and pans be PRISTINE. No scorch marks, no scratches, no gunk in the corners.

And the dishwasher can't do that. And I know, I know, why do you have to put something in the dishwasher if it's already been hand washed? I don't know. It just does. I never said I made sense.

And lastly, the dishwasher. Loading the dishwasher takes a very long time.

First you have to make sure there's no cheese on any of the plates or silverware (and omfg, there's always so much cheese). Then you need to have everything organized so that everything is orderly, and arranged properly by shape and color, that the silverware is evenly spaced and separated by category.

One should look in their loaded dishwasher and feel calmed. "I have taken the chaos of my gross kitchen and I have tamed it. I am in control of my life."

I wash my hands less often than a person with OCD, but suffice to say that there's a reason why I keep jumbo-sized hand soaps next to all of my sinks. If I stuck to the standard-sized soaps, I'd be changing them out every few days.

—But this works in my favor! Because if you keep the cheesy dishes in the sink, there can be water and soap running on them every single time I wash my hands! So, most dishes look perfectly clean before I even start thinking about loading the dishwasher.

Enter my kid and his partner. First of all, they're kids. They have absolutely no concept of how many tiny little tasks parents do, because they haven't fully lived on their own yet and experienced what it's like when nobody else comes along and wipes down the counters or deals with the sticky spot on the floor. And you really can't teach that, it only comes when you live on your own, and yesterday's cat puke is still in the same spot, and all of the socks that you wadded up and tossed in the laundry basket, come out of the dryer still wet, dirty and gross, etc.

And, unfortunately, I only remember to tell them to clean the kitchen when I'm angry, and so it's, "GODDAMIT WILL YOU CLEAN THIS FUCKING KITCHEN," and not, "Guys, I know you love your late night cooking dates, and yes, it's all very sweet, but I have to insist that you scrub every pot and pan, scrub the cook top, unload and reload the dishwasher, take out the trash, get all your fucking wrappers off the counters, put all the fucking recycling in the fucking recycling containers, take out the compost, wipe all the fucking drips off the counters, WRITE THINGS ON THE FUCKING GROCERY LIST WHEN YOU FINISH SOMETHING, and, for fuck's fucking sake, just *treat the kitchen like your mother has crippling anxiety, and try not to trigger it every single day!*

Ahhh, okay! That's better!

They're such nice kids. But holy balls, they need their own kitchen. And their own bathroom. And their own mudroom.

Head pats and there-theres only please. I'm already pissy, I don't want to bite more peoples' heads off who don't deserve it.

Thursday, December 12, 2019 12:28pm

TFW you fill your coffee cup too full, and you walk back to your chair and realize you've been dripping the whole way, but there's no doggy following behind you to clean it up.

Tuesday, December 17, 2019 12:27pm

I feel like all cults, religious and otherwise, boil down to the sentence, "We're not lying to you, everybody else is lying to you."

Sunday, December 22, 2019 3:04am

Kiddo and Billie came home, and he said, "We're both fine! But I hit a deer."

He was able to drive the Vibe home but the lights and the grill look ...like it hit a deer.

I'm *beyond grateful* that they're all right. But with Curtis (and Curtis' car) in North Carolina for a week, the timing's just awful.

We'll figure it out. I actually think that, rides-wise, we'll be totally fine. The bigger stressor is going to be deciding if we should total the car or fix it. Alas, I'm no expert, and I had a migraine long before they got home, I still have it, and everything can wait for morning and beyond.

They're okay.

Monday, December 23, 2019 8:04pm

$3700. to fix a car that KBB says is worth less than $500.

Sounds about totaled.

2020

Thursday, January 9, 2020 7:23am

I'm grateful for every picture and video I took of my doggy, but sometimes they just break my heart into a million pieces.

Wednesday, February 12, 2020 10:17pm

Someone on a corgi Facebook page shared a pic of her doggy tonight, and he was too skinny, and his little face was starting to sink like Chester's did, and it made me so very sad.

They're beautiful their whole lives, but a bony/sinking face is the first detail I see now.

Tuesday, February 25, 2020 3:40am

I did something real damn stupid.

Of the "home improvement" variety.

I replaced the old-time 'springy' toilet paper holder with a new, hook-style one.

I had been intending to ask Curtis to deal with it, but his jobby-job has been super intense for a bunch of days, and I decided to watch a YouTube and give it a try on my own, and save him some work.

It did not go well.

Literally no part of the task went well.

It looks -awful-. And it'll be a miracle if the thing is even still attached to the wall come morning.

I may be investing in one of those tall tp holders that stands on the floor.

I deserve to have some hot-tempered man come scream, "WHAT THE HELL WERE YOU THINKING????" at me.

Curtis was describing a conflict between two of his co-workers:

"Person A is like an artist. He writes code that I'm literally envious of. It's beautiful and it follows all the best practices, and I'm always asking him questions so I can learn from him, since I'm new to this specific programming language.

And Person B, ... well, imagine if HGTV had hired Shelly Duhn to come into a grand mansion they were flipping, and had her hang the toilet paper holder....."

(I was laughing so hard I didn't even get my feelings hurt)

To celebrate the life of the great Kenny Rogers, I just spent the last hour+ learning *Lady*. I love songs that let singers take the lid off and project their voices all the way up to the rafters and back to the lobby. So that's basically what I was doing.

I'm sure all the people in this house were like, "You know, normal people don't sing at 4am, Shelly!"

But 4am is the BEST time to sing!

(I didn't record it because, like every other song I play, by the time I got to the end, I was playing it so fast, all the meaning was lost.

So, *Lady* is all passion and sex and soaring violins. ..except when I play it. Then it's more like if the Duke boys were singing it as they jumped their car over a creek.)

215

Tuesday, March 24, 2020 4:31am

[Headline: Texas Lt. Governor Dan Patrick suggests that he and other seniors are willing to die to get the economy going again]

Dear grandparents: Everybody wants you living and whole and doing whatever you damn please with your money. Please don't martyr yourselves at this altar.

And please, PLEASE, enthusiastically invite this dude, and all the dudes just like him, to eff right off with this nonsense.

Sunday, March 29, 2020 11:46am

I've seen a meme shared a bunch of times, showing the president looking very serious, and it said, "Pray for the president. He has the weight of the world on his shoulders."

And you know, just that: if I believed for a single second that he felt the weight of *even just his own voters'* needs and expectations, I'd feel so comforted. If I thought he wanted to save even just Red State lives, not just because he enjoys the feel of their tongues on his asshole, but because he could see the worth of their existence even when their tongues are inside their mouths, I'd feel better.

Sunday, April 12, 2020 4:52pm

My mailman cried over Chester twice: When we put the ramp off the front steps, and when Doggy died. He genuinely loved my dog. And my dog adored him.

My mailman told me that being part of sending postcards to my nephew Jack every day when little Jack had cancer last year was one of the greatest honors of his career. He cried for Jack too.

Postal carriers are awesome. Buy some stamps. #savethepostoffice

Saturday, April 18, 2020 11:03pm

Please don't get yourself killed to own the libs. It doesn't make you a free-thinking individual, it makes you *dead.*

216

Strap on your fancyass gun and march around your backyard if it makes you feel strong and in control. But stay home.

The people telling you this is a choice between the economy and Grandma are either idiots or they're evil.

You can get through hardship if you're alive.

So stay alive.

Friday, May 1, 2020 12:12pm

Living with a young man mostly means that every screw-top re-usable water bottle in the house requires superhuman strength to get open.

Tuesday, May 19, 2020 10:58pm

I just finished watching the end of Avatar's Season 1 on Netflix. Where Princess Yue becomes the moon, and the last few seconds of the episode are where we see Princess Azula for the first time, and It's. So. Omgggggggggg!!!

And I flashed back to the first time I watched that episode, and Milo was almost 7 years old, and he got so excited, he ran outside and did a lap around the house in his jammies (because it was a night-time show), and he could barely stand it that he'd have to wait MONTHS for the next season to start. Happy memory.

Sunday, May 24, 2020 9:07pm

In a perfect world, the president would constantly repeat, "I'm listening to the experts, and you should too,"

and not *"Why aren't you being nicer to me???"*

I'm proud to be a New Yorker. Our state government certainly hasn't gotten everything right, and they're going to have to answer for some big missteps. But there's one certainty that I have: They're trying to get this right. They're trying to see the big picture, they're listening to people who know stuff, and they're doing their best.

Saturday, June 6, 2020 2:14am

I was cleaning up the kitchen, nearly ready to go up to bed. Curtis came downstairs and said, "Good morning!"

Me: Oh, I didn't know you were sleeping!

Curtis: Yep, I slept great! How are you?

Me: Ugh, miserable! I'm too hot and I can't stop sweating, and I have a headache, and the cats are on my last nerve! It's pretty much just gloom, despair, and agony on me.

Curtis: ...

Me: Deep, dark depression, excessive misery

Curtis: ...

Me: If it weren't for bad luck, I'd have no luck at all!

Curtis: *Whoooooa!*

Tuesday, June 9, 2020 12:25pm

When people handwring that no one wants to hear from police leadership on the subject of reimagining police work, it's a lot like how no one wants to hear from Catholic bishops on the subject of pedophilia.

Oh, you're sad because no one considers you a trusted expert anymore? Well, whose fault is that?? And how much more time do you need to get your shit together? 10 years? 50?

Sunday, June 28, 2020 6:20am

A little green Honda Civic just drove by, and I thought about Plain Gramma and how she used to put bandaids over the rust spots on hers.

Tuesday, July 7, 2020 10:00am

Greatest Hits

This photo appeared in my Social Studies textbooks. I assume it appeared in yours, too?

I keep coming back to 45's Fourth of July speeches, about how 'The Radical Left wants to indoctrinate your children.' But let's just use this picture as an example: How would different history books describe this photo?

Because if one American History book teaches its children that we took a weird looking mountain and carved the faces of our most beloved founding fathers into it, and we should feel great pride..

..and a different American History book teaches that the US broke a treaty with the Lakota to take their mountain, already named Six Grandfathers, and carved white presidents' faces into it, is that indoctrination?

Or is that just holding the mirror up?

Does it perhaps give us more context about why present-day protests about pipelines are so fraught? Does it make us look at the photos of excavators parked on sacred lands today to build 45's monument to racism, and feel anything at all?

Because if we only teach American children that the US is great, that the US must never be questioned, that the US is "the good guy, period!," then we end up with a bunch of really shitty people who are the exact opposite of great.

We end up with a bunch of really shitty people who lack empathy, who never need to have a hard night of the soul, who never feel called to Make America Do Better.

219

Nobody alive today had anything to do with the broken treaty that gave us Mount Rushmore. Nobody alive today carved those faces into that mountain. You don't need to feel like an asshole because that vandalized mountain exists.

But if you only feel defiant, belligerent, *Eff You* pride when you look at the faces on Mount Rushmore, who, exactly is the indoctrinated one?

Monday, July 13, 2020 4:12pm

Me: My headache came back. It was a little better but now it's bad again.

Curtis: That really sucks. Can I do anything for you?

Me (sulking and grumpy): NO.

Curtis: Should I feel sorry for you?

Me: YES.

Curtis: Should I kiss your forehead?

Me: PROBABLY.

Curtis: (comes over and gives light-light-light little forehead kisses)

Me: Harder.

Curtis: (blows noisy raspberry on my forehead)

Me (giggling): That actually helped!

Friday, July 17, 2020 4:06pm

I'm usually pretty good at completely ignoring angry-mediocre-white-man horseshit, but last night, I stupidly read a copy/paste post that asserted that mask mandates were created by dictatorial Nazis and are designed to turn the populace into frightened sheep.

And even though I keep reminding myself to consider the source, even though I have exactly zero respect for anyone who thinks that belligerence is an appropriate response to a fucking worldwide pandemic, that post is still rolling around in my brain.

Human beings are being literally harmed, literally intimidated, and literally unprotected with the blessing of the Trump administration. I don't feel personally unsafe, but my dread and worry for already vulnerable populations grows bigger and bigger by the day.

Wednesday, July 29, 2020 5:25pm

I live the *suburban dream* in a lovely, quaint little village.

It's a very curious place because some of the houses right in the heart of the village have been fully renovated and sell for a small fortune.

And some of the houses, like mine, need a lot of attention and can be bought quite cheaply.

Realtors call them "starter homes," because they don't expect young families to be able to afford anything fancy until they're older.

You know. Because of the low income.

Oh! You know, now that I think about it, I think maybe he meant a different kind of *low income*? Hmmmm, I wonder what kind of "low income" he could have meant? Maybe we'll never know.

Friday, August 28, 2020 5:49am

Holy buckets, between forcing his elderly supporters to cram together for relentless hours on a miserably muggy August night during a raging pandemic, and then forcing them to run the gauntlet of non-violent but extremely loud and absolutely furious protestors without the benefit of crowd-dispersing tear gas, it's almost as if the president actually wanted all of his strongest supporters to have the most unpleasant night of their lives.

What an absolute shitshow.

Friday, August 28, 2020 3:16pm
My kiddo's moving out, and our days of unlimited take-out and errand running are over.

Sunday, August 30, 2020 6:58pm
They're protesting police violence and inadequate consequences for police violence. That's it.

Even the usual empty words we've heard for decades would cool some heads.

Instead, President Stable Genius threatens to send in tanks.

It's the "I'll give you something to cry about!" method of presidenting.

Friday, September 11, 2020 1:20pm
This is 100% true.

(I can't remember if this took place on 9/11/01 or 9/12/01)

There was a candlelight vigil in Raleigh NC, near where we lived back then. Like every other earthling, I felt grief-stricken and shocked by the attack on NYC.

I brought Kiddo with me. I made a sign and taped it to his stroller. It said, "Let there be peace on earth and let it begin with me."

I got a few sad smiles and nods. But mostly I got offended and/or truly infuriated looks.

"We all came together as Americans back then" is a towering load of horseshit peddled by the exact same people peddling that exact same magical thinking today.

Sunday, September 20, 2020 11:13am

Just like how when the first snow falls, you have to teach yourself to drive again,

the first night that you sleep under your winter blanket, you have to re-learn the art of not dutch-ovening yourself.

Saturday, September 26, 2020 9:16pm

Be a real shame if you lost your healthcare during a pandemic and had to celebrate that loss of care because someone told you your death would be a win for Life.

Sunday, September 27, 2020 1:06am

I'm so grateful we don't have to experience e-learning, I actually feel guilt about it.

The gulf between the folks who 'are a bit inconvenienced' and the folks being swallowed whole by stress is really easy to see with regard to COVID.

Wednesday, September 30, 2020 4:17pm

I'm as comfortable calling for "law and order" as conservatives are saying "black lives matter."

Conservatives know perfectly well that when folks say, "Black Lives Matter," we mean "Police must stop killing black people who aren't threatening them. _Policing_ must change."

And folks who fall on the side of anti-fascism know perfectly well that when folks say, "Law and Order," they mean, "Police can do any goddamn thing they want. _Protesters_ deserve everything they get, whether they're setting fires (completely against the law) or holding a sign (totally A-OK)."

Friday, October 2, 2020 1:38am

Here's the thing. If Trump ended up in the ICU, face down on a bed, with a diaper covering his asscrack but open on the sides, and a ventilator breathing for him, and someone took his picture like that, it would save so many lives.

We can't do anything at all for the people he already killed with his penis-pumped bravado. We can't save the people who thought if they hung a big enough flag off the back of their truck and 'made the libs cry,' they'd be immune from the latest Democratic hoax. We can't save those peoples' vulnerable loved ones.

But we could save the people who have only stayed negative so far because of luck and not caution.

Fuck Donald Trump. Whether he finds his way into the lake of fire today, tomorrow, or ten years from now, we can all rest assured that (if such a lake exists) it will welcome him with open arms.

Wear a mask. Wash your hands. Stay home when you can. The fewer people out existing in public, the safer it is for those who have to exist in public.

Monday, October 5, 2020 2:23am

It's been a week since we learned Trump doesn't pay any taxes.

It's been five days since Trump told the Proud Boys to stand back and stand by.

It's been four days since we heard Melania say, "Who gives a fuck about Christmas?"

It's been four days since we learned Trump has COVID.

It's been two days since we got confirmation that Trump knew he had COVID and went to his fundraiser at Bedminster anyway.

So yeah. This is fun.

I get that Kamala's got a tightrope to walk, and she can't rock the boat.

I know we're trying to pick off Republican women, who also hate being treated like brainless *Little Ladies* by the shittiest, stupidest men on earth... but jeeeeeeez. Giving Pence the upper hand on climate change??? Fuuuuuuuuuuuckkk!

Greatest Hits

There is a Pepto Bismol commercial on TV, and every single time I see it, without fail, I think of my brothers.

Jamie is two years older than me. And when we were little, and Jamie felt like getting me in trouble, he would lean over and say, "Poodle."

That's it.

"Poodle."

There is no reason at all why this would be funny, except that it was *die laughing* funny. Every time. *Especially* in church.

And there I'd be, snorting, shaking, sputtering, and generally making an enormous spectacle of myself as I tried, and failed, again, to not completely crack up.

Then there's my brother Joe, who's five years younger than me, who could make me laugh just as hard by singing the line, "God blessed Texas," like the Little Texas country song, as if he was enormously constipated and pushing (I literally just cracked myself up, TWICE, remembering the face Joe would make, flat smile, eyebrows raised, worried eyes, as he sang, "MMMmm, GOD blessed Texas." ..make that three times).

225

So every time I see that Pepto Bismol commercial, with the perfect catchy way the man sings, "Diarrhea!" I get the giggles, then I picture my brothers making me laugh helplessly. And then I imagine the siblings who are children right now, bored senseless in church, making each other laugh until they can't breathe, just by mouthing/singing, "Diarrhea!"

Sunday, November 8, 2020 6:53pm

Calling out to all the sheeple, all the indoctrinated soy boys and beta cucks, the snowflakes, the cancel cultists, the virtue signalers, the COVID hysterics hiding in their basements, the feminazis, the #metoo liars who aren't hot enough to rape, the antifa supersoldiers, the radical leftist mob, the destroyers of suburbs, the killers of Christmas, the SJWs, the triggered pants-wetters, the safe space needers, the men in dresses lurking in public bathrooms, the cancers on our once great nation, the baby killers, the freedom haters, the pizza parlor pedophilia supporters, the lamestream media, the politically correct, the gun grabbers, the looters burning down all the cities, the election riggers, the Mexican caravans, the corrupt mailmen, the persecutors of Christians, the demon-rats, the lobster eating welfare queens, the Martin Lucifer Kings, the latte swillers up in their ivory towers, the libtards, and, of course, George Soros:

The Right would like you to show grace, civility, and humility while they mourn the election results and experience the fear of us that they've created in their heads and fantasized about for decades.

You should.

If you can, it's better for you if you can turn the other cheek. It's better to go high. It really is. You'll live longer and be happier.

If, however, you would rather invite them to go snack on the biggest, gnarliest bag of dicks they can find? Yeah, that works too.

Sunday, November 15, 2020 5:32am

I'll feel comfort someday when this conversation I had with Curtis pops up in my Memories:

S: I wanted to ask you. I don't think we're going to end up taking the euthanasia route with Mary. I think we're just going to find that she's died some morning, probably soon. So then, will I just call the vet to have her cremated?

C: That's one option, I suppose.

(Mary [Who's still fairly perky most days if not hungry] climbs out of bed and comes over to see why we're talking about her. She jumps up on my lap and settles in).

S: What are the other options?

C: Well, we always buried our cats when I was a kid.

S: Oh. No, I don't want to do that. Mary's earned her way onto the shelf with Mika and Chester. Even if she was a bad cat.

C: Yeah, that's true. And I've got news for you. Mary's not a bad cat.

S: You're right. Mary is a good cat." (Snuggles the purring cat.) "A very good, BAD cat.

C: I've known bad cats. Mary's not a bad cat.

S: (singing to Mary): I don't kno-ow! You're pretty terrible!

(Mary purrs louder and gives headbutts of love)

Sunday, November 29, 2020 4:42pm

Omg you guys, I just had the CUTEST pizza delivery driver.

So, I like to order and pay online, and my special instructions are, "Strong preference for no contact, please leave pizza on the side steps."

We have a covered front porch with no sidewalk leading to it <East Aurora. shrug>, and the side steps are closer to the back of the house.

I had a notification from Amazon that there was a package delivered today, so I happened to be out on the front porch picking up that box, when this old Toyota clunker with a roaring muffler pulls into the driveway. The kid sees me and points and waves. So even though I'd said "side steps," and there's no walkway to where I was standing, I stayed put and waited for the kid.

Omg, this kid.

Other than the mask, he was straight out of the 1980s. He was wearing a ball cap, but I still think he must have had a mullet, because non-curly hair doesn't flip out in all directions like that when the sides are long. Seriously, he looked like every kid on my big brother's high school soccer team, circa 1987. Under that cap, I'm sure he had the half-assed suburban high-schooler version of the young Agassi haircut.

He had a long trench coat on. Remember how, before Columbine, trench coats were kind of cool? Like, Judd Nelson in Breakfast Club?

So, he marches toward the steps. He wasn't a big guy, but he had a big guy voice. "Hey! Thank you SO much for the tip! That was awesome!" (There was nothing special about the tip, lol, he was just exuberant).

I bumble through my "You're welcome! You can just leave the pizzas right there...."

So he sets the boxes down, and then shoots me a thumbs up. "Hey. GO BILLS!"

And then he swaggers away with all the confidence of someone who is definitely having sex with the entire drama club. He gets to the car, whips off his mask, tosses it on the passenger seat, and roars off.

It made my day.

228

Monday, November 30, 2020 4:23pm

I think it's telling that 45 made Melania deal with all the White House Christmas stuff alone, even though she's on (unauthorized) tape saying, "Who gives a fuck about Christmas?"

He could have handed that job off to the Pences (who, I guarantee you, love Christmas, and love showing off how *their* love for Christmas is just a little bit more meaningful than *your* love for Christmas), or he could have brought Barron in to walk the halls with Melania. He even could have turned off his television for three minutes and been in those pictures with her.

But he didn't. He let Melania shoulder that humiliation all on her own.

And I know. Melania's every bit as much of a birther piece of shit as her husband. But, holy buckets. It's been months since we all heard that recording. There's been enough time passed now that tempers should have cooled and "lawfully wedded spouse" Donald Trump should have had the decency to turn the heat down on her 2020 Christmas debacle.

If he gave a fuck about Christmas.

Or his own wife.

Tuesday, December 8, 2020 4:56am

It's 4:30am, the middle of the night before we say goodbye to Mary Kitty. Curtis had a long call with the vet today, just one more of sooooo many long calls with the vet (who has been lovely and kind and patient with us), and they both agreed that she's just too sick to keep trying new ideas. That it's okay to let go. That euthanasia would be kinder than waiting (possibly) weeks for her to go on her own.

It's been a horrible back and forth for Curtis and me these last few weeks. We couldn't seem to get on the same planet with regard to how much treatment is appropriate at the end. Seriously, there's only been one other time in our marriage where we just could not reach consensus, and that was when Kiddo was a pre-teen and he wanted to play video games that had violence in them.

So. When you can't get on the same page, you have to just wait it out. And Curtis didn't want to give up on her. There were still things to try. The vet said, "Maybe this will help." "...Okay, maybe this will help." "We could still try this.."

So he's been giving her stacks of pills every twelve hours, and he's tried to hand feed her since she won't go near her food bowl. He's brought out bowls of warm water and washcloths to clean her up when she's puked all over herself again (We've both done that). Fresh towels for her heated bed so we can just change them out and she doesn't have to lay in her sick. We've given her subcutaneous fluids every day. And other than a few flukey bites of food here and there, she's still gotten worse. She's just wasting away.

And finally, *sadly,* now there's consensus. It's what I wanted. It feels horrible.

Her appointment is at 3pm. Milo's coming over to say his goodbyes before that.

Nobody can sleep.

We should sleep.

We are sad.

Wednesday, December 9, 2020 7:23am

Flashback to 2019, when Milo and Billie put party hats on the cats to celebrate my birthday. Every picture of Mary that's older than, like, four months... I'm just gobsmacked at how big she was. She was terrifyingly frail and skeletal at the end. I was so afraid to pick her up. (The kids and Tildy have their own place now, and that's good for everybody, but this picture makes me feel extra sad and also happy but mostly sad).

Sunday, December 20, 2020 1:03pm

Republican leaders who are fine with your parents dying alone, hooked up to a machine with only sedatives to keep them from dying of terror first, should be so far at the back of the vaccination line, they shouldn't get to celebrate in-person Christmas next year either.

Tuesday, December 29, 2020 6:50pm

Since Kiddo moved out, Curtis says some version of this sentence to me nearly every week:

"Um. Well, I feel like I should preface this by saying that I *FULLY* support your attempts to have our house make more sense. But, um, where do we keep lightbulbs now?"

Wednesday, December 30, 2020 6:27am

We submitted an application for two kittens!!! Omggggggg!!!

Wednesday, December 30, 2020 8:28pm

Abject terror.

Wednesday, December 30, 2020 10:07pm

Welcome to our world, Chopper Chips and Sean! Chopper is white and Sean is orange. And they're not loving on us yet, but they're very playful and FUNNY. Oh my goodness. Cuteness overload.

2021

Saturday, January 2, 2021 4:15am

Greatest Hits

Aurora Republicans: "Look, clearly we aren't racist, because saying "Opposed to multiculturalism" is nothing at all like saying "Blacks aren't welcome." We merely think Christian white men should be favored and centered in every way, and if you think clinging to that worldview in this century makes us less relevant than a steaming fetid pile of runny horseshit, that just means you're a socialist or a communist or antifa, whatever that is.

Our sincerely held beliefs are just good old common sense.

Your sincerely held beliefs are identity politics and we absolutely can not have that, little lady.

If you think someone as important as the Aurora highway superintendant could ever, and we mean EVER, think that a woman should make her own medical decisions without input from some biologically-penis-equipped MAN, then you are responsible for dividing our country. Also, don't say 'penis;' whatever happened to civility?"

Republican Committee Reaching Out for Potential Candidates

The Aurora Republican Committee will interview candidates for local offices during the month of January. The offices that will be on the ballot in 2021 include the town supervisor's post, a two-year term. The committee will also interview people for the four-year seats that include: town clerk, highway superintendent, and two town council seats.

The Aurora Republican Committee will consider individuals that share its philosophy of small government, lower taxes, pro-life, support the second amendment, believe in legal immigration and are pro-police. Aurora Republican Chairman Earl Jann noted in a news release that the group is "opposed to multiculturalism, including identity politics and socialism/communism as we believe these policies are responsible for dividing our country."

Interested candidates may send their resumes to Aurora Republican Committee, P.O. Box 892, East Aurora, NY 14052.

Let Us Deliver Right to Your Door
Call 652-0320 to start your subscription today!

Greatest Hits

[I'm not actually going to submit this. It's just a satire piece, which is good, because people know where I live, and I have no idea how to scrub broken eggs off windows)

Letter to the Editor

Friends and neighbors, my name is Shelly Duhn, and I'm running as the Republican candidate for Aurora Highway Superintendent.

I am a middle class, hardworking, regular joe with small-town, heartland values. I love my Chevy truck, I love my guns, and I love my god. I love this country. I love the flag. And you betcha I'm opposed to identity politics!

First, let me discuss my support for States' rights. I mean, LOL, not New York State's rights (gah!!), but Ohio, Idaho, Michigan...you're catching my drift, here, right? States where you can protect your family from all the illegals and BLMs and Democrats (Or Demon-rats, amiright? Ha! I love to kid. I'm a kidder. But you know. Not really).

Pro-police. My friends, like you, I've noticed a massive influx of uppity urban thugs and hoodie-wearing antifa supersoldiers roving the streets of our beloved village. Once I saw a riot nearly break out in the hidden craft supplies room in the back of Vidler's. -It was just a few kids all needing the same item for the same school project due the next day, but who can tell the difference between students and rioters when they're all dressed like that? I certainly can't!

The point is, the police have an incredibly difficult job, knowing the difference between who's an animal deserving an immediate execution, and who's just a standard speeder who forgot to slow down before they passed the speedtrap outside Sammy's.

It is not our job to question the police, or even notice if they go a little too far sometimes. In healthy societies, police are given free rein to do as they please, and even their own bosses shouldn't ever tell them to ease up on the infliction of violence upon unarmed, terrified young people. After all, if only good guys were cops, only cops would be good guys. Or something like that. Just go with it. Cops are great. Never wrong. The end.

Small government and pro-life. My friends, the average uterus in an average human woman's body measures 3-4 inches by 2.5 inches. That is exactly what size the United States government should be. If it can't adhere snuggly and safely to the inner wall of any random uterus, that government is simply too big. It might try to take away my right to keep a military-sized arsenal in my basement. It would be like Venezuela all over again. But here. In East Aurora.

Which, of course brings me to legal immigration. Neighbors, we've all noticed it. Back in July of 2019, the US Census Bureau stated that the racial makeup of our fair town was 95.8% white. But you've noticed it, haven't you? If they checked again, I venture it would barely crack 95.7% white.

But my friends, that is okay. It's okay!

I personally went to the household of the one black family that moved to EA this year, and they were all able to prove to me, with long-form birth certificates (-the real ones!), that each family member was born at a Buffalo-area hospital. The parents were both born at Mercy, and the children were born at Children's. Ergo, they immigrated legally. The law worked! God bless the US Constitution! Which I clearly have read and even understand some of.

But I must admit that I have a small amount of ignorance, too.

Socialism and Communism and Multiculturalism are all words I do not understand. I'm pretty sure they come after the LGB in that whole alphabet soup the woke young people keep using. Like Tick Tock. I do know that they're very bad, and that if you support (or understand) those things, you are responsible for dividing this country. It also means that you're the ones persecuting me, a white

Christian man with nearly $500,000.00 in personal wealth. You can't imagine my suffering.

My own children were indoctrinated by the BLM this year, and now they've been persecuting me too. Whatever happened to civility? I remember when this country used to care about a person's feelings. How far we've fallen, huh.

And now for the last talking point. The important one. What you're all thinking about. Lowering taxes. Well, brother, it's time to celebrate. You can shrink those taxes right down to zero if I'm elected, because I will never notice or care if the snowplows are running! That pothole outside your house that dozens of cars hit every day? That sucker can just grow and grow and grow. It can join with all the other smaller potholes around it, until driving over it reminds you of hopscotching children, if hopscotching children were able to destroy axels.

--That's a word, right? Axels? Funny story, I don't actually know anything about large vehicles or how they operate. Thank God none of that was in the job description! Here I thought I was unemployable, but it turns out, I just needed to have an opinion about other people's pregnancies and whether the Blue Lives Matter flag is more badass than the original American flag. -Well, and the right skin color. And the long list of grievances. And the twig and berries. And a pickup truck.

This. This right here. This is why I'm a Republican. We do things the way we've always done things. And the way we've always done things is good enough for me, Shelly Duhn. Your next Highway Superintendent.

Wednesday, January 6, 2021 4:12pm

Why do women need the absolute right to an abortion? Because men exactly like the ones storming the Capitol on TV right now think whatever they want is exactly what they deserve.

They'll hold you down and scream "I'M THE GOOD GUY" until you repeat it back to them: "You're the good guy! You are! You're the good guy! Please stop! You're the good guy! The good guy! You're the good guy!"

And eventually they lose their boner and lose interest because it's only fun for them if you're fighting.

And eventually they go away, absolutely certain they've won the argument.

And then we do what we have to do to start healing.

Thursday, January 7, 2021 11:03pm

In case you're curious, I just read the EA Advertiser's letters to the editor. They were all concerning the EA Republican party's stated desire for all candidates to be opposed to multiculturalism. The letters were all earnest and very much wishing that we could all get along, in this, our great melting pot, yada yada yada.

Not one single letter was snarky or bitchy or had cuss words. That's probably for the best, but I came away sooooo disappointed, LOL

Saturday, January 9, 2021 8:08am

"Oh hey! Yes, we DO love the $85 cat tree! It's *NEAT!* ....use it? .... but, but... here's a laundry basket..."

Friday, January 15, 2021 1:58pm

I had to use an Etsy artist for Mary's urn because my dear potter friend isn't taking commissions right now and I wanted Mary to have her own special urn too. I think it turned out so pretty. It fits her, I think. Quirky in a good way.

Wednesday, January 20, 2021 11:15am

Anybody else feel like you're not going to take a deep breath until after the ceremony is over and all those people have dispersed a bit?

Wednesday, February 3, 2021 2:48pm

Today I learned that Tartar sauce (which I HATE), and Remoulade sauce (which I LOVE) are the exact same thing.

Yep. Still a sucker for fancy words. *sigh*

Saturday, February 20, 2021 11:28am

Anybody who thinks Cancel Culture is something new has never spent any time branded a slut.

Feb 07, 2021 11:08:47pm

TFW you yell at feral kittens for being too wild.

Saturday, February 20, 2021 6:43pm

They're so precious I can barely stand it.

Monday, February 22, 2021 8:01pm

I think people understand "Privilege" better now, in the context of COVID. Because privileged people are able to stay home and isolate; privileged people's jobs can be done from anywhere; privileged people's jobs still exist and they're still paying their bills with the exact same ability that they had a year ago; privileged people aren't raising school-aged children and having to keep them on task and progressing academically, privileged people aren't being demonized or used as pawns in political fights (ex: teachers, restaurant workers, etc).

Does that mean that these COVID-privileged people have no problems? Of course not. They're still losing loved ones, they're still grieving, they're still missing their friends, they're still experiencing mental health crises from too much isolation, they're still putting off regular or needed healthcare, they still have pain. But you can see how one batch of people is having a vastly different experience than the folks in the other batch.

Saturday, March 6, 2021 3:36pm

That poor toilet paper holder I "hung" will remain at a 330 degree angle, with a hardened glue-drip stretching nearly a foot down the wall, and a screw sticking out about a half inch (because my drill wasn't charged enough and quit), until the day we gut this poor house and reimagine the whole thing. ..or die of old age, whichever comes first.

Monday, March 8, 2021 3:52am

Greatest Hits

You know what I've been thinking about a lot lately? Video games.

When I was a teenager in the mid-80s, (– late middle school/early high school years/pre-driver's license years), it was extremely common for kids to go to the mall on Friday night. "My mom can drop us off if yours can pick us up," etc. And if you had some young teenager version of a boyfriend, that's where you'd see them: at the mall, on Friday night. Then you'd walk laps around the mall, holding each other's sweaty hands. Feeling simultaneously proud and mortified as you looked around at all the other promenading teenagers to assure yourselves that you were properly participating in the peer parade.

Okay, so we're in that context: Teenagers at the mall.

In that context, NOTHING pissed me off more than when my boyfriend (or anybody's boyfriend. All the boyfriends did it) would take me into the video game arcade and play a game while I was expected to stand next to him and just exist. Like a sulky hood ornament.

Remember – this was the 1980s. Long before cell phones. Standing in the video game arcade with their paramour du semaine, that girl couldn't call a friend, couldn't text a friend, couldn't scroll through Instagram. She couldn't talk to anybody around lest she cause him to lose focus on the game. She had to stand there and look bored facing the game or stand there and look bored facing the room.

I often carried a book in my purse, but that usually offended the boy if I started reading. A better girlfriend would think his prowess at freaking Galaga was riveting enough, you know. I wasn't this crass as a kid, but I know once I hit my college years and the subject of video game arcades came up, more than once I said that I would so much rather watch my boyfriend jerk off than play a video game, because at least then I'd know he'd be done in a reasonable amount of time (And that's also something I could be sincerely impressed with and interested in for a few minutes anyway).

And now, fast forward a few years (LOL, Okay FINE, fast forward a generation, gahhh), and there are countless people -and not all men! - making millions and zillions of dollars on Twitch and other forums, playing video games for massive (interested!) live audiences. It absolutely boggles my mind.

And this is why the internet is great: You want to watch a guy play a video game? Here you go. You want to watch a guy jerk off? Right this way. You want to do something that requires your own participation and input? We have that too. You want all of it at various times? Hey, that's just being well-adjusted, friend!

It's the future! There's something for everybody!

Saturday, March 20, 2021 6:49pm
Greatest Hits

Years ago, when we were on an (Awesome! Amazing!) Alaska cruise with my inlaws, a tour guide pointed up at the trees and said, "Do you see all those white things that look like golf balls up there? Those are all eagles." And it was so cool, because once I knew to look for "golf balls" in the trees, I saw them everywhere.

Fast forward to today, and I saw what looked like a golf ball in the trees over the creek. I watched it for ages, but I never was sure if I was looking at an eagle or if it was just the sun hitting some other breed of big bird just right. Eagles are pretty rare in Western New York, so I'm more inclined to believe the latter. It was really cool, no matter what it was.

So yeah, that's why this popped into my head for the zillionth time: Eagles.

The night of the 2020 election, when Joe Biden was the projected winner, he came out and gave a lovely speech. At one point, he quoted a popular Catholic song, "On Eagles' Wings."

Joe Biden's words from the speech: "In the last days of the campaign, I began thinking about a hymn that means a lot to me and my family, particularly my deceased son Beau. It captures the faith that sustains me and which I believe sustains America," he said. "And I hope it can provide some comfort and solace to the 230 thousand Americans who have lost a loved one through this terrible virus this year. My heart goes out to each and every one of you. Hopefully this hymn gives you solace as well. It goes like this: And he will raise you up on eagles' wings, bear you on the breath of dawn, make you to shine like the sun, and hold you in the palm of his hand."

Most people in my social media didn't mention it, but the few who did were put off that he quoted something so blatantly religious. They took it as a sign that he'd bring his religion into the job.

I'm an ex-Catholic turned Agnostic/Atheist (I don't know if there's a god but I doubt it), so I'm usually pretty cynical with most things pro-religion, particularly in concert with politics. But when Biden quoted that song, it didn't bother me a bit. Actually, I liked it and I felt it fit with the general tone of the speech.

So then I wondered if it's just because I know the song and I always loved singing it?

No, that's not it.

I finally know why it didn't bother me. Because he wasn't proselytizing, he wasn't judging, he wasn't placing his beliefs above anybody or anything. He was just quoting a song he knows and finds comfort and truth in.

If he'd said, "There's an old Irish saying that goes...." Or "The Native Americans have a song about..." no one would have had a reaction to it. But it was the Christian/Catholic-ness, specifically, that put some off.

So why is that? Well, it's because we are so accustomed to having Christianity wielded like a club at us. --From strangers literally knocking at our doors to tell us about Jesus (as if there's an American alive and living in America who hasn't heard allllllllllllllllll about Jesus), to politicians (and popes) insisting that our gay friends' lives mustn't be blessed, to companies holding firm that they shouldn't have to offer health insurance to slutty bitches who think they deserve the right to decide how many children is right for them, to preachers telling generations upon generations of harmed wives to keep the marriage together no matter how hard hubby hits the children, to men everywhere believing that their ~missing rib~ means they're smarter and better and wiser and more moral than women.

Truly, my first reaction to most political discussions that bring up religion is always, 'Oh just fuck right off with your all-too-convenient-and-obvious use of horseshit piety. I'll believe you're a Christian just as soon as you stop bending over forward and backward for the money changers.'

Back to the speech and the song: "And He will raise you up on eagle's wings, bear you on the breath of dawn, make you to shine like the sun, and hold you in the palm of His hand." It's not really a song I would choose to quote for a speech, because it doesn't feel so BIG without the gorgeous melody, but it's still quite nice.

Biden quoting this song in this way is actually what I hope the world could someday be, it's the unity that I might someday sort of trust. He didn't place his religion above anybody. He didn't need to make YOU feel bad so that HE might feel good. He just took his place in a world full of different people with millions of different beliefs and needs, said "I like this," and then continued on without a sales pitch, without a smug, 'God says I deserve all these millions.' And without any of the passive aggressive (and overt) language we're so accustomed to from televised and elected Christians (and "Christians") who seem to think they're doing us a favor by laying it on so relentlessly.

Anyway. I might have seen an eagle over my creek today.

Thursday, March 25, 2021 3:30am

Greatest Hits

Tonight as I was playing Feather Toy with the kitties, I was reminded of a scene from my childhood that wasn't funny at all, but when the cats reenacted it, was hilarious.

I think most people, at some point in their lives, wonder if they were switched at birth to explain how they got stuck in their family. But most people aren't still wondering when they're 48. Alas.

My dad was always very busy with work and his weekend band. Us kids were always busy with all the suburban bullshit that some kids love and some kids just fucking loathe: dancing lessons, piano lessons, T-ball, soccer, CCD. Just go go go go go go go. And I can't even tell you the number of times I heard, "You already read that book! Stop sitting there like a bump on a log, go outside and play!"

And because we saw so little of my dad, my mother insisted that my dad would play ball with all of us in the backyard some summertime evenings.

After dinner, we would be a FAMILY, and there were mitts and baseballs and bats. And, literally, 100% of the time, I held my mitt out in front of me, the ball would go someplace other than directly to me, and then Dad would yell at me that my feet aren't planted in the ground.

But, jeeeeez, I did not give a shittttttttttt about playing ball. It was hot and the setting sun was in my eyes and all my friends were outside where I could see and hear them, and I had to stay in our yard and get yelled at because my feet aren't planted in the ground.

And how dumb is it that when you play ball, you're supposed to stand still and bored until suddenly it's time to RUN.

Always, within the first ten minutes or so, it wasn't just my dad yelling that my feet aren't planted in the ground, it was everybody.

And, how in the hell did I end up in that family? There we all were. Everybody else RUNNING to the ball, CATCHING it even! Go go go go go go!

"Look at Jamie! See how he runs right up to where the ball's going to land? That's what you do! Here it comes! RUN TO IT! RUN TO IT! YOUR FEET ARE NOT PLANTED IN THE GROUND! --Oh perfect, now she's crying. That's it, go inside and pout."

So then I'd go crying up to my bedroom, which overlooked the backyard, and I'd watch them all actually play ball and *run to the ball* and do things like get runs and tag each other out and laugh.

You can tell when people are enjoying themselves. My family was always truly enjoying themselves. And I'd think, "I wonder if my real family is out there somewhere, watching TV in the daytime and reading the same books over and over and over."

--That's not true. Mostly I just thought that everything about me was WRONG because I wasn't fun, and I hated most "fun" things.

The cats. How it all of this like the cats playing Feather Toy?

Well, Seany is a Mason, through and through. He is CHASING that feather! Up the cat tree, down the cat tree! On the couch! In the cat bed! On the table! Jump! Jump higher! "I GOT ITTTTTTTTTTTTTT!!!!!"

And Chopper? Well, Chopper will chase it for a little while. Maybe a minute. Then he lays down on the floor with one arm out, lazily batting at nothing, while Sean jumps over him and sometimes steps on him and pretty much loses his ever-loving mind trying to get that feather toy. Seriously, Sean is almost scary, how ferociously he HUNTS that thing.

And watching them be so utterly and completely THEMSELVES, I felt such affection for them both, but I also said out loud, gently, "Chopper, your feet aren't planted in the ground!"

No need for a pouting though, since nobody was bothered by the play dynamic as it existed.

245

Sunday, April 4, 2021 12:48pm

This is 100% true:

Last night I dreamed that Curtis and I were standing in a screened-in porch, and Milo was on the other side doing some kind of gardening. And I said, "Kiddo, I think I see some bees..." and then thousands upon thousands upon thousands of bees swarmed around him, and Curtis and I were screaming "Cover your ears and nose!" And "Don't run!"

And I woke up before they started stinging him, but yeah. Don't have to dig too deep to find the symbolism there.

Monday, April 5, 2021 11:27pm

One of my favorite things in the world is when you've got a snoozing kitty who's sort of in the process of waking up, and you pick them up, and they give this massive, awesome full body stretch, and your arms start vibrating, and you feel like He-Man.

Monday, May 31, 2021 3:08am

Greatest Hits

Sometimes these kitties are so obnoxious and exasperating, I feel like water getting ready to boil.

My NC shrink always told me that when something extra-extra bothers me, there's usually a memory from my past that coincides with the emotion. And I found the memory in an instant:

I babysat for one of the Buffalo Bills' kids (well, two Bills actually, nobody famous), and he and his wife were these omg, hottest-humans-on-earth types, and they had all of these awesome CDs. -Like the kind of CD collection you'd have if you got paid an NFL salary: Just go into the record store and drop a few hundred at a time, just based on whatever mood you were in. And then do it again and again.

246

And ALL I wanted to do was sit in their living room, with my homework books open, Anita Baker singing on the CD player, and daydream that this perfect life with an unlimited CD budget, cable tv with pay channels, and a gorgeous house that was 'super nice but not formal' could be mine.

But, ugh, I was there to, blah, BABYSIT, and the kid was THREE, and the child of JOCKS, and he was always so BORED, and I'd try so hard to be nice and steer the kid toward something that didn't require my full attention, and though I tried not to show it, I know the kid knew I was annoyed by him, and I'm sure it took no time at all before I became the babysitter the mother called only after every other babysitter had said no.

That's it. That's the memory. Constantly stopping the music to deal with the kid, who couldn't help that he was a baby jock and fundamentally incapable of sitting down and coloring.

~Back to the present~

I love my new furniture, I do. Love it. We just got new power recliners. Classiest shit ever. Sit down, push a button, RRrrrrrrRrrrRrrrrrr, feet up. Amazing.

Now picture me, happily reading in my chair. Spotify playing. Content. So content.

..goddammit, what's that cat doing now? "SEAN!!"

RRrrrrrrRrrrRrrrrrr [feet down, gets up]

"Ugh, what even is that? No, kitty, not for kitties. Give it to me."

(Sits back down) RRrrrrrrRrrrRrrrrrr (picks up kindle) (reads with determination)

[CRASH]

"MOTHEREFF!!!" RRrrrrrrRrrrRrrrrrr [feet down, gets up]

"Chopper!!! Leave Daddy's headphones alone!"

[Sits back down] RRrrrrrRrrrRrrrrrr (picks up kindle) (reads with sense of acute persecution)

[though no one's at my computer, it begins making the Windows complainy noise]. BauBUM BauBUM BauBUM My computer is remotely connected to Curtis' PC in the other room. The kitties are doing something they shouldn't be able to.]

(From my chair): "CUT IT THE FUCK OUT!!"

BauBUM BauBUM BauBUM

"Jesus, god, fuck, dammit.."

RRrrrrrrRrrrRrrrrrr [feet down, gets up]

Yep. That's my night.

Sunday, June 13, 2021 12:54am

Sean and Chopper with the feather toy are so very funny. Imagine Sean as the 7th grade volleyball player who's so good they make him captain of the JV team. He's all eagerness and joy, hollering "I GOT ITTTTT" at every wild serve the other team gets over the net. It doesn't even matter if they hit it out of bounds, he's going to outrun that thing and hit it back in.

Chopper is the kid whose mother insists that 'video game friends aren't real friends, and in this family, we know that real character comes from playing TEAM sports. OUTSIDE. In a UNIFORM.'

--And he'd never admit it, but Chopper/the kid actually enjoys sports just fine. He's terrible at them, but he'd like to be good. And he really tries, even though his teammates all groan every time the coach puts him in the game.

And there's Seany. He's so skilled and so loving, you don't even have to tell him to let Chopper have the easy ones. You don't have to explain to him that Chopper has other special gifts, but that his body just doesn't move the way that Seany's does. Seany knows.

248

So, the game starts. And Chopper's under the table, watchful and wishful.

And THERE GOES SEAN! Up to the top of the cat tree! Down below the table! Back up to the top of the cat tree! HE'S HERE! HE'S THERE! HE'S EVERYFUCKINWHERE!

And then I plunk the feather down in front of Chopper. He backs up two paces. Wiggles his butt. Backs up two more paces. Wiggles his butt.

And Sean waits. He's so good and so loving. He waits.

Until Chopper backs up two more paces, and then Sean slowly but deliberately walks up to the feather, picks it up, and walks away with it.

BACK TO THE ACTION! Sean's up the cat tree! He's in the floofy cat bed! He's under the table! He's back up the cat tree! He! Can! Do! This! All! Day!

Finally, Chopper emerges from under the table. Sean has made it all look so fun and so easy; Chopper wants to try. Sean backs off.

I leave the feather toy on the floor. Chopper marches over it and drops his full girth down on top of the feather. THUD.

Okay! Let's do this! Okay Chopper, can you get up to the first level of the cat tree? Yes, Chopper can get the feather from the first level of the cat tree. Good Boy!! Chopper takes the feather toy and goes over to the floofy cat bed.

Okay! Can Chopper get to the second level of the cat tree? Chopper has seen Sean jump from the floofy cat bed to the second level of the cat tree. Chopper believes he can do this too.

AND HE DOES IT! OMG! --Not quite as gracefully as Sean. No, only Chopper's front paws make it all the way to the actual cat tree, and it takes a minimum of five seconds to hoist the rest of himself onto the platform, but he does it! Good boy Chopper! --Oh, you need a rest? Yeah, that makes sense.

AND HERE COMES SEAN!

Wednesday, June 16, 2021 8:58pm

I needed to pick up a prescription yesterday, and since I was already braving the outdoors and Curtis's claustrophobia car, I decided to continue on to Left Coast Tacos, because, duh. One has to bribe oneself with tacos in order to pick up a prescription (I don't make the rules but I do follow them).

So, okay, went to Rite Aid, got my prescriptions, went to Left Coast Tacos, got my food. I folded myself back into the car, turned it on, and began backing out of the parking space. It's a fully electric car, so it doesn't make any noise upon starting, but it makes soft, pleasing 'bing bing bings' when you back out.

If you're familiar with East Aurora, you know that Left Coast Tacos is next door to Larwood's pharmacy.

So there I was backing out of my parking space. A maskless man walked out of Larwood's to his truly massive, dually pickup truck. Under his baseball cap, his hair is a bit Hulkamania. His caucasian skin is the brown leather of someone who spends the entire day, every day, laboring in the sun. He's wearing a yellow Hi-Viz muscle shirt. He walks like his biceps are unusually heavy. He also has a pristine vaccination bandaid on his shoulder that practically glows next to his skin.

He's looking at my car because it's making a strange noise, and he notices me noticing his bandaid.

As one, we both grant each other genuine, whole-face smiles.

You know, it ain't much. But it did feel like a more neighborly, unguarded exchange with an other-side-of-the-aisle stranger than I've had in years.

Sunday, June 20, 2021 4:58pm

One of the things they never tell you about having cats: Sometimes they'll leave you a lovingly crafted popcorn garland.

Only the popcorn is made of poop and the string is your hair.

Sunday, June 20, 2021 5:56pm

One of the added benefits of widely available birth control and women's autonomy, is that you see so many more fathers who genuinely seem to love and appreciate their role. Happy parents are among the best things in the world.

Thursday, July 1, 2021 9:13am

Greatest Hits

I'm in a mood (100% humidity. Expect me to be in a mood until late October at least), and I just saw the clip of Tom Cotton and Chuck Grassley doing pushups on stage while Joni Ernst counted for them.

I had a burst of righteous anger on her behalf, and I so enjoy writing down my bursts of righteous anger. So without further ado, and with a content warning for many incoming F-bombs, please enjoy:

This is my interpretation of Joni Ernst's inner monologue as she counted while Chuck Grassley and Tom Cotton did push-ups:

"I am a fucking United States fucking Senator. I'm their fucking equal! But now I have to count while these two fucking jagoffs prove their manhood to each other? Should I give them both handjobs, too, since obviously we're all still fucking fourteen?

You know who wouldn't have to do bullshit like this? Fucking AOC. Why do the men in AOC's party treat her with collegiality and respect while I'm over here counting while these two fucking testosterone-poisoned fucking TODDLERS try to beat each other at doing fucking PUSHUPS for Christ's fucking sake. Fucking Pushups!!

And it's not like I'm not some Palin or Bachman clone. I fucking KNOW things! I was in the fucking National Guard! I have a goddamn fucking Master's degree! But here I am, gamely fucking COUNTING while these two old farts play 'Mommy Look At Me! You're Not Looking At Me Mommy! Mommy, Are You Watching?' all fucking day. Jesus fuck.

You know, they say feminists hate men. But feminists are smart enough to stay the fuck away from men like this. You know who really hates men? The ones who have to stand here like a fucking HOOD ORNAMENT and fucking COUNT while their fucking "equals but with a penis so actually somehow better though no one can explain why" do fucking PUSH UPS FOR FUCK'S SAKE!!! GAAHHHHHHH!!!! FUCKKKKKKKK!"

Monday, July 5, 2021 11:04am

I have spent the last two days fretting over a friend request I received because on the one hand, there's no way she knows what she's in for, but then on the other hand, most of my posts are set to public, but then on the other hand, all of her public facing posts are of American flags and Jesus, but then on the other hand, I don't want her to think I'm rude and have it reflect poorly on my mother, but then on the other hand, won't it reflect poorly on my mother if this lady sees all my fuck fuck fucks and fuck shitty mens and fuck Christianity, and gahhhh.

IT IS SO HARD BEING ME.

Tuesday, July 6, 2021 1:19pm

I just finished filling up my first Morning Pages journal. I started it last fall, and I've been pretty terrible about maintaining the habit even though I love it and find that it's helpful for both creativity and mental health.

But mostly I'm happy to start a new notebook because one day last year, I was writing my Morning Pages, and Curtis came into the room with his phone, and he'd been speaking to the vet, and they had some questions about Mary Kitty that he wasn't sure about the answers to.

So that was the scene: Me sitting in bed holding my morning pages, Curtis sitting on the end of the bed talking to the vet, and us not being able to reach consensus about what Mary's end-of-life care should be. I was ready to say goodbye and Curtis wasn't. And we were like two parallel lines. It was the worst feeling.

And the vet was busy, of course, and she said that she needed to go but that we could email her any time and she'd do her best to get back to us that day. And I had a pen and paper in my hands, so I wrote down her email on the back of my Morning Pages book.

And since then, every time I've closed my notebook, my eye has fallen on that email address, and it's made me so sad. Sad because I miss my Mary Mackey, and sad because, while we often forget the words in disagreements, we never really forget the emotions. And not being able to find common ground over the life and death of our beloved cat was just the worst feeling I think I've had in years. It was all of these bad emotions compounded into one, and there was no bad guy to be mad at, and just, sad sad sad.

And, like, I'm writing this down now, so I'm sure it seems like I've been thinking these thoughts for a long time, but really, it's just been these little heartbeats of sad, every time I close the book. Then I forget it's there until the next time. Then another heartbeat of sad. Then I forget it's there until the next time.

it'll be nice to put those heartbeats of sad into a drawer.

Saturday, July 10, 2021 4:38pm
Life with Seany

Me: (looking at my ipad)

Seany: (stalks up my Boob Mountain)

Seany: Woah, TRUST FALL! (THUD)

Me: Ugh!

Seany: It's funny because you have to catch me.

Me: Yes, it's very funny Sean.

253

Seany: (snuggles in tight, face right in the cleavage) I love you Mama.

Me: I love you too, Bee. You're a good snuggler.

Seany: Yes. You know what else I can do?

Me: Oh, please don't.

Seany: I can fold myself in half and clean my butthole!!

Me: Gah. Stop it. Go someplace else!

Seany: It's actually a sign of great trust that I'm doing this! You should be flattered!

Me: I am. I'm very, very flattered, Bee. Please go someplace else.

Seany: (climbs down) Oh hey! There's a sandwich crust on this plate!

Me: No. Sean. No. Not for kitties.

Seany: It smells like it's for kitties....

Me: I appreciate that. But it's not for kitties.

Seany: (stalks back up my Boob Mountain) Whoooooa, TRUST FALL!!!!!

Monday, July 26, 2021 8:36pm

Them taking the earnest and sincere, pro-woman line, "My body my choice," and bastardizing it so that it means *Freedom Sneezing* or whatever the fuck, is so ugly and shitty and unoriginal and enraging.

Friday, August 6, 2021 2:57am

TFW you don't feel right in your soul because you thoughtlessly pointed out a Daddy Long Legs spider to the kitties, and they went ahead and gave him the full kitten treatment.

Monday, August 23, 2021 2:21pm

Something I love about Seany: When he's asleep someplace, and he decides he wants to keep sleeping and also be held, so he approaches me with his eyes open about 5%. "I'm sleepwalkin Mama!"

Monday, August 23, 2021 7:29pm

Greatest Hits

FACEBOOK MEMORY FROM 9 YEARS AGO:

FRIDAY, AUGUST 23, 2013 7:50PM

SHELLY DUHN ADDED A NEW PHOTO.

NICE ENOUGH FOR AN EVENING STROLL AT HUNTER'S CREEK PARK!

~~~~~~

Today:

I'm in a really bad headspace, and it's fine because (all together now), "I've been here before, and I know this feeling is temporary." Also, it's August, and fuck August.

So, when I'm in this bad headspace, I ask myself questions like, 'Okay, so is this ugly thought just my mental illness being a dick, or is this an actual truth I don't like to face?"

Well the "truth" that always pops up in my mind lately is that, not only am I not fun now, but I've never been fun, I've only been better at hiding how not fun I am.

--But also, I think maybe I've never been particularly good at hiding it. So the choice for my loved ones has always been, 'Leave Shelly at home and go have a nice time,' or 'Take Shelly along, and she'll make everyone in her vicinity suffer.'

Which brings me to this picture. Looks so nice, doesn't it? Out for a walk in the park with my doggy and my teenager. So nice, so normal, such a good family, doing what good families do, have outdoor fun in the summertime.

Except that I remember that evening. I was mmmmmmmmmiserable. I was sweating profusely, and I had twisted my ankle on a tree root (because if I didn't hurt myself on any given day, was I even alive?), and at one point, I thought I heard a swarm of bees, and before my brain could work out what I was *actually* hearing, a man going a zillion miles an hour on a mountain bike came roaring around the corner we were approaching, and he nearly ran both Chester and Milo over, and I screamed. Then I lost my shit at the man who nearly ran over my kid and my dog. He didn't stop, but hollered back, "Pay attention!" over his shoulder, and I'm sure I screamed, "Fuck you!" at him, because I was nothing if not always a good role model for my child.

So then we were walking back to the car, and I couldn't shake it off. I was sweating balls, and my ankle hurt. I was so furious that a man on a bike had nearly crashed into my kid and my dog. --Like, if they'd collided, everybody would have been injured. And I was kicking myself because, who the fuck mistakes a bike sound for a swarm of bees? I had heard him coming! But instead of pushing my child and dog off the path, I stood there and thought, 'Gosh, that sounds like a huge swarm of bees!'

256

And the whole time, Kiddo was just rolling with it. Like, 'Yep, Mom loses her shit sometimes. She's not mad at me, so just leave her be.'

But like, you look at the picture, and you think, "Oh how nice. Out with their doggy, enjoying nature. So healthy! So normal! What a good family. Getting a little exercise. Being part of the community. These are good people."

But I hated it. And we never went to Hunter's Creek again. Kiddo went with his friends often, once he started driving, but I haven't been back since. Because I'm not fun. And I only like nature in photos (that someone else took).

So yeah. Anyway. Fuck August. Fuck this headspace. I know I won't feel like this forever, but man, I hate when I'm in the thick of it. No advice please. Head pats and 'there theres' will do.

Friday, August 27, 2021 7:44am

I always always always miss my son because he's funny and sweet and delightful to be around, and so talented and loving.

This post is not about that.

This post is about how much I miss my son because when he lived here, I could pay him and he'd take care of the house when I couldn't do it myself. I can do most things, but not when my whole body is this locked up, and definitely not when I'm this heat-overwhelmed.

If kiddo were home, I would ask him to name his price to have him give me an afternoon where I just say, "Okay, now the dishes, please." "Okay, now the cat box please." "Okay, now a load of laundry." "Okay, now get my prescriptions and pick up Left Coast Tacos please." "Please put together this rolling stool I just bought so I can sit down and unload the dishwasher when you're not here." "Please put ten cups of cool water and a big scoop of Epsom salts in a plastic pan and put it in front of my feet." "Now take it away and rinse it out and put the pan back in the cupboard." "Please brush the cats." "Please vacuum up the hilarious amount of fur that's everywhere."

And on and on and on and on.

Curtis always says he can do anything I need, but between his sleep disorder and all the constant stress at work, he needs at least as much caretaking as I do. I asked him to take the garbage down to the road Wednesday night, and then asked him to bring the cans back up Thursday night, and he was *completely* fine with it, but I felt like such a dick just asking: "Honey, I know you kill yourself all day to give us this nice life and, in return, I barely make sure you have enough clean underwear....but can you do even more, and I'll do even less?"

Anyway. It's a pandemic. I'm plenty freaked out just having Instacart drivers put things on the mudroom floor, so I really don't want a non-resident in the house, including Kiddo. We're all vaccinated, but we've never been bulletproof, health-wise. I don't want to tempt fate.

I've been here before. I know it's temporary. We'll get a cool night sometime and I'll feel a bit of life re-enter my body. But yeah. When Kiddo lived here, he handled the bad times so they never got so bad.

Monday, August 30, 2021 5:52pm

Well it's been a day (Milo's typing, as I have screen restrictions, but I really am fine) Milo and Curtis will read me any messages or comments. I'll write more in a day or two.

Commenter Friend:

- Oh, no… I'm sorry you aren't well. Explanation please? Unless it's a private problem.

Shelly Duhn

- me, private? LOL

Curtis Duhn

- Shelly asked me to share what's going on.

Last night around midnight Shelly realized that her speech was slurred. She alerted me that something was wrong, so I asked her to try smiling, and only one corner of her mouth went up. I called 911, and they took Shelly to Mercy Hospital by ambulance. Milo joined us there for a long, scary night in the ER getting lots of tests, culminating in an MRI, which confirmed that she had experienced a stroke affecting part of her motor cortex in the right side of her brain.

The hospital admitted Shelly for observation, but didn't have any beds open in the stroke ward, so she spent the rest of today in the ER, where she was evaluated further by doctors, nurse practitioners, physical therapists and a speech therapist. Fortunately her most obvious deficiencies seem to be fairly isolated and manageable. She has some weakness in her left arm, slightly slurred speech, and a tendency to accidentally bite her tongue and lips. She has some facial asymmetry when she smiles, although her speech therapist noted that when she laughs or "smiles from her heart", that asymmetry goes away. Shelly's mind is sharp. She has no problems understanding written or spoken language. She's not missing words from her vocabulary. Her memory seems fine. She can do math in her head. She can stand up and walk around without support. It's hard to feel lucky in such a scary situation, but we all know it could have been much worse.

Tonight a room finally opened up in the stroke ward, so Shelly is settled in there for the night. Her doctors will be doing an ECG and more blood tests to try to understand what caused this. Then they'll prescribe medications and other steps we can take to minimize the risk of recurrence, and they'll start guiding Shelly on a journey of rehabilitation.

I don't think Shelly is going to be eager to have visitors while she's in the hospital, but I know she'll appreciate all your messages of love and support. We'll keep you updated.

I'm grateful to the doctors, nurses, and therapists at Mercy, to Milo for being there by her side with me, and to our families for their eager support. Most of all I'm so proud of Shelly for being brave through an ordeal that has subjected her to many of her greatest fears.

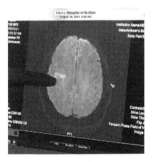

Tuesday, August 31, 2021 5:58pm

Well here we are. I'm fine, but my left hand and arm don't work so good. The occupational therapist said that ai'm going to need to re-teach myself to type so my brain can do it again. Holy balls, typing this is taking forevefr. All I want to do is just give up and type with my right hand only. But. I care about typing. I care about ukulele. So, I'll take the time and get there when I get there.

Other than the extreme arm annoyance, I'm really okay. Thank you so much for all your prayers and good wishes. I really needed them. I love you all. I'm nog sure yer fi i'm going home tonight or tomorrow. But I'm not hooked up to any machines anymore, so they're not worried about me. Yay!!

Wednesday, September 1, 2021 2:17pm

I am home!

Thursday, September 2, 2021 4:42am

I'm doing a TON of glorious, in-my-own-bed sleeping, but I'm also up in my brain, thinking about writing, writing, writing, and I'll post something long and mostly misspelled soon (although, my typing fingers are doing a whole lot better than yesterday).

But for now, here's my big victory: today, I can pull my hair into a ponytail and fasten the clip.

I so rock!!

Okay, I've been downstairs for a little while, and I ate some food, and read the headlines (and then decided I needed to not even look at headlines for a while), and now I'm ready for more sleep in bed.

It's weird how much I want to sleep, but it also feels right. Like, I can't stop my mind racing unless I'm sleeping, so better to sleep.

I'm steady on the stairs, though going up stairs is exhausting. I go slow and I'm not scared, but I get to the top and it's like I want to find a park bench to rest on before I make my way to the bed. Walking down the stairs is totally fine.

I'm so grateful for all the love, but I need a little bit of patience right now. I'll put it this way: Earlier this summer, I went and got my eyes checked, and then five weeks later, I had the mental capacity to leave my house again and go pick up my new glasses.

Imagine what an ambulance ride followed by a CT scan followed by an MRI followed by another CT scan followed by followed by followed by, etc. It's going to be a little while before I stop feeling like a gong that's eternally boy-yoy-yoy-yoy-yoy-ing.

One quick anecdote: I had just arrived in the ER, and I was desperate to pee, and I wasn't allowed to get up and use a toilet, so the ER nurse put this longish blue contraption right up against my business and told me to go ahead and relax, that the contraption had suction and my pee would magically get whisked away, so I relaxed, and unleashed a full bladder's worth of piss all over myself and the bed.

So the nurse was horrified and apologetic and she and Curtis helped me out of bed, and she had me leaning against Curtis while she cleaned me and the bed up, and Curtis - who was every bit as terrrified and panicky as I was - whispered in my ear, "I promise we're going to laugh about this someday."

Saturday, September 4, 2021 2:33pm
One of the ten crapzillion tasks I'm supposed to be doing to get my coordination back, is stacking coins. Just pour some coins out of your wallet and use your left hand to pick them up and stack them on top of each other.

OMG, it's SO HARD!!

...not because my fingers don't work, but because of these daggone CATS.

My strength is pretty good. It's hard to explain what I feel in my arm and fingers. It's like there's just this physical hesitance. I can do everything, but there's this itty bitty little pull that I have to get past.

My face, on the other hand, is really bugging me. You find out just how vain you are about your looks when your mouth isn't the right shape anymore. :(

Sunday, September 5, 2021 11:32am
The thing about my Seany is that he is always in trouble, and he's also so darn likable.

262

Sunday, September 5, 2021 11:35am

Yesterday, I learned that I can still whistle. Today I learned that I can NOT close my left eye without also closing my right eye.

Sunday, September 5, 2021 7:51pm

Greatest Hits

(Written Saturday and Sunday. Writing is exhausting.)

I guess I'll write this up today since I really am supposed to be typing a lot for hand and arm strength. And my typing speed is pretty great, but my brain gets so tired. Weird to say that typing is exhausting, but here we are.

My hospital stay was, overall, pretty wonderful. I'll maintain forever that if you might be pregnant and need a hospital, stay the eff away from a Catholic hospital, since they consider any contents of your body to be more deserving of rights than YOU, but since my own uterus has sat purposefully and pleasantly empty (well, except for IUDs) for the last 22 years, that wasn't a concern.

I did ask the EMT if I should be going to Gates Vascular Institute instead, but he said that Mercy was closer and every bit as good, so I accepted his advice.

But yes, like I said, overall, my experience was excellent. My caretakers were competent and loving, and they did everything they could to keep me calm and present – not an easy task with someone like me. They heard me when I asked a question, they took me seriously when I said I needed something, etc. Truly, I got the care anybody would want.

But it's a whole different world during a raging, worldwide pandemic, and when remaining unvaccinated has become a way to "express your patriotism and devotion to freedom."

And my experience would have been entirely perfect, except for the last night I was there. There had been all this talk about possibly letting me go home on Tuesday, but for whatever reason, the discharge orders never came in. -But like, on Tuesday night,

I wasn't attached to any machines. I changed out of my hospital gown because my room was roasting and I'm pretty sure that gown was made of a combination of wool, flannel, fleece, and maybe a few self-heating pads for good measure. So yeah, I spent my last night hanging out in my roasting room in my street clothes, with the IV port still in my arm, but not attached to anything.

I'd had a roommate (she was mad as a hornet, younger than me, and she'd had one stroke last week and a second stroke this week. I'm still panicky about the possibility of a repeat) who was discharged Tuesday afternoon. So, for quite a few hours, I was alone in that room. I was hoping that it would stay that way, but the nurses had warned me that anybody could get moved in at any time.

Finally, around 9-9:30PM, a worker came in to clean that side of the room. He was young, probably mid-20s, mask around his chin, and chatty chatty chatty. He told me he's a writer, but he really wants to direct, and that he's interested in stories that 'don't put any punches for the pussies.'

Like, I know. I've just got one of those faces. People always think I'm nicer and more interested than I actually am. But then, because I'm at least a little bit nice, I let him continue telling me how Quentin Tarantino is his hero and that, no, he didn't study English in college, he just knows how to talk, and that everyone always tells him he's a genius, and that this job is only temporary, but at least it's union.

That's fine. It's not like I was busy.

But then. (Oh, you knew a 'but then' was coming). Then, after he'd been farting around in the room for a good 45 minutes, he said, "So, are you vaccinated?"

Me (suddenly more terrified than I'd been since the MRI machine): "Yes... Are you?"

Him: "Nah. I mean, I've thought about it, but you just don't know who to listen to, you know?"

Me, Silent: *Experts! Listen to the fucking experts who went to college and studied and mastered actual complicated sciences and didn't believe their friends when they blew sunshine up their asses and called them geniuses!!! Fucking listen to those people!! Fucking Jesus humping Christ, how the fuck do you work here???"*

Anyway, after no doubt noticing me gazing longingly at the mask on my bed table that I wanted to put on but didn't want to offend HIM (UGH), he finally decided that he'd spent enough time in the room "cleaning" and he left. (What I was told, was the rule for patients in the hospital is that you can have your mask off in your room, but any time you're in the hallway or in a public area for testing, you have to wear a mask)

I turned out the lights, closed my curtain, put on my eye mask (because even with the lights off, the room is almost fully lit) and tried to sleep. I did not sleep.

At some point, I heard a new patient coming in and the nurses talking to her. "Are you in pain," "do you feel dizzy," the usual questions. And then one said, "Have you been vaccinated?" And the woman (who, yes, was frightened and vulnerable and had just had a stroke, so I should be more generous and loving with her), said, with all the friendliness of a school board meeting anti-mask protestor, "NO!"

So, there I was, completely losing my shit. I grabbed my medical mask and put it on.

I had the curtain closed, so I didn't know if she had a mask on or not. I don't know if the rules were the same for her as for me. I was allowed to have my mask off, but was she? I thought it was 'any patient in their room can be unmasked.' But does that include the deliberately murderous and/or suicidal patriotic superspreaders?

I texted Curtis. As always, God bless Curtis.

"My roommate isn't vaccinated."

He replied, "WHAT THE FUCK. I'm getting you out of there now."

Anyway, first he called the hospital to see if I could be moved or if he could come get me. They told him that they can't discharge neuro patients early, and that they'd look into moving me somewhere.

The nurse, who was very nice, and stayed two hours past her usual quitting time trying to help us, came in at one point and gave me a Xanax. She tried to ease my mind by saying that the other woman was wearing a mask and blah blah blah, and she asked me if I was okay, and I said that I wasn't okay, I was terrified, but that I was resigned to being stuck in a room with an unvaccinated person.

Anyway, the Xanax conked me out good, but Curtis and this nurse spent the rest of the night going back and forth about how to get me moved somewhere else, and at one point, there was talk that one patient had needed to go into quarantine, so they'd clean that room right up and move me there, and Curtis was like, "Wait - into quarantine because of COVID? You want to move my wife into THAT room???"

Anyway, I slept through the whole shebang, but when I woke up, someone was in the room cleaning, and shortly after that, a new roommate was wheeled in. A new nurse came to my bed and said, "It's okay, she's fully vaccinated. You can keep sleeping."

So between the hours of, like 11pm and 4am, Curtis and this nurse managed to move the unvaccinated woman someplace else and let me and the next stroke patient hang out with our own worries and fears around our individual circumstances, and we were able to relax (as much as one can in a hospital) about the threat of a deadly virus.

Anyway. I'm home. So far, I'm not experiencing any breakthrough COVID symptoms. Obviously, I have no idea if the unvaccinated lady was infected, though, until all this is over, I will assume every unvaccinated person IS infected.

As far as the unvaccinated roommate, I know the hospital was in an impossible situation – and they moved Heaven and Earth to make it right for me.

As far as the unvaccinated room cleaner, hell, I don't know. It's not like he's the only hospital employee in all the land who listens to shitty "just asking questions" assholes and pretends he's sticking it to Big Pharma or whatever the fuck they're claiming as their this-time-totally-reasonable-reason-for-being-terrible today.

Yep. Anyway. I'm back in my house. I like it here. I'm staying. And I feel just awful for the rest of you who have to navigate this horrific shitstorm every day. It's terrifying. Masks save lives, vaccines save lives. Viruses do not care at all about your news sources or your "news" sources. Real patriots care about their communities and do their part to stop the spread.

I'm probably going to call my doc on Tuesday and ask if we can change my nighttime anxiety med from my usual Buspar to Xanax, at least for a week or two. All day long, I'm strong, solid, unafraid, and easy-breezy. But as soon as nighttime rolls around, every phantom sensation freaks me out, every moment feels like the next attack will be here any second. And I know it's not reasonable, but knowing it isn't reasonable doesn't help me stop it from happening. And my sleep is terrible. I wasn't going to write about this part, but I know quite a few of my Facebook friends are dealing with health crap right now too. And maybe it'll help us all feel less alone to know that others are feeling especially frightened and mortal too.

Thursday, September 16, 2021 2:18am

One of my friends praised me and said I had a whole book's worth of material in my funny Facebook posts, so I've been eagerly combing through my Memories every day, so that I can share another old chestnut and get more praise, since I pretty much live for praise.

Anyway. I've been on Facebook for 13 years. And I haven't been funny a single time in any early September in 13 years.

Thursday, September 30, 2021 5:34am

"Mil- ugh!

267

CHES- augh!

SEANNN!!"

Tuesday, December 7, 2021 3:59am

[eating dinner]

Me: You know, most of these heart healthy recipes are close enough to good tasting that I don't get too pissy about it, but this one just feels like punishment.

Curtis: Oh, I really liked it! …Of course, I added a few ingredients..

Me: Yeah? What did you add?

Curtis: Salt and cheddar cheese.

Me: Mmhmm. Yeah, that sounds about right.

Saturday, December 11, 2021 4:17pm

The thing you don't really think about when you buy a power recliner, is that, when the power goes out, you're gonna have to get real acrobatic when you want to stand up.

2022

Thursday, January 27, 2022 7:02pm

I just tried a new recipe in the instant pot - a pasta dish with garlic, spinach, and grape tomatoes. It was great, but I had cooked chicken breasts beforehand and then used the same pot again without washing it first. Some of the pasta got a little burny and stuck to the bottom of the pot. —Still perfectly fine except for the noodles that stuck.

Anyway, now my house smells like Grandma Mason's house. I don't know what specifically it is that reminds me of Grandma's house, but as soon as I smelled it, I was instantly transported.

And I keep giggling at the idea of Grandma up in Heaven being like, "You burned your dinner and it reminded you of me???"

Saturday, February 19, 2022 9:37pm

Seany the cat's not nearly as bad as Chester Doggy was, but, omg, I swear Sean's part raccoon and part goat and part seagull. The objects that cat has puked up have freaked me out to no end.

Mary Kitty wouldn't eat anything that wasn't heated to the perfect temperature, and she frequently changed her mind about foods she'd liked in the past. Seany's like, "Hair ties? Bread ties? Plastic bags? Potato chips inside of plastic bags? Yes please! Om nom nom nom nom. And soapy dirty dishwater to wash it all down!"

Thursday, March 3, 2022 9:56am

One of my friends wrote a vulnerable post about their creative existential crisis, and their mom replied, "I hope you figure it out sweetie."

And, as both a creative and the mother of a creative, this interaction made me spontaneously combust.

Sunday, May 8, 2022 1:50pm

We had the most lovely day! We've paid our deposit and we're getting our house painted later this spring. IT NEEDS IT, OMG, WE'VE BEEN SUCH TERRIBLE VILLAGERS.

Anyway, we've been playing around with the Sherwin Williams ColorSnap app, trying on various different colors, but it's not been going particularly well - mainly because when we look at one color on a computer screen, it looks radically different from how it looks on the phone screen, and that looks radically different from how the in-person paint swatch looks. So we've been floundering a bit, not even sure what Step 1 is.

Finally Curtis had the brilliant idea that we should drive around the village and really pay attention to house colors and see what we're drawn to. I agreed, and today was the day!

We are really not "leave the house" kinds of people, and actually we were thinking that the last time we'd left the house together for a non-medical reason was Christmas of 2019. But I just remembered that I picked Curtis up recently when he was helping Milo and Billie moved out of their apartment back at the end of November. But yeah. We really, really don't go places. Which I know sounds freakish and embarrassing, but it doesn't feel freakish and embarrassing, so SHRUG.

Anyway, we drove around and had a genuinely delightful time together. Just poking around being "Sunday drivers" on side streets is really a pleasant way to spend a day. I kept marveling at the whole process. I was like, "It just seems so weird to care about the color of a house! I thought it would be like, 'slap some brown or gray on it and call it good!'" And Curtis said, "Who knew?! It turns out we have preferences!"

I felt a whole lot of sad nostalgia because Chester and I walked nearly every single village side street zillions of times back when we were both healthy. Curtis said that he felt the same way when he looked at those old hallway pictures he found in the basement recently. One of the pictures is my dad and Milo in a toy store, and Dad's pulling Milo in the wagon they bought that day. It made Curtis sad because at the end of Chester's life, when he couldn't walk more than a few steps, Curtis would take him for walks in that wagon. So yeah, lots of Chester energy around us today.

Anyway, it was calm and happy and, dare I say, *date-like*, driving around, taking pictures of houses and being suuuuuper judgy about house colors. Like, put yourself in that mindset - look at every single house around you and ask yourself the question, "Would I put those colors on a house on purpose?"

But then! The very best and lightest moment of the day was when we pulled into our driveway and looked at our house with those same judgy eyes, and we both burst out laughing. Like, it was the most spontaneous simultaneous crack-up ever. Omg, our house is so dreadful. Paint peeling everywhere.

Apr 09, 2022 7:53:07pm

I could never live without Siri doing basic math for me. When I had my stroke, they wanted me to do math in my head, and I was like, "Ma'am, I haven't been able to do math at any point in my life. Ask me song lyrics or something instead."

Thursday, May 26, 2022 8:27pm

Apparently, gas prices are no problem for the local coal rollers. They're out all day every day.

I have a snoring recorder app on my phone, and I had one "epic" snore register last night, in the middle of an otherwise pretty reasonably "light" snoring night.

When I played the recording back, it wasn't me. It was just closing time at Leo's Pizza across the street, and it was prime redneck mating-call time.

Thursday, June 16, 2022 2:48am

I'm watching the hearings, and it should come as no surprise that, as usual, the most descriptive threats of violence were geared toward women. They were eager to 'come for' Jerry Nadler and 'hang' Mike Pence, but they couldn't wait to "rip all the hairs out of Nancy Pelosi's head."

Patriots, man. They fucking terrify me.

Friday, June 17, 2022 1:23pm

The thought I can't get out of my head, days after the Jan 6th hearings, is that, while I saw a bunch testosterone poisoned jackasses, easily duped by the real-money Republican Party, Black folks saw a literal lynch mob, eager to haul living people outside to destroy their bodies in the street. And sure, some in the mob would have only watched and cheered, but plenty of people were in place, full of absolute, self-deluded certainty and ready to kill.

It was a different sense of horror for me and other white folks - who were mostly embarrassed and ashamed and disgusted - than it was for people whose ancestors were forced to cower in terror while people with skin like mine hunted them down.

We weren't just the monsters in the barbaric "old days" when we supposedly didn't know any better.

Saturday, June 25, 2022 7:59pm
Greatest Hits

Leaving the church was easy. Like, easy-easy. There were two points that I was never going to reconcile. Abortion was #1, of course.

Like all indoctrinated Christian children, I was "pro-life." I even had a pin of "Precious Feet" tacked to my purse flap. I remember, because that stupid pin was tacked to my purse when, as a 15-year-old, I had a pregnancy scare.

Oh, it's a funny story; I've told it often: After months of my boyfriend's obnoxious begging, I relented just to finally get him to shut up about it. He picked me up for a date an hour or so later, so I wouldn't have time to change my mind. The night I lost my virginity, we were supposed to go see the movie Broadcast News (which I've still never seen), but instead we went back to his house. He cranked up the Whitesnake so his parents wouldn't hear us, and then pushed his way in after no foreplay at all ("But it's a lubed condom!"). He didn't go slow.

Because he wasn't a complete monster, I have to think maybe he was just doing that thing – like when you see an injured animal, you're supposed to kill it quick, so you don't draw out its suffering. (It was before the internet, and you just don't know what you don't know).

The second time we had sex was exactly the same, except that A. I didn't bleed as much after (though I still bled some), and B. The condom broke.

I knew exactly what a broken condom meant. And though I had somewhat irregular periods, I knew that my real period (and not just my vagina-smashing injury) was due any day. I immediately and wholly believed that I was pregnant.

I stared at those Precious Feet on my purse a lot in the following days. Where I had once never questioned that abortion was murder, suddenly I saw a picture that was so much bigger – like in the Wizard of Oz when the picture goes from black and white to color, only the image was gruesome not beautiful.

Oh.

I saw my future clear as day: Tied forever to this person I didn't even much *like*. Tied forever to this person who regularly put my life in danger with his reckless driving – who thought it was hilarious when I was scared (and who literally died in a motorcycle accident years later. I suspect that was his aim all along). Tied forever to this person who was an ASSHOLE. Tied forever to a child who would surely be just as much of an asshole as its dad.

It was immediately clear: Call it anything you want, but I will be god-damned before I have this baby. Those fucking fly-sized feet on my purse were not more precious than my own.

There's not much more to the story. Unlike so many other people, my period was only late. So, I never needed an abortion. But my mind was made up. I would have done literally anything – I would have stolen from loved ones, I would have sucked two or three dozen randos' dicks for money, I would have harmed my own body. I would have *happily* done anything at all to not carry that dude's baby.

One of the first things I did when I got my driver's license was go to Planned Parenthood and get on the pill. They were wonderful to me. I asked my embarrassing questions, and the doctor very patiently reassured me that, even though my vulva didn't look exactly like the pencil drawing in my health textbook, my body wasn't deformed at all. -I mention that because violent anti-abortion extremists love to target 'the butchers' at Planned Parenthood. But all I found at Planned Parenthood were respectful and caring professionals.

I don't recall the Catholics being so hung up on fetuses when I was a little kid. But holy buckets, in the 1980s (and I assume "the 80s, 90s, and today!"), every week at church became the Fetus Fandom Hour. After my pregnancy scare, all that "Mary said yes" horseshit rang pretty empty. Mary didn't get to say a goddamn thing.

So yeah. Although I didn't leave the church until sometime in the earlyish 90s, it was clear that there would never be a compromise between me and the church on exactly when my life's sanctity had ended.

My second reason for leaving the church might not sound as serious to you, but it was very much a deal-breaker for me: That women can't be Catholic priests. Hell, I'm a better writer and speaker than most priests I've ever endured. I have more charisma than most priests I've ever endured. But I still need someone with a cock to interpret the bible for me? SURE JAN.

And it's not even like I wanted to be a priest. I've always thought I'd make a good homilist, but there's a whole lot of reverence and solemnity and ceremony involved in priesting, -all things I'm terrible at (I will never have the patience for the Stations of the Cross. I just won't).

But this insistence that any stupid man would make a better priest than any smart woman, or that an angry, orgasmicly-constipated man should be counseling couples about real and valid problems in their marriages (and that their advice would always be 'Shut up, woman') – it just made my skin crawl.

So, with regard to abortion, I had this kind of eye-rolling, 'Yeah yeah, Butchers at Planned Parenthood, we *know*. You've *told* us.' -And maybe that's because I knew Catholic girls who'd had abortions and weren't ashamed. I suppose it felt similar to how kids drink, and their parents get mad, and then those kids grow up and become parents, and then their kids drink, and they get mad, and then those kids grow up and become parents, and then their kids drink, and they get mad.

Like, sure the *people in charge* have "rules," but when we want to, we'll ignore those rules.

But it's not like a parish somewhere could ever hire a lady priest and let her say the mass and baptize the babies and officiate the weddings and bury the dead. It's not like that's a rule we can all ignore while sticking our tongues out at the old farts in the rectory.

So yes. Leaving the church was easy. [It's only hard for me when people die. Catholic funerals when you're an Atheist feel wrong. -Like, you want to honor the dead in the way they want to be honored, but you also want to honor the dead in a way that feels sincere. And those are some pretty parallel lines (So I do what everybody does. Be there, be loving, blend in. It ain't about me).]

Becoming an Atheist was different, and it came much later. It happened in the years after 9/11. You remember the Judas Priest song, "Screaming for Vengeance?" That's what America felt like to me. It felt like a loud, manic, boiling sea of crosses and flags demanding the blood of any body from any brown country. It felt like there was no suspected Muslim who shouldn't be tortured on the whims of the US Government with the full backing of every faithful Christian.

My Atheism and my anti-patriotism were born at the same time. They were born of this desire to separate myself from the aggression and ugliness that I watched swallow so many mainstream white folks who look just like me. Truly, it felt like I had been raised in peace among a nationwide sleeper cell of genial deer hunters who got their orders and changed on a dime.

I'm so embarrassed that I didn't understand what I was seeing until after 9/11. In retrospect, the mainstream bloodthirst and racism and woman and LGBT hatred were always there, and not even hiding. But because everybody was so nice and funny and kind and eager to help each other out, I couldn't imagine that those people really meant it when they told that kneeslapper joke about why black people don't like lawnmowers.

It reminds me of the Dar Williams song, Teen for God, about a kid at church camp:

Help me know four years from now

I won't believe in you anyhow

And I'll mope around a campus, and I'll feel betrayed

All those guilty summers I stayed and

Then I'll laugh that I fell for the lure

of the pain of desire to feel so pure

And I'll bear all the burdens of my little daily crimes

Wish I had a god for such cynical times

Far from today

Anyway. I've been sitting here for a while, trying to figure out how to wrap all this up and give it a point, but I guess there really isn't one.

Leaving the church is easy when they show you the door. Staying away from the church is effortless when they try to call you back with offers of more singing, smiling community, delicious baked goods, and all the patriarchal white supremacy you can pretend to not see.

I set out to write a post about abortion, and this obviously isn't that. It's about me and my selfish sadness, and my intense fear for all the millions more people who find themselves helpless to stop a pregnancy they can't afford, helpless to stop a pregnancy they don't want, helpless to stop a pregnancy that could kill them, helpless to end a miscarriage that won't expel on its own.

When I was 25, and ready, and insured, and had the right partner, I got to have a celebrated baby. It was wonderful to enter parenthood that way. I had one child, and decided that was enough for me, and then had IUDs for the rest of my fertile years. I wish that freedom for everybody. I don't understand people who would curse their own daughters and grandchildren to lives of poverty, abuse, and unhappy relationships, just so they can please their made-up jerk of a god. Thanks for listening to my homily.

And now, let us stand for the Profession of Faith. We believe in one god. The father the almighty. Maker of Heaven and Earth. Dee da Dee da Dee da da da.

Tuesday, June 28, 2022 12:27am
The cats would like to remind me that I am allowed to store exactly one thing in the treat cupboard. And it ain't infrequently used cooking utensils.

Saturday, July 16, 2022 9:42pm
The best thing about eating a peach: Peaches are delicious!!

The worst thing about eating a peach: The next batch of hours, where you're constantly singing, "Movin to the country, gonna eat a lot of peaches. I'm movin to the country, gonna eat me a lot of peaches."

Saturday, July 23, 2022 12:09am
Me interacting with the kitties:

Oh my heavens, look at your sweet little face!

Oh, my precious, precious beebee, how did I get so lucky?

Oh, look at your beautiful belly!

Oh my goodness, that's such a big stretch!

Let's brush this furry little monster!

Let's feed these hungry hungry hippos!

Oh my goodness, these starvin marvins have been patient long enough, huh?!

Me interacting with my husband:

Mornin!

I heated up fish sticks!

Okay, Sleep tight!

Friday, July 29, 2022 9:34am
Greatest Hits

This is very long:

It's been (not quite) 11 months since my stroke. and I've lost (not quite) 70 pounds. I weigh myself once a week, and the last time I checked, I was down 67 pounds. Yay! I very sincerely don't want to have a *conversation* about it, but I do want to write about it.

278

I saw a friend the other day – not anybody close, but someone who sees me in-person sometimes, and he said, "Hey you look great!"

It was that simple. Nothing besides a pleasant noticing: "Hey you look great!"

And because it felt safe and like an emotion-free zone, I said, "Thanks! I'm almost to 70 pounds!"

I've told Curtis the number at various points. I told Milo once. But while I care a lot about the number, I'm so conscious of the fear: "If they know I've lost xxx pounds, then if I gain it all back, they'll know that too. Better to act like there is nothing to see here and pretend my shorts have always fallen off my ass when I put my phone in my pocket (it is a weirdly heavy phone).

This friend (who's also big and also has health issues, which is why the conversation felt so perfectly safe in the first place) said, "What's your secret?"

And, AGHH, I didn't have an answer prepared, and so I went to a negative, self-deprecating place: "I track everything I put in my mouth, blehhhhhh."

And then we had the conversation that's expected:

"Oh, I can't do that, I'm too lazy."

"Yeah, it really sucks."

"I could never remember to write it all down."

"Oh, it's an app. It's actually pretty easy."

"Yeah. Meh."

"Yeah. Meh."

The end.

But here's the thing: I don't think food tracking sucks. No lie, I think food tracking is the most empowering thing I've ever done.

But I'm getting ahead of myself.

I have been fat for a really long time. Most of my life. And I've said a million times that the best piece of advice I ever got was when, long ago, my shrink said,

"Does hating yourself make you stop eating?"

Me (sobbing): "No!"

"When you call yourself disgusting, does it make you feel less hungry?"

Me (sobbing harder): "NO!!"

"Then why not just give yourself permission to enjoy the food?"

Seriously, that was one of the most meaningful moments of my life. Someone pointing out that all this flagellation was getting me nowhere, and that since I was eating the food anyway, I might as well delight in how delicious it is..it was just staggering. It changed my mind in a way that nothing ever had before.

Food is delicious, so feel happiness at the deliciousness. How simple! How revolutionary!

And, of course I wanted to be smaller. Mainly because it was clear that the larger I got, the more trouble I had moving my body, and the more pain I had all the time. I couldn't prove that my pain would go away if I was just smaller, but it seemed like a safe assumption. But I didn't try very hard to get smaller. Oh sure, when my body felt strong-ish, I'd walk more. When the stars aligned just right, I'd cook more (instead of ordering takeout). But the combination of pain and depression is a hurdle that I didn't believe I could ever get over. I thought maybe there'd be a pill someday that could fix me. But mostly, I had decided to just accept reality: I am a big person who suffers with mental health issues and chronic pain. Other than those things, I have a really nice life.

[Actually, the main reason a fat person wants to be smaller is because of chairs. Seriously, Step 1 in my agoraphobia was the ever-shrinking number of public places that had chairs that I trusted.

And if you know or love a fat person, have a thought for chairs before you ask them to go someplace new (or old. Stately old theaters are abysmal places for fat people). The literal only thing they'll be thinking about is whether the chairs will hold them or if the arms on the chairs will cut off the blood supply to their legs. When I've referred to someone's house or a public place as a "safe space," for me, that means there are multiple chairs there that I trust. I don't have to be lucky or fast enough to get 'the good chair.' All of the chairs are good chairs.]

But then I had a stroke.

This was the second near-death experience I've had (and actually, the less grave one). Just before Milo was born, I developed pre-eclampsia and HELLP Syndrome, and both of us were dying. I couldn't understand why the doctors had let me get so shockingly sick, and Curtis explained that it was like a mathematical equation the professionals were doing with us: The faster they took Milo out of my body, the worse it was for *his* survival. But the longer they left him in, the worse it was for *my* survival. So they intentionally allowed me to get sicker for days, which gave the steroid shots they'd injected to strengthen Milo's lungs time to do their work.

My experience of that was kind of like the 'frog boiling' myth. By the time I realized how dire things were getting, I felt like I was watching my own death from a detached place. Like, "Wow, this is really scary." And, "Isn't that strange? I don't think I've ever seen Curtis cry like that.."

(I was in the best hospital in the area, hooked up to every machine. They weren't going to let me die. But they did let me get a whole lot sicker than I would have preferred).

The terror came later, after the threat to my life had mostly passed.

With my stroke, the terror happened almost immediately.

I've always been a hypochondriac, and I spend a ridiculous amount of time telling myself I'm fine. "You're fine. Just get out of the sun." "You're fine. This is just anxiety. Let's count blue things." "You're fine. You've had migraines before. It'll go away." "You're fine. You know what depressive episodes feel like. This is nothing new."

So when I had the stroke, I tried to "You're fine" my way out of it.

But something definitely wasn't fine. I felt, I don't know...slow. Confused. But not confused like, "How many fingers am I holding up?," Confused like, "Did I just die? Am I still alive?"

I picked up my Kindle and tried to read out loud. My reasoning was, 'if I can read words that I didn't write myself, I'll know I'm fine.' But the words came out buzzy and slurred. I thought, I think I have to go to the hospital. And I stood up and put clean clothes on. I put my ipad, phone, Kindle, and water bottle into a bag to take with me, and went downstairs.

Part of me still thought I was making it up, until I got downstairs and spoke to Curtis. I don't know what, exactly, he saw, but his eyes got ENORMOUS, and after about .03 seconds of pure panic, he grabbed his phone and dialed 911.

And that's when I got scared.

Being rushed to the hospital in an ambulance while conscious and alert is just about the worst thing imaginable for a fat person with both agoraphobia and claustrophobia.

Strapped down, too tight to move, on a narrow gurney in a freakishly rickety ambulance.

The hydraulic system that lifts the gurney whines loudly and jostles.

Panicking and trying to rip off my mask as they're putting me in for a CT scan while a very patient but firm nurse wrestled with me and repeated, "Your mask protects me" until it sunk in and I nodded and stopped fighting.

Spending an hour in an MRI machine with tears running into my ears, thinking, 'if I was just a little smaller, this wouldn't be so scary. Maybe if my arms didn't touch the sides, this wouldn't be so scary."

So yeah, it was bad, and I was pretty darn raw already, when one of the doctors woke me up the next morning to say, "We don't know why the stroke happened, other than..." and he waved dismissively at my fat body.

He spoke words words words, which I didn't hear because I was both still half asleep and completely rocked by his mean-spirited insult.

But as he left the room, he said, "So yeah, just lose fiftysixty pounds and watch your sodium." He said it in a tone that made clear he knew I would not be losing *fiftysixty* pounds or watching my sodium, and that he'd be seeing my fat ass back in his ICU again sometime in the near future.

I have spent a lot of time in the last year reading/watching/listening to people on weight loss journeys. And they all say one thing or another: "Why can't I just START?" or "Why did I take so long to START?"

In my case, the answer's easy: I started because I had a life-threatening traumatic experience, then an authority figure in a white coat told me it was because I was fat, and then suddenly any food with salt in it felt like a weapon to me.

The first few months of my journey were desperately terrible. I couldn't dial back my anxiety. I felt so sick and scared and MORTAL. I couldn't soothe myself with the foods I loved. The learning curve for eating enough-calories-but-not-too-much-salt was shockingly steep (bread?? Carrots?? MILK???). I felt so much guilt. That I had harmed myself, that I had known I was harming myself and did it anyway, and I deserved every bad thing that was happening to me.

At the beginning of my journey, I did not believe that losing weight would be possible for me. Like, I didn't even consider the possibility. Zero chance of success, I'm not even going to try.

But I was pretty sure I could cut my sodium. I was pretty sure that ice cream doesn't have a lot of sodium, so since I could still eat ice cream, I could live with cutting back on other foods. That was the whole starting plan.

And that's how I started. Calories, fat, sugar, carbs, etc, are all triggering words for me. But "sodium" and "salt" aren't. After all, I know zillions of people with high blood pressure, and they're every size imaginable – fat, skinny, and in between. So watching sodium numbers didn't feel as fraught as watching those other numbers.

I downloaded an app called My Fitness Pal, and put my info in. It forced me to enter a goal weight, which annoyed me because I wasn't trying to lose weight. But I entered 50 pounds just for shits and giggles and because that's what the cardiologist told me to lose. But seriously, as I entered that 50, I was thinking it would be as likely for me to barf up a unicorn as it would to lose 50 pounds or even one pound.

But I had to enter that goal weight along with my present weight, age, and height so that it could tell me how many calories to take in (--*You want to eat as many calories as you possibly can and still lose weight. If you cut your calories too radically --even just over the course of your day, you get too hungry and end up bingeing. It's why 'eat less move more' never worked for me. Until I started weighing and tracking my food, I didn't understand how to stagger my food/energy intake so I never get so tremendously hungry*).

For me, that was 2070 calories a day. I also had to change the suggested sodium number in MFP from 2300mg to 1500mg, to follow a true, low-sodium diet.

I cannot emphasize enough how much I hated the first few months of this. I was only "caring" about my sodium numbers, but of course the app shows all the numbers. Calories, carbs, fiber,

284

protein, sodium, sugar, fat. So I could see all the numbers either way.

There were plenty of my favorite foods that I knew would be out of the question. Bar Bill chicken wings, Wendy's spicy chicken value meal, etc. But it was the foods that I'd always assumed were perfectly neutral that upset me so much. I used to eat a turkey sandwich with chips, and carrots, and blue cheese every day.

I knew I'd have to cut out the chips. Okay, fine.

But 2 slices of Sahlen's turkey breast + 1 tbsp mayo, + 3 tsp dijon mustard, + one slice Lacy Swiss cheese, + 2 slices Healthy Multigrain bread, + 3 oz baby carrots, + 2 tbsp Marie's Chunky Blue Cheese = 1451mg sodium. The single meal that I thought I'd cut the salt down enough on still had my full daily allowance of sodium. The chips? A single serving bag of chips would have only added another 360mg of sodium.

I learned that there is no deli meat that fits in a low sodium diet. There is no store-bought bread or flour tortilla or pita or wrap that fits in a low sodium diet (I make my own no sodium white bread in the bread machine or I have corn tortillas). There is no frozen food dinner, including Lean Cuisine and Amy's Organic that fits in a low sodium diet. And, unless it says "No salt added," there is no canned food that fits in a low sodium diet.

So how in the motherfucking FUCK does one eat a low sodium diet?????

I can't even tell you the number of times I'd get to the last meal of my day and still have 700 calories I could eat, but no sodium allowance left. The number of times I ate a puny couple of servings of unsalted cashews. The ABJECT MISERY and feeling of utter hopelessness that I was just going to die of another stroke because this was just not going to work.

And yes, I heard the advice to call a nutritionist from a zillion different providers.

But I don't cook.

I *WON'T* cook.

Or, I might cook if I'm feeling strong and feeling like I have the capacity to deal with dirty pans and heat sources, but that ain't going to be every day. And humans need to eat every day.

So where I finally found relief was with a meal delivery service. I've tried three different services. I started out using Metabolic Meals, and they were my favorite by a mile. But I finally decided to cancel them because I wanted to eat two Metabolic Meals a day, and that was too much sodium. It didn't leave me enough for my other meal or snacks.

Then I tried, for one week, Silvercare by BistroMd. Omg. Remember what hospital cafeteria food used to taste like? This wasn't as good as that.

Finally I found Fresh N Lean. I've been eating two Fresh N Leans a day since...probably sometime in January. They're not particularly interesting, but they're good, and they're enough food.

Then for my other meal, I usually eat chicken tacos [3 oz Instant Pot chicken breast + 3 corn tortillas + a bunch of grape tomatoes + 1 oz Extra Sharp cheddar cheese], or 2 servings of Frosted Mini Wheats with 12 oz Silk Unsweetened Coconut Milk. My snacks are, nearly 100% of the time, Mint Chocolate Chip Yasso frozen yogurt bars. Sometimes I eat one serving of unsalted pretzels + one serving of Peanut M&Ms. The pretzels are flavorless, so they take on the taste of the M&Ms, and it's like you're eating more M&Ms.

I have a few cookbooks that I've bought, and one that I really like is Jeffrey Eisner's Lighter Step by Step Instant Pot (I always leave out the salt).

I'm getting ahead of myself again. Back to the Fresh N Leans: They're expensive. $160 a week for 14 meals. But they're enough food, decent nutrition, and I don't have to think about them. I like them enough to eat them long-term.

From months of reading the labels on the Fresh N Leans I figured out the rule of thumb that works for a low sodium diet: If the sodium amount is within 100mg of the calories, then the food is worth it.

So many foods are perfectly fine calories-wise every now and again – a Whopper, a hot dog, a fish fry. But the sodium makes it unacceptable. Look at the label on a can of Cambell's soup sometime to see what I mean. Just look at the calories vs sodium. (Now that I've been at this a while, and my blood pressure isn't hanging out in FREAK OUT territory, I might possibly allow one of those things every month or so. I ate a piece of pizza two months ago and I didn't worry about it. It was AMAZING).

This is a biggie. I'm reading my words and thinking what it would be like if I'd read a 'changed lifestyle' post like this from one of my peers a year ago. I know exactly what I would have thought: Well, I'm not going to do *that!*

The answer to the question, "Why didn't I start sooner?" was, for me at least, that something truly terrible had to happen first. It wasn't until I fully understood that I could die, and soon, and had the traumatic hospital experience to back it up that I was able to start.

--And I hate it, but I *needed* that recent trauma to keep me going through those miserable, super-steep-learning-curve, intensely depressing months before I started to notice changes and feel better.

I remember feeling straight-up PISSED that every woman-targeted ad and magazine article has always promised that if I just ate right and exercised, that I'd feel good. Well, it was MONTHS before I felt good. I felt like dogshit those first few months.

I started out with food. Exercise was a lot more difficult because of balance and anxiety issues. I have an elliptical machine that I bought when Milo was little, that is weight-rated for 325 pounds (if you're fat, only buy weight-rated furniture. Google everything. No furniture impulse buys, ever). But I didn't like using it because my balance is screwy and there was a big step up to get on it.

I solved that problem by buying one of those aerobics-class steps and setting it next to the elliptical. YAY! Problem solved! (-- And added bonus that when my anxiety makes me start to feel like I'm falling, I can put my foot on that step and collect myself! Awesome!)

Except that when I look out the window, the cars going by make me super dizzy.

Okay, close the blinds!

Except that now there's nothing to look at and I'm bored and all I can think about is how much I hate this. Also, I hate closed blinds. Haaaaaaate closed blinds.

Okay, distract yourself. Maybe an audiobook? I like audiobooks!

Nope. Not when I'm exercising.

Okay music! I used to like fast music, I could make a playlist of fast music!

Yeah, that works!

...for a few weeks. Now I'm bored again. Bored bored bored bored. And so much of the music, even the fast music, doesn't push me along. Why is it so hard to find music that PUSHES me?

Google google google. Workout Remixes?

Ohhh! Yes, that's exactly what I wanted! And playlists with the BPM listed? PERFECT! OMG!

But I'm still bored. Yes, exercise is getting easier, but I really need something to look at.

Okay. I have lots of devices. The elliptical, just by luck, faces a closet door. So I bought a book holder than hangs over the door and put my ipad on that. I can watch anything. I can watch movies!

Nope. Hated that. Movies don't push me like music does.

I'm not sure what I searched for that landed me on virtual running videos on Youtube, but when I found them, it was the greatest thing ever. I've (virtually) run the Grand Canyon, I've run through fields with giant fluffy sheep everywhere, I've run along countless lakes, oceans, and fjords, I've run up mountains, I've run over scary narrow bridges. I learned that I don't even like *virtual* crowds, so Death Valley, Central Park, and a resort in Hawaii were all unpleasant and I won't do them again.

Lately, I most prefer state parks out west that are too inclimate for me to ever put on a bucket list. I keep coming back to Bryce Canyon and Zion National Park. They're just unbelievably cool places.

I found a Watkins Glen hike recently, and I put the playback speed at 1.25 (to imitate a run), and did that. It was gorges (lol)! Then I had a nice little daydream about buying a GoPro and videoing trails at Letchworth Park. It obviously wasn't a serious intention, but it was nice to think about all the same.

Fairly early in my journey, I started following a weight loss guru named Chris Terrell. I can't explain why what he says sinks in for me, but it does. I loathe cheerleaders, and I straight-up despise drill sergeants, but Chris just talks and says simple, pragmatic things. Like, "You do *not* have to lose 150 pounds. You have to lose *one* pound. ..Okay, you lost one pound? Fantastic!! Let's see if you can do it again!

He makes a big deal about completely reinventing your relationship with food. As in, there are no good foods, there are no bad foods, there are no forbidden foods, it's all just food. There aren't even any cheat meals, because again, there are no bad foods, and 'cheat' suggests you're doing something wrong.

He says that people who need to lose a lot of weight should never try a diet like Keto, because Keto is a temporary diet. We are not on a diet that we can go "off" of. We are reinventing our entire relationship with food.

He makes a big deal about what happens when you hit maintenance (He doesn't use the word Goal Weight very often). He says that most of us have no trouble at all losing weight.

Our problem is with not gaining weight.

So we have to have a plan for what we do when we hit maintenance.

In his case, once he got near his goal weight, he stopped tracking his food and began "intuitive eating," which is a buzzword for how we're all supposed to eat. I aspire to be an intuitive eater. He continued weighing himself once a week. He had a five-pound range that he allowed himself to fall within. And if he stayed at the top of the five-pound range for two weeks in a row, then he had to go back to tracking his food. But mostly, when he noticed that he was gaining, he'd try to change his habits a little bit without getting super strict with himself.

And he's had to go back to tracking a few times. But because he had that five-pound limit, he's been able to continue his journey without falling into the trap of self-hatred and hopelessness that's so depressingly normal for people who've lost weight and started gaining it back.

I should mention, because he mentions it, that he had his own weight loss guru. And his weight loss guru gained the weight back. That's not to discourage someone from starting. It's to keep us clear-eyed about this journey.

I had a really interesting thought recently. Like, I'm all-in with Chris's advice about this being a forever journey, and that you really can't ever go "off" the diet. That's fine for me because I know I have to continue with Low Sodium to stay alive. That's a forever journey. So I haven't been falling into my own previously common pitfall of being like, "Oh, I just can't wait until I can eat Pasta Carrabba again!"

I already know that I can eat a few bites of someone else's Pasta Carrabba, but I will not be ordering my own plate ever again. Okay fine.

But recently, I was up on the elliptical, running some trail, pushy music in my ears, chewing bubble gum, doing all the things I do to make it less miserable, and I thought, "Ugh, I can't wait until I can stop doing this all the time!"

And I got kind of excited that I noticed it. Because exercise isn't a temporary thing either. Exercise is why my balance is better. Exercise is why I feel stronger and less terrified all the time. Exercise is why my back isn't constantly spasming.

Eating less food is why I weigh less. But exercising more is why I feel better.

All right. So, what else?

Before I started going to physical therapy, I followed a Tik Toker named Justin Agustin. He's so loving and wholesome and kind. Exactly the sort of person I'm drawn to.

I might have even written it here before that I've known I needed help with movement for a few years, but I felt like I needed to get better before I could be well enough to start physical therapy. Which, I know sounds ridiculous. You should start PT whenever and wherever! Except that wasn't true. I knew that PT was going to mean breathing hard and sweating. I knew that PT was going to mean effort and difficulty and embarrassment and awkward positions, and vulnerability. AND IT WAS ALL OF THOSE THINGS.

Justin Agustin is one of the reasons I felt strong enough to start PT. He has you do things like sit on the edge of your couch and do 5 leg lifts. He has you do things like the arm movements from jumping jacks without any of the jumping.

I know this won't mean anything to a lot of you. But I know a few of my followers might be helped by him. Folks who aren't traumatized yet, -who would love to not be traumatized, but who are disabled to the point where you don't know how to even get strong enough to start PT. Go on TikTok. Follow Chris Terrell for weight stuff, and Justin Agustin for mobility stuff. They'll help you too.

Okay, that's it. Thanks for reading this far. I know it was long AF.

I haven't set a specific goal weight. I'm going to keep losing, but I'm already at a point where I can move more comfortably, and my body doesn't hurt so much. So I won't mind if my pace slows down a bit. My journey is long, and like all journeys, it's been bumpy, and it'll keep right on being bumpy. I'm at the point now where weight loss feels like an emotion-free, mostly simple process. And that's how weight loss is supposed to feel!

It's never been like that for me before, and if you're heavy, I assume it's never been that way for you either. It's like there is a mountain of vulnerability and guilt and self-hatred to climb first. And because that mountain is so steep, you never really start, and if you do start, you never get to the point where weight loss is as simple as eating less and moving more.

It's like the female orgasm. If you've never had an orgasm, you feel like everybody else must be lying. But then you figure it out by accident one day, and you're like, *Holy shit, they're real! omg!!* That's kind of what months-in weight loss is like: Calorie deficit, regular exercise, lose weight! Holy shit, it's possible!! --And again, it was adding a food scale and a food tracking app that removed the emotion and self-sabotage, and turned this process into something straightforward and mechanical. For me anyway. I know these kinds of things are so radically individualistic.

If you want to talk more about this, DM me. I have an easier time 1:1 on this subject than I do any other way.

I still don't like leaving my house. I still hate sunshine and heat. I feel pretty good that I've found the tricks I'm using. I've discarded at least a million others.

12/8/19: Dippy Selfie:

2/7/21: With Seany (seven months PRE-stroke):

4/9/22: With Curtis (Seven months POST-stroke:

9/30/22: In my old but never worn before dress:

The Story of Trisha the Puppy

Oct 04, 2016 2:19:14am

{{This is the bedtime story I used to tell Milo when he was younger. He loved Trisha and he always had a million questions about being a baby in the hospital. ...And he could NEVER fall asleep. This was the story I would tell after books, after love yous, after lights out, after I'd gone back downstairs. Then he'd come get me, tell me he couldn't sleep, and would I please come back up and tell him the Trisha the puppy story? I haven't told it in many years, but I think I've remembered it pretty closely.}}

Once upon a time, there was a tiny little stuffed animal puppy named Trisha. Trisha lived at a toy store, and she was very sad. Someone had dropped her in a big, clear plastic bin filled with great big stuffed animals. And poor Trisha had slipped between all those great big toys and was now stuck on the bottom. She didn't think anyone would ever take her home.

One day, a short lady with a pretty face came into the store. And Trisha watched as the short lady wandered between the big bins, picking up all kinds of different stuffed animals and then putting them back down.

The short lady wandered around and around. Finally, she stopped at Trisha's bin. Trisha watched as the short lady stood on tippy-toes to reach the different toys inside. But none of them were right for the short lady. Finally, the short lady backed away from the bin. She looked disappointed.

But then the short lady saw Trisha! She looked right at Trisha and smiled! She leaned in closer, and Trisha heard the short lady whisper, "This one's perfect."

The short lady was too short to reach Trisha, so she found the tallest man in the store, and he dug through the bin to get Trisha. Trisha was so excited!!

The lady carried Trisha to the checkout and said that Trisha was going to be a present. She asked if Trisha could be put in a box and wrapped with pretty paper and a bow.

Trisha was the happiest little puppy! She wondered if she was going to be a present at someone's birthday party. She'd always wanted to go to a birthday party! She wondered if she was going to live with a little boy or a little girl. She couldn't wait to find out.

But poor Trisha had to wait a long time in that box. She didn't know how long it was, but it felt like forever.

Finally, Trisha was taken for a ride in a car. The moment was finally here! She hoped it was someone's birthday party!

But instead, when her box was finally opened, there was a different lady. And this lady looked sad and tired.

The lady smiled at Trisha and said, "Oh, how sweet! Milo will love her, I'm sure."

Trisha was more confused than ever. The tired lady held Trisha while the short lady visited. When the short lady left, the tired lady carried Trisha to a baby crib and set her inside. Then the tired lady stood at the crib and cried for a few minutes. Then the lady left the room.

The crib reminded Trisha of the toy store. Once again, she was surrounded by much larger toys. Great big stuffed teddy bears, and a panda bear, and a koala bear, and dolls, and so many other toys. And they were all so big. Trisha felt like crying too.

Days went by, and more toys were added to the crib. And once again, Trisha was lost and forgotten underneath bigger toys.

She knew this was a crib, not a toy box, but nobody ever put a baby in the crib. They only put toys inside.

One day, the tired lady came back, and she wasn't carrying a toy this time. Instead, she went to the crib, picked up each toy, and then set it down. She did this with every toy in the crib. Because Trisha was the smallest, the lady didn't notice her right away.

Finally, the lady noticed Trisha. And just like the short lady, the tired lady smiled at Trisha and said, "This one's perfect."

The lady picked Trisha up, and Trisha hoped she'd be put back in a box and wrapped like a present and taken to a birthday party!

But instead, the lady carried her to a car, and they went for a ride.

The car stopped, and the lady carried Trisha into a huge, noisy building. There were people everywhere. They rode in an elevator, and they got out on a very quiet floor.

There weren't any people at all on this floor. The lady pushed a button on the wall, and a sliding door opened. The lady set Trisha down on a table, and she went to a sink and washed her hands and her arms.

The lady counted, "One Mississippi, two Mississippi." She counted Mississippis for a very long time. Then the lady dried herself off and picked up Trisha. Then another sliding door opened, and they walked through.

It was like a different world. They were in a room filled with brightly lit, clear plastic boxes in rows. And there were beeping machines next to each plastic box. As they walked past one plastic box, Trisha saw there was a baby inside the box.

There were babies inside all the boxes. And they were all so small.

They were small like Trisha.

Finally, Trisha understood. These were sick babies. She was a present for a sick baby. And maybe the reason that the ladies had chosen her was specifically because she was small enough to fit in one of those boxes with a baby.

Trisha was so scared. She had never seen a sick baby before. She was afraid she'd do everything wrong.

The tired lady stopped to talk to another lady wearing blue clothes. The nurse talked about Baby Milo. She said Baby Milo had stopped breathing a few times, but that the machines had gone off and that the nurses had been able to 'bring him back around' just by rubbing his chest.

The way the lady and the nurse were talking, Trisha knew that Baby Milo stopped breathing often. She was terrified.

Finally, the nurse noticed Trisha. "Oh, how darling!" she exclaimed. She took Trisha, sprayed something stinky on her, and then set her in the plastic box with Baby Milo.

This was Trisha's first good look at Baby Milo. He was so small! He was laying on his side, propped up with blankets. His skin was red and wrinkly. There were wires attached to his feet, his arms, his mouth and his nose. He was very, very scary to look at.

Trisha spent many weeks inside the box with Baby Milo. She watched him grow. She heard him cry.

Baby Milo opened his eyes all the time. Sometimes she thought he looked right at her. She noticed how each week, Baby Milo needed to have fewer wires stuck to his body.

The tired lady and a tired man came to visit Baby Milo every day. Nurses and doctors came to see Milo every few minutes.

It didn't take long for Trisha to stop being afraid of Baby Milo. Pretty soon, Trisha began to love Baby Milo. She was so glad that she was small like Milo.

Finally, Milo and Trisha were moved from their plastic box to a crib in that same room in the hospital. Trisha knew that when babies moved to a crib, that meant they were strong now, and that they would go home soon.

Milo didn't forget to breathe anymore. But he did cry a lot.

And then they got to go home! Milo's daddy put him into a car seat and tucked Trisha next to him. His mommy and daddy hugged every nurse and every doctor. Then they left the room with all the babies in boxes, and they walked to the elevator.

The elevator doors opened, and there were many people inside. When the people saw Milo, they all gasped. One person said, "Oh my god." Another person said she'd never seen such a small baby. Trisha wanted to laugh and say, "You should have seen him two months ago! That was a small baby!"

When they got back to their house, Trisha assumed that she would spend all of her time with Milo still. But she was wrong. As soon as they were home, Trisha was tossed into Milo's crib with the other toys. She wasn't special anymore. She was just a tiny little toy who was lined up with some of the other toys at one end of Milo's crib. She got pushed to the back and forgotten.

But Trisha didn't mind. She had been Milo's when Milo needed her. And she got to see him whenever he slept in his crib. That was enough, she decided.

Milo got bigger. And he wiggled, he hollered, he laughed, he sang, and he scootched around in his crib.

One day, Milo was awake in his crib. Usually, he would start bellowing as soon as he woke up, but today was different. Today Milo scootched over to the side of the crib where the toys were. And even though most of Trisha's body was hidden behind bigger toys, Milo kept scootching until he found her.

When Milo's mom came into his room, she could hear him singing his la-la-las, and she saw his legs sticking out from under his toys. "Oh my goodness!" she exclaimed, and she ran to make sure he wasn't stuck. She pulled his little body out from under the toys, and Milo held on to Trisha.

"Oh hey! I remember this little puppy!" Mommy said.

"Shh Shh," said Milo.

"She's a puppy. Can you say pup-py?" (Mommy knew Milo couldn't talk yet, but for some reason, both she and Daddy were always asking Baby Milo to say words.

"Shh Shh," said Milo.

"Pup-py. She's a pup-py."

"Shi Sha," said Milo.

Mommy laughed. "Did you say Trisha? Is your puppy's name Trisha?"

"Shi Sha!" said Milo.

"Okay then! Does Trisha the puppy want to have some lunch too?"

Trisha did.

Trisha and Milo were inseparable after that. She slept with Milo every night. She was the toy Milo first crawled to. She was the toy Milo first walked to. She rode in Milo's backpack when they went to sleepovers at Gramma Sonie's. She rode in Milo's Thomas the Tank Engine rolling suitcase when they took airplanes to visit Gramma Sally. She was Milo's Show-and-Tell for preschool, and again for kindergarten.

One day, Milo seemed more excited than usual. "Today's my birthday party!" he whispered to Trisha.

Trisha remembered all those years ago, when she lived at the toy store, and more than anything in the world, she had wanted to go to a birthday party.

Maybe Milo understood that she wanted to go to the party. Or maybe she was just so special that Milo couldn't imagine having a party without Trisha.

Milo gave Trisha her own party hat to wear, and he sat her right next to the cake.

She got to hear all of the children sing Happy Birthday, and she watched as Milo opened present after present.

And after the party was over, Milo left the presents on the floor, and he carried Trisha upstairs for their usual nap. And Trisha the puppy was the happiest puppy ever.

Milo with Trisha:

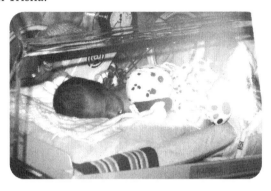

Thank you so much for reading!

Lots of people write books -and that's wonderful- but it's nearly impossible to draw attention to individual works.

There are thirty three million different books for sale on Amazon, and customers are only shown a miniscule fraction of them because, regardless of their quality, they won't catch the algorithm's attention.

One way to help books get noticed is to leave a review on Amazon.com, goodreads, or any other place where books are discussed. The algorithm notices reviews. Enough reviews will cause the system to put this book higher up in the results section when shoppers enter Memoir or Essay or humor, or any other applicable search terms.

That's a great thing! It's better for a shopper to see my book and decide yes or no, than for them to never see it at all.

Word of mouth helps a lot too. And the holidays are coming up! This book would make a lovely gift!